An Erotic Philology
of Golden Age Spain

An Erotic Philology
of Golden Age Spain

❞ • ❞

Adrienne Laskier Martín

Vanderbilt University Press

NASHVILLE

11 10 09 08   1 2 3 4 5

This book is printed on acid-free paper made
from 50% post-consumer recycled paper.
Manufactured in the United States of America
Design: Dariel Mayer

Publication of this book has been supported by a generous subsidy
from the Program for Cultural Cooperation between Spain's
Ministry of Culture and United States Universities.

Library of Congress Cataloging-in-Publication Data

Martín, Adrienne Laskier.
An erotic philology of Golden Age Spain /
Adrienne Laskier Martín. — 1st ed.
    p. cm.
Includes bibliographical references and index.
ISBN 978-0-8265-1578-0 (cloth : alk. paper)
ISBN 978-0-8265-1579-7 (pbk. : alk. paper)
        1. Spanish literature—Classical period, 1500–1700
—History and criticism. 2. Eroticism in literature
3. Sex in literature. 4. Symbolism in literature. I. Title.
PQ6066.M29 2007
860.9'3538—dc22   2007022440

For Will, Mikey, and Chloe

Contents

Acknowledgments

An Erotic Philology of Golden Age Spain has been a rewarding extended journey. I am grateful to a number of accomplished friends and scholars in the United States and in Spain whose stimulating conversation, debate, and wit have enhanced and confirmed my conviction regarding the quirks and merits of erotic literature. Foremost among that exceptional group are Anne Cruz, who has been a formidable interlocutor for many years; Steven Hutchinson and Mercedes Alcalá Galán, companions at numerous international conferences and generous hosts in Andalucía; and J. Ignacio Díez Fernández, model collaborator on several projects, whose own work and interests parallel and have helped refine my own. Frederick de Armas, Diana de Armas Wilson, Emilie Bergmann and Christopher Maurer read the manuscript at various stages and their keen observations are greatly appreciated. José J. Labrador Herraiz and Ralph A. DiFranco could not have been more generous in providing poetic texts and timely suggestions.

At the University of California at Davis, Cristina Martínez Carazo, Marta Altisent and Sam Armistead, whose willingness to share thoughts and articles is boundless, are superb colleagues. Fellowships at the Stanford Humanities Center and the U.C. Davis Humanities Institute provided the opportunity to exchange ideas with fellow early modernists. Many thanks are due my excellent graduate students, several of whom are now scholars doing compelling work in Golden Age studies.

At Vanderbilt University Press, I thank Betsy Phillips for her extraordinary enthusiasm and guidance in bringing this book to press. I am also indebted to Dariel Mayer, Joan Vidal, and the original readers for their discernment and attention to editorial detail. All have improved the manuscript immeasurably. Fragments of Chapters Two and Three first appeared as "Góngora: 'Poeta de bujarrones,'" in *Calíope* (8.1 [2002]: 101–20), and "The Mediation of Lesbian Eros in Golden Age Verse," in *Lesbianism and Homosexuality in Golden Age Literature and Society*, edited by María José Delgado and Alain Saint-Saëns (New Orleans: University Press of the South, 2000, 343–62). I appreciate the editors' permission to incorporate revised versions here.

The members of my family, each in his or her own way, have contributed enormously to this project, and I dedicate this book to them with love and gratitude: to my parents, Dot and Jim Laskier, *in memoriam*, to whom I owe everything; to my husband, Will Corral, for his intellectual rigor, encouragement, and unqualified support; and to Mikey and Chloe, peerless canine companions, for the fun.

Preface

Gerard Ter Borch the Younger (1617–1681), creator of the painting that graces the cover of this book, was not only one of the finest northern baroque Dutch portraitists but also an exquisitely refined artist of daily life. In 1654 he produced this magnificent genre painting first known as *Paternal Admonition.* In it a father admonishes his daughter; the mother casts her eyes downward in embarrassment and silence. The effect produced by the dazzling conjunction of luxurious fabrics, the complex play of light, and the natural air of the man's rather quizzical expression reveals the influence of artist Diego Velázquez. (The painters, who were contemporaries, undoubtedly met when Ter Borch visited the Spanish court in the 1630s.)

But what is the true image reflected on this canvas? By the post-Victorian mid-twentieth century, art historians no longer saw in it a commonplace domestic scene; instead, they saw a representation of a high-class brothel (Kettering 2004, 114). Renamed *The Gallant Conversation,* the painting is thought to depict a military officer/client possibly proffering a coin, an elderly woman/procuress, and a young woman who could be a courtesan. Adding to the complexity of the probable messages of the work, a dog turns its back on the group gathered around the bed to conduct (according to the new view) a presumably sordid business transaction; the animal appears burdened with shame. To what do we owe, we might wonder, this change in perception?

As a result of this revised perspective on the part of viewers, *The Gallant Conversation,* sensual and enigmatic, presents a myriad of tantalizing interpretive possibilities. Its portrayal of sexuality is nuanced and highly expressive: the candor of the girl's exposed neck, the blatantly sensual folds of her shimmering oyster satin gown, the officer's extravagantly feathered hat and oversized foot seemingly poised to penetrate the female space, the old woman's dainty grasp of the wine glass. The central figure in the painting has her back to the onlooker, her face averted, in a gesture of demureness or aloofness, perhaps shame or powerlessness, or quite probably resignation.

Indeed, *The Gallant Conversation* can serve as a general metaphor for the types of texts that compose the raw material of this book—which feature a still unheralded sexual and erotic content—and for their unsettled and until now incomplete critical reception. These works, whose marrow is sexual alterity, have also been avoided, veiled, and misrepresented, and their subject matter has been outrightly rejected, reactions that are surely related to not only the social, cultural, and historical spheres of their time but also our rather prim critical tradition. In recent years, precisely because of changes in artistic interpretation, an upsurge in serious scholarly interest in previously marginalized or willfully misinterpreted literary works has been recovering them for, and therefore changing our conception of, Spanish literary history. Like Ter Borch's painting, the works discussed in the chapters that follow can be elusive and ambiguous; their revelation of the complexity of erotic behaviors and prevalent attitudes of their age poses challenges that this book takes on.

It goes without saying that pleasure, desire, and sexuality are tenacious components that shape literature and our lives in fundamental ways. At the same time, popular and critical receptions of works riveted on sexuality and eroticism—that is, the depiction of the physical aspects of sexual passion and love—have swayed between fascination and revulsion, revelation and restraint, exclusion and production, especially when those texts revolve around non-normative sexualities. In spite of historical reticence and prudery, however, the efforts to study sexual practices as integral parts of literary, cultural, sexual, and historical processes can be productive in the revision of what Frank Kermode has called critical "used thinking," in order to arrive at a greater understanding of early modern mentalities and literature. In an essay on sodomites and Western culture, Randolph Trumbach argues with respect to a subsequent historical period:

We ought to study the historical forms of sexual behaviour not simply because they are interesting in themselves, but rather because *sexual behaviour (perhaps more than religion) is the most highly symbolic activity of any society.* To penetrate to the symbolic system implicit in any society's sexual behaviour is therefore to come closest to the heart of its uniqueness (1977, 24; my emphasis).

Sadly, in hispanism, critical inquiry into sexuality in literature, especially the types of "deviant" practices examined in this book, has traditionally been considered a somewhat distasteful and unworthy scholarly endeavor best left to historians of the Inquisition. The reasoning behind such censorship can no longer be sustained in this century, however. In the past decade several essay collections have broached the topic of sexual otherness (especially homosexuality) and the erotic with respect to pre- and early modern Spanish texts. This revisionism is present, for example, in the essays included in *Queer Iberia* (1999), edited by Josiah Blackmore and Gregory S. Hutcheson, and *Lesbianism and Homosexuality in Early Modern Spain* (2000), edited by María José Delgado and Alain Saint-Saëns. In Spain, two books from the late 1990s also contain essays or discussions of early modern sexualities: *Sexo y razón* (1997), by Francisco Vázquez García and Andrés Moreno Mengíbar, and *El sexo en la literatura* (1997), edited by Luis Gómez Canseco, Pablo L. Zambrano, and Laura P. Alonso. With respect to specifically erotic texts, my edited collection *La poesía erótica del Siglo de Oro: Crítica y antología* (Martín 2007), the compilations co-edited with J. Ignacio Díez Fernández—*La poesía erótica de Fray Melchor de la Serna* (Martín and Díez Fernández 2003), *Venus venerada: Tradiciones eróticas de la literatura española* (Díez Fernández and Martín 2006), and *Venus venerada II: Literatura erótica y modernidad en España* (Martín and Díez Fernández 2007)—and Díez Fernández's *La poesía erótica de los Siglos de Oro* (2003) are revitalizing research on Spanish literary eroticism.

This book is different from earlier studies, however. *An Erotic Philology of Golden Age Spain* focuses specifically on the representation of a variety of unorthodox and eroticized figures—prostitutes, homosexuals, lesbians, transvestite female warriors, and sexual tricksters—in order to explore that particular uniqueness to which Trumbach refers. The approach of this book is greatly, although not exclusively, informed by the sociology of deviance (see Ericson 1964), which defines certain behaviors as normal or anomalous based not on any inherent qualities of the comportment but on the social audience's reaction to them. As a corollary to this approach, the exploration of non-normative sexualities (perversions for some in the Golden Age) illuminates how such stigmatization functions as an ordering principle in the law, in society, and consequently in literature. In other words, deviance is an expression of conflicts, desires, expectations, and inner impulses that can produce a social (and literary) chain reaction that is clearly evident in the texts examined herein. The purpose of this study is also to elucidate the symbolic universe and historical referents that inform the representation of those characters in a variety of poetic, prose, and dramatic texts and to center on the complex signifying system by which they are portrayed. In sum, the goal is to enhance the burgeoning field that might perhaps be called erotic philology and, in so doing, to bring sexuality out of the historical and legal closet. It is the contention of this study that literary sources can reflect social attitudes and sexualities that are vastly more complex than those projected, and severely repressed, by the official arbiters of public morality during the Golden Age.

In an effort to preserve the presence of the diverse genres examined (as well as the schools or movements to which these texts might belong) in its holistic reading of the erotic vein in early modern literature, this book discerns how the manifold sexual practices and practitioners were constructed via literary expressions that depend on a particular type of discourse. The issues addressed include what the works mean, both literally and figuratively; how they function as literature; what sorts of sociocultural conditions explain the attitudes that determine and control the reception of certain sexual behaviors and assign them to categories of normativity or deviance; and finally, and most important, what is their lasting aesthetic effect and significance.

It is a truism that any literary study tells us as much about ourselves and our own mentality as it does about past beliefs. This effect is especially true with respect to the erotic in art. The specificity of Spanish Golden Age culture, whose human values are examined herein, serves as a mirror, reflecting back on the reader the ways in which we, too, in our discomfort (and in an attempt to safeguard our own social and sexual identities) assign symbolic meanings to "deviants" and transgressors. At the same time, that textual glass offers up to scrutiny both the material culture of desire and the mercurial poetics of eroticism.

CHAPTER ONE

Prostitution and Power

Es lícito permitir las rameras, en la República, por evitar otros
males mayores.
  —Enrique de Villalobos, *Manual de confesores*

[It is licit to allow prostitutes in our Republic, in order to avoid
greater evils.]

In his 1625 handbook for priests who were charged with administering
the sacrament of confession, Enrique de Villalobos grapples with the
institutional, social, moral, and humanistic concerns that surround sex
for sale. His endorsement of prostitution as a remedy against graver and
unspoken sins (homosexuality) reveals that the trade did not always
occupy a well-demarcated or stable socioethical territory. As a source
of ongoing preoccupation for the church, theologians, moralists, and
civil authorities, "the oldest profession" also surfaces in an inordinate
number of medieval and early modern literary texts.

In his *Pragmática que han de guardar las hermanas comunes,* Francisco de Quevedo, one of seventeenth-century Spain's greatest satirists
and no stranger to prostitutes as objects of representation, addresses
prostitutes as follows: "Y porque sabemos la suma desorden que se ha
introducido en vuestros alojamientos, mandamos que nadie llame a
vuestras posadas, casas, sino tiendas pues todas sois mercadería" (quoted
in Profeti 1994, 204). [And because we know of the great disorder that
has been introduced into your dwellings, we order that nobody call
your lodgings houses but shops, since you are all merchandise.] Such

1

diminishment of women into marketable flesh (and a source of social disorder and disruption) is a necessary discursive step in the process of exclusion to which the structures of power and control in early modern Spain attempted to submit prostitutes by enclosing them in licensed brothels. In *Sexo y razón,* Francisco Vázquez García and Andrés Moreno Mengíbar point out in this regard that

> el status forzado de la ramera, definido claramente por las ordenan-
> zas, es el de la *extraña,* exterior al orden de la ciudad y al orden de
> las alianzas. . . . La manceba es, pues, arrojada a la exterioridad de
> la ciudad, entendida ésta como colectivo y como espacio, pues la
> mancebía se ubica siempre en las afueras, lejos de los barrios popu-
> losos. . . . Es extraña, extranjera, elemento singular en un universo
> que se ampara en la colectividad, la que lleva sobre su figura y sobre
> sus ropas la tacha de la diferencia, de lo otro. (291–93)

> [The forced status of the prostitute, clearly defined by legal ordi-
> nances, is that of *stranger,* outside the order of the city and the order
> of alliances. . . . The prostitute, then, is cast out of the city, which is
> understood as a collective space, since the brothel is always located on
> the outskirts, far from populous neighborhoods. . . . She is strange,
> foreign, a singular element in a universe that protects itself through
> community, one who carries on her person and clothing the mark
> of difference, of the other.]

In spite of her social marginalization, however, the prostitute is a popular literary subject in Spain's Golden Age. *La Celestina, La Lozana andaluza,* and *La pícara Justina* are the obvious templates, and the greatest prose writer of the period, Miguel de Cervantes, was not only well aware that prostitution thrived but also knowledgeable of the long literary tradition that centered on the problems elicited by venal love.[1] However, his complex and alternative take on the sex trade differs substantially from the overwhelmingly misogynistic socioliterary norm of the time. His more tolerant view of working girls can be appreciated in the brief novella *La tía fingida* and in the memorable character Maritornes, the servant girl and occasional prostitute at Juan Palomeque's inn, from *Don Quijote de la Mancha* (1605).

La tía fingida is an enigmatic and intriguing novella receptive to a wide variety of critical approaches, from traditional sociohistorical or philological/stylistic analyses to the most recent theoretical methodologies that serve as an interpretive palimpsest for the twenty-first century. Paradoxically, most critical studies of this brief yet complex narrative have, up to this writing, neglected its content to focus exclusively and obsessively on resolving the inevitable and persistent question of its uncertain authorship. This focus has sidetracked other possible interpretations that would locate the text within the abundant current of Spanish literature that centers on sexual traffic. By attempting, above all else, to prove or disprove the novella's attribution to Cervantes, critics have paradoxically provided closure or foreclosure for a text that calls out for an amplification of its context and nuances.[2] Thus, it is not without irony that this story—which, among other literary constructions, questions truth, social legitimacy, and power relationships—has been the source of biographical fallacies that derail the text. As noted in subsequent chapters of this book, the critical emphasis on exteriority is a result of the normative nature of Spanish literary history as written to date. This fact notwithstanding, and although it is not my purpose here to engage in the authorship debate, I find *La tía fingida* to be overwhelmingly Cervantine. Its content, themes, style, and tone clearly identify the author as Cervantes. In fact, the protagonist of this novella embodies one more species of prostitute among the diverse cast of *semi-doncellas* who populate the prose and dramatic works of Cervantes and who are discussed in the following pages.

Discourse and the Poetics of Transgression

Given the critical dead-end mentioned previously, it seems more fruitful to excuse the authorship question for the moment in order to concentrate on the conceptual ramifications of the story itself. In a way, I find myself at the formalist crossroads of revealing the device without totally obliterating the author. To this end, my own reading of this provocative story draws more from the generally poststructuralist notion of Cervantine discourse than from the author-ity of the empirical Cervantes. Therefore, I analyze prostitution in his works within the general framework of Foucauldian notions of discourse and the Peter Stallybrass and Allon White theory of transgression posited in their study *The*

Politics and Poetics of Transgression (1986). As a consequence, I view the narrative fiction of *La tía fingida* as a mediated reflection of the high/low dichotomy that Stallybrass and White explore in the symbolic socioliterary hierarchies of the time. Throughout my text, "discourse"—the totality of relationships, units, and operations understood as utterances that involve subjects who speak and write—represents a central human activity and not a general text or universal. These discursive practices are interwoven with social practices by the circulation of power. It should come as no surprise, then, that in *La tía fingida* discourse is constituted by the antagonistic relationship between a desire for openness and the institutions that support the notion that discourse is formed through constraint and control.[3]

Despite my initial proviso, I should mention that in their study Stallybrass and White discuss the origin of the notion of the classical author. This idea cannot be applied very satisfactorily to the Cervantes of the Renaissance, but it can be illuminating for current critical receptions of his texts that incorporate prostitution and for works discussed herein. According to Stallybrass and White (1986) and Curtius (1973, 249–51), the notion of the "Classic author" derives from ancient taxation categories, which separated the elite from the proletariat. Under this system the citizens of the first taxation category, called *classici*, formed the model for literary categories. In effect, authors and works of literature were classified according to their social rank. Stallybrass and White note that

> the ranking of literary genres or authors in a hierarchy analogous to social classes is a particularly clear example of a much broader and more complex cultural process whereby the human body, psychic forms, geographical space and the social formation are all constructed within interrelating and dependent hierarchies of high and low. . . . The high/low opposition in each of our four symbolic domains . . . is a fundamental basis to mechanisms of ordering and sense-making in European cultures. . . . Cultures "think themselves" in the most immediate and affective ways through the combined symbolisms of these four hierarchies (1986, 2–3).

As occurs with the human body and geographic space, these socio-aesthetic poles of high and low are never totally separable. The early bourgeois subject, Stallybrass and White continue, defines and redefines itself constantly by excluding what it designates as "low" in terms of filth, repulsion, noise, and contamination. This very act of exclusion is constitutive of the bourgeois subject's identity, since it internalizes the low under the sign of negation and disgust. However, because repugnance always bears the imprint of desire, the expelled domains return as the object of nostalgia, longing, and fascination (1986, 191). Thus, the exclusion necessary to the formation of social identity at the level of the political unconscious is simultaneously a production at the level of the imaginary (193). It is for this reason, Stallybrass and White argue, that what is socially marginal is so frequently symbolically central to the construction of subjectivity. As we will see, the negotiation of this exclusion/dependence dichotomy (aided and abetted by power relationships) in society and literature is fundamental to a proper interpretation of *La tía fingida*, whose very title codifies the presence of disputed conceptual territories.

Stallybrass and White conclude that the poetics of transgression reveals the disgust, the fear, and the desire that inform the dramatic self-representation of a given culture through the contemplation of the "low Other" (1986, 202). This theory can be observed at least in all Western literatures that represent society's marginal sectors (among these the prostitutes, transvestites, homosexuals, and sexual tricksters who are the object of study of this book) and in a particular manner in *La tía fingida*. The prostitute and the literature of prostitution—the social and literary frames for the texts examined in this chapter—are obvious examples of the low socioliterary category, but, as indicated by Bubnova 1996, it is impossible to separate the prostitute and her historical referents from ideological state apparatuses such as the church, the state, and the university. This socioliterary sphere of the prostitute is also inseparable from legal discourses, as we will see. More pointedly, the prostitute commercializes the lower part of her body; precisely that which is farthest from the head, the spirit, reason, and the soul composes the center of her existence and her literary portrait. In that regard, following the transcription of the Francisco Porras de la Cámara manuscript, which Juan Bautista Avalle-Arce used in his edition of *La tía fingida* (1982), the subtitle—which reads "cuya verdadera historia sucedió en Salamanca el año de 1575, y demuestra quanto perjudican las terceras" [whose true history occurred in Salamanca in the year 1575, and shows how much harm is done by go-betweens]—not only codifies a way of reading but also grapples with the notion of fact versus fiction.[4]

Woman as Marketable Flesh in La tía fingida

Unlike most canonical Renaissance works, *La tía fingida* has been marginalized in part because its fable is relatively unknown. The novella is a particularly lively narrative, which, according to the subtitle, actually took place in Salamanca in 1575. In a way, it can be said that Cervantes is providing a ripple to the notion of the Italian Renaissance *cortigiana onesta,* generally an "honest," high-class prostitute who worked at home rather than in a brothel, whose services were expensive, and who was selective in her clientele.[5] Thus, Cervantes's tale begins when two young Manchegan students come upon a known house of ill repute, whose blinds, curiously, are drawn. The students learn that the house is inhabited by a certain venerable old woman and her beautiful young niece and imagine that the two are courtesans. When the old woman (Claudia) and her niece (Esperanza) arrive, the students are captivated by the niece's beauty. They enlist the help of a young ne'er-do-well gentleman friend, Don Félix, who agrees to conquer the damsel for them at any cost (the exchange and symbolic value of this attitude does not escape the reader). Don Félix subsequently bribes Grijalba, one of Claudia's *dueñas,* and she reveals the truth: Esperanza has already been sold three times as a virgin.

A feeble cloak-and-dagger strategy is enacted when Grijalba hides Don Félix in Esperanza's room that evening, explaining that she and the niece have arranged a liaison without Claudia's knowledge in order to avoid having to share the profits with her. In the meantime, in an adjoining room, Claudia launches into a litany of advice about how her niece can make a more profitable career of prostitution. Esperanza insists that she will not succumb to the needle and thread repair that Claudia intends to make to the young woman's hymen in order to sell her "virginity" for the fourth time.[6] (This situation, of course, echoes back to the most famous hymen mender in Spanish literature, Celestina.) The craft of repairing a torn hymen allows for the ultimate deception and pretense in Golden Age society and its literary representation, by restoring a woman's most treasured and valuable asset: her virginity. Thus, the hymen mender wields a discourse of profoundly subversive power. Consequently, perhaps, Esperanza finally accedes, agreeing to do as her aunt wishes. At this point in the narrative, Don Félix experiences an inopportune sneezing fit and is discovered by Claudia, who indignantly protests his presence in her house. Don Félix informs Claudia that he has overheard her previous conversation with Esperanza and is willing to pay any price for her niece. Grijalba excitedly places Esperanza's hand in Don Félix's. An altercation ensues between Claudia and Grijalba, and the racket attracts the local *corregidor,* who marches Claudia and Esperanza off to jail. At this point in the text, the gathering of voices common to early modern narratives (again reminiscent of *La Celestina*) and the intersection of gossip, rumor, and hearsay come to the fore.

The two Manchegan students witness the arrest of the women and manage to free Esperanza and spirit her away to their lodgings. There the men argue when one attempts to claim the fruits of his labor, to "gozar" [rape] Esperanza. When the other man prevents the would-be violation, threatening to kill his companion if he persists, the first man resolves the impasse by offering Esperanza his hand in marriage. Esperanza delightedly accepts, and the student carries her off to his father's home, where they are married. It is finally revealed that Claudia was not really Esperanza's aunt; she is then charged with sorcery and pandering and is sentenced to the corresponding punishment: four hundred lashes and caging in the town square. The tale ends happily with Esperanza winning over her father-in-law with her discretion and beauty, even though he has been duly informed of her shameful past. The story's moral pleads for similar punishment for evil women such as Claudia and highlights the fact that few prostitutes experience the same good fortune as Esperanza. As I argue with respect to other texts examined herein, the type of narrative used in *La tía fingida* is too orderly for comfort and seems constrained by the very Cervantine ending in which the "innocent" female protagonist is rewarded by acceptance into the wider community. Her past misdemeanors are overlooked, thus concealing the social disorder that she embodied as an itinerant prostitute. The moral, of course, has nothing to do with the truth of the situation. In fact, it could be interpreted as nothing more than the writing of power, which Michel Foucault ("The Discourse on Language" [1972]) prefers to see as the violence that we do to things or, in any case, a practice that we impose on them.

It is evident that the fictional narrative embodied in *La tía fingida* plainly underscores the simultaneous existence of disgust and fascination as poles of a process in which a political imperative to reject and eliminate the low in society and in literature (represented in this supposedly exemplary tale by a prostitute and an aunt who exploits her) conflicts powerfully and unpredictably with the desire for this "low Other" (the young and desirable courtesan). Claudia and Esperanza, differentiated embodiments of the low, are situated on the periphery of early modern Spanish society. And, in the mapping of Salamanca in terms of dirt and cleanliness, it is not difficult to ascertain which pole they represent. In spite of her marginalized status, however, Esperanza is not only *the* object of desire for the men who compose an important sector of that specific fictionalized society—the Salamancan university—but also the symbolic nucleus of the novella.[7]

Nonetheless, desire may not always motivate and justify actions, since the characters are forever trapped in a dialectic between the fantasized and the socially acceptable. The result is a conflicting fusion of power, fear, and desire in the construction of Esperanza's subjectivity. In *La tía fingida* the tripartite fusion is actualized through the protagonist's complete reification, which, following Foucauldian precepts, would be part of one of the procedures for mastery. Esperanza is consistently characterized by a marked excision between body (flesh) and spirit wherein the former totally eclipses the latter, along the lines of the historical outline of dominance. The young prostitute is perceived by others as a simple object: a commercial pawn for the women and a sexual pawn for the men. From the first moment, even before Esperanza and Claudia appear, they are presented as dwellers of a "tienda de carne" [meat market], a description that is self-evident and devoid of any metonymic value.

Subsequently, the flesh motif reappears often in *La tía fingida,* linked always to Esperanza's degradation as a totally disempowered being. The protagonist is reduced to "carne humana" [human flesh]: young, tender, and displayed for sale at a high price in spite of her "tres mercados" [three sales]. Salamanca, in turn, becomes the Renaissance marketplace that is variously festive, therapeutic (mainly for men), and orderly yet permeable, a living creature that can be grasped only in the sketched impressions for which the genre of the novella is an ideal textual space, especially if its topic discloses the transgression of institutionalized power relationships. As Foucault argues throughout his texts on discourse, claims to objectivity made on behalf of specific discourses are always spurious. Esperanza's discourse is not measured in terms of its truthfulness but in terms of whether or not it is powerful. The discourse employed to describe her is powerful indeed, in the sense that it reduces Esperanza to a one-dimensional sex object upon whom acts of violence are freely perpetrated. For example, when Esperanza is introduced for the first time, the two Manchegan youths who pursue her have the inclination "de los cuervos nuevos, que a cualquier carne se abaten" (Cervantes 2001, 629) [of young crows that swoop down on any meat]. Esperanza is the "nueva garza" [new heron] whom they attack "con todos sus cinco sentidos" (629) [with all their five senses]. The only objection that Esperanza raises against her fourth resale as a virgin is the "sensibilidad de [sus] carnes" (641) [sensitivity of (her) flesh], a perception that contrasts with Claudia's idea of human flesh as simple "mercadería" [merchandise]. The single moment in the narrative in which Esperanza's body and spirit are united is when she alleges this tenderness of her flesh. This prostitute maintains a separation between her inner self and her lucrative being—the body/merchandise whose most intimate part she later describes as "negra de marchita" (642) [withered and black]. Bodily sensation and the self thus provide Esperanza with a sense of objectivity and corporality, since her identity, character, and morality really depend on her core emotions and the limits that she places on her ideals and not on her real erotic preferences, to which we are never privy.

It is not necessary to resort to theoretical models generally foreign to the sociohistorical specificity of Spain to reveal that in this work Esperanza is rarely depicted as a whole human being capable of rational deliberation or conscious of her legal inefficacy.[8] Her innermost conscience, which remains untouched by lucre, is ultimately unknown and thus enigmatic, except in those brief moments when she comments ironically on her situation. For example, when Don Félix, after being discovered in Esperanza's room, argues with Claudia, who defends against all odds her niece's purported virginity, Esperanza distances herself from her body to observe it with apparent objectivity: "Por cierto, bien limpia soy—dijo entonces Esperanza, que estaba en medio del aposento como embobada y suspensa, *viendo lo que pasaba sobre su cuerpo*—y tan limpia, que no ha una hora que con todo este frío me vestí una camisa limpia" (645, my emphasis). ["To be sure, I am very clean," said Esperanza, who sat perplexed in the middle of the room, contemplating what was happening to her body, "and so clean, that even with this cold I put on a new chemise not even an hour ago."]

Given the typical procedure in erotic literature of using words with opposite equivalences, it is difficult to interpret without irony the young courtesan's use of *limpia* as meaning "clean" or "without stain." Nonetheless, the first description of Esperanza initiates a marked textual insistence on her physical appearance, and details abound regarding her dress and stereotypical beauty (a young woman eighteen years of age, with dark almond-shaped eyes, shapely brows, black lashes, and a rosy complexion). Naturally, this discourse of an early system of feminine fashion and beauty both reifies bodily surfaces and codifies the reactions of those who observe the signifying values of those surfaces. This is precisely the system that Cervantes will parody with his unforgettable character Maritornes, who is analyzed later in this chapter. Given the emphasis on Esperanza's physicality and the fact that the text does not locate a moment of precise physical and mental convergence, it is not surprising that descriptions of Esperanza's character are scarce, except the few brief mentions of her "rostro mesurado y grave . . . ojos al descuido adormecidos . . . ademán grave . . . mirar honesto" (628) [composed and grave expression . . . drowsy eyes . . . sober expression . . . honest glance].

With respect to her spirit, only an absence exists, an emotional/textual void that engulfs her as she withstands, for the umpteenth time, the aunt's counsel regarding how she might increase her "honor" with her sexual transgressions: "Estaba a todo lo dicho la dicha niña Esperanza, bajos los ojos y escarbando el brasero con un cuchillo, inclinada la cabeza sin hablar palabra, y al parecer muy contenta y obediente a cuanto la tía le iba diciendo" (640–41). [The child Esperanza listened to everything that was said, with her eyes downcast, poking the brazier with a knife, her head inclined without saying a word, and seemingly very content and obedient to everything her aunt was saying to her.] Esperanza ascends to the level of true subject, and not simple object, only once in the novella—when she initially refuses to permit her hymen to be mended for the fourth sale. No matter how great the profit, she will not allow Claudia to torture her once again. But even now her reification is undiminished. Esperanza subjects herself to objectifying metaphorization (alluding to her aunt's possible pleasure in physically abusing her) when she eloquently appeals her case as follows:

> Deje, señora tia, ya de rebuscar mi viña, que a veces es más sabroso el rebusco que el esquilmo principal; y si todavía está determinada que mi jardín se venda cuarta vez por entero, intacto y jamás tocado, busque otro modo más suave de cerradura para su postigo, porque la del sirgo y ahuja, no hay pensar que más llegue a mis carnes. (642)

> [Aunt, stop digging through my vineyard, since the search is sometimes tastier than the harvest; and if you are still determined that my garden be sold for the forth time as whole, intact and untouched, find another more gentle way to lock its door, because needle and silk will not touch my flesh again.]

Here the conventional garden of love motif is transmuted, and the body of the text becomes the text of the body in the most direct way. But Esperanza, seemingly powerless before an impossible situation, finally succumbs to her aunt's insistence and obeys, thus observing one of the maximum early modern female virtues. In this regard, numerous theological premises served at the time to justify women's subjugation to masculine authority. For example, in his 1566 marriage treatise *Saludable instrucción del estado de matrimonio*, Fray Vicente Mexía states that the wife is neither slave nor servant and is the mistress of her husband's house and estate but is always subordinate to him (see the discussion in Perry 1990, 60–66). The obvious and ideologically charged difference in the case of this novella is that the prevailing authority comes from a woman—the false aunt.

As I have stated, the notion of buying and selling is transparently associated within the text with that of woman as marketable flesh. Moreover, *La tía fingida* is constructed around the theme of merchandise and of transgressive commerce in women's bodies. In the opening passage of the novella, the two students roaming the streets of Salamanca are surprised to find the shutters of Esperanza's house closed, "porque la gente de la tal casa, si no se descubría y apregonaba, no se vendía" (Cervantes 2001, 625) [because if the people in such a house did not put themselves on display and advertise, they could not sell themselves]. If one resorts to the historically based axiom that women are the traditional objects of the male gaze, in this instance the narrative can be construed as a textual variant, especially given the fact that these two particular women make their living off the various male ways of seeing. This focus notwithstanding, the only home that appears in the work is identified as a shop window displaying female flesh.

The type of liminal space that Esperanza and Claudia inhabit was, of course, prohibited by law. Although many did not, urban prostitutes were expected to remain enclosed within public brothels or to restrict their business to certain streets, and numerous city ordinances prohibited them from plying their trade or spending the night outside, since these practices could result in public disorder remarkably similar to that which occurs in *La tía fingida*. For example, a 1553 Seville/Ronda ordinance required that prostitutes remain in the brothel at night "porque ay muchas en la dicha mancebía que tienen palacios alquilados fuera de ella, donde se van de noche a dormir con hombres fingiendo ser mugeres de mas calidad y engañándoles y llevándoles por ello muchos dineros, de lo cual se ha recrecido e puede recrecer muchos escándalos, muertes, heridas y otros graves incombinientes" (quoted in López Beltrán 1987, 22) [because many women in said brothels rent houses outside, where they go to sleep with men at night, pretending to be women of quality, deceiving and cheating the men out of their money. Many scandals, deaths, injuries, and other serious problems have arisen from this].

It would not be stretching an argument to view the construction of such a space as an elaboration of what feminists within the politics of traditional Marxism see as the form of alienation that has become the paradigm for women's oppression. Moreover, it is not difficult to appreciate throughout the novella a corresponding insistence on the language of commerce, and I reiterate that this choice of vocabulary is not gratuitous. Thus, Don Félix offers to conquer Esperanza for the Manchegan students "costase lo que costase" (Cervantes 2001, 635) [at whatever the cost]. In order to do so, he bribes Grijalba with a silk shawl and tries to similarly bribe Claudia with a gold chain (an object full of Celestinesque reminiscences). But the price seems low to Claudia, who angrily rejects the proposition. As a point of comparison, in Seville brothels a young and attractive prostitute could earn as much as four or five ducats per day; older or less attractive women might earn only a few *maravedís* (Sánchez Ortega 1995, 141). Out of her earnings, the prostitute would have to pay brothel-related expenses, which were established by law. For example, a 1570 Ronda ordinance stipulated that prostitutes could not be charged more than one silver *real* daily to rent a room furnished with bed, sheet, blanket, and pillow. The same rate was charged in Córdoba (López Beltrán 1987, 12). Assuming that Don Félix's chain is real gold—unlike the one sported by another Cervantine frequenter of prostitutes, Alférez Campuzano from *El casamiento engañoso* (2001)—his offer is actually quite generous.

In our story Don Félix reacts as befits an anxious buyer, desperately bettering the terms of his offer by affirming, "Sólo por la muestra del paño que he visto, no saldré de la tienda sin comprar toda la pieza. . . . Quisiera yo ser el primero que esquilmara este majuelo o vendimiara esta viña, aunque se añadieran a esta cadena unos grillos de oro y unas esposas de diamantes" (645). [Simply because of the sample I have seen, I will not leave the shop without buying the whole piece of fabric. . . . I would like to be the first to harvest this vine, even if a pair of golden shackles and diamond handcuffs were added to this chain.] Don Félix ends up offering the price that would most likely persuade Claudia—the vain promise of occultation and pretense. Even at this critical juncture in the well-known views of symbolic exchanges, it is worth restating Marc Shell's view that language and money produce value because they provide a means of exchange or define the difference between falsehood and pious economy in sexual production (1993, 93–101). In this case, the prevarication that surrounds the young prostitute both enables and establishes her worth.

Returning to the negotiation that has preceded Esperanza's kidnapping by the students, we see that this has been nothing more than the preparation of the textual space for the final purchase of Esperanza's body. In the novella's denouement, the Manchegan student who has snatched Esperanza from the clutches of the authorities discovers that his friend will not allow him to enjoy what has cost him so dearly. In other words, there is, perhaps, another buyer on the horizon whom the student must outbid by offering the highest possible price—commitment to the institution of matrimony. The commerce of societal power continues, but at this point it escalates into high finance. In the context of woman as merchandise, the student who offers marriage (institutional power and the discourse that it enacts) would be the highest bidder. This is reification in the most Lukacsian of terms, since readers encounter an economic process whereby human relationships and actions take on the appearance of relationships among objects or things. Tangentially, Esperanza's dilemma (by implication, given the role of the church in society) does not evolve out of a moral-religious problematic but out of moral-sexual and economic determinations.

Recent studies of the historical period that this story mimetizes have, with greater certainty and beyond expectations, proved that intimate relationships between women and men have varied over the years, that social class affects norms of sexual conduct, and that the relationships between the sexes reveal both power positions and mentalities in the larger social order (Perry 1990, 8). Within the temporal frame of *La tía fingida,* the bases for the literary representation of women were their supposed physical, moral, legal, and political inferiority (see De Maio 1988). This is evident in such Spanish Renaissance moral treatises on women as Juan Luis Vives's *Formación de la mujer cristiana* (1947) and Fray Luis de León's *La perfecta casada* (1992), which have become increasingly pertinent in the study of early modern transgression after the establishment of sexuality studies in the 1980s and 1990s. In addition, such institutions as the church sought to punish those who undertook extramarital and/or nonprocreative intercourse for pleasure. The process by which Esperanza is "courted" circumvents such restrictions because it conceals its symbolic center: her "virginity." Vives defines the social function and formation of women in a strictly subordinate fashion, classifying them solely by marital status as *doncella, casada,* or *viuda.* As Anne Cruz argues in "Studying Gender in the Spanish Golden Age" (1989b, 196–97), Luis de León establishes a model for the ideal married woman based on an irrefutable ideological truth—that woman forms part of a divine scheme that reaffirms male power. In her study of Spanish humanist discourses on women, Mar Martínez-Góngora (1999) also explores how the model of women promulgated by Spanish humanists responds to the bourgeois man's expectations of female domesticity, subordination, and control as a means of preserving his own masculinity.

Cruz's point had been formulated before in an analogous fashion by Foucault. For him, our perception of man as subject is engendered in an expressly male ethics:

It was an ethics for men: an ethics thought, written, and taught by men, and addressed to men—to free men, obviously. A male ethics, consequently, in which women figured only as objects or, at most, as partners that one had best train, educate, and watch over when one had them under one's power, but stay away from when they were under the power of someone else (father, husband, tutor) (1990b, 22).

This ethics is really an apparatus that produces sexuality as a form of discourse in which the will to know our desires serves as the main mechanism through which individuals such as Esperanza, and those who want her, are subjected to control.

Prostitution as Social Prophylaxis

It bears repeating that in Golden Age Spain women fulfilled roles of vital importance to the patriarchal order, symbolizing both virtue and evil. At the same time, they provided a negative foil against which men could define themselves, permitting a justification for male authority (Perry 1990, 5). The people of the early modern period had at their disposal a common cultural inheritance made up of beliefs and traditions that were intimately connected with a single religion. And, as Chapter Four argues with respect to Catalina de Erauso's *Historia* (2002), the process of adaptation of religious constraints to areas such as the New World was infinitely difficult. Within this context, and back in the Old World, religion and matrimony provided the most respected and the only really acceptable states for women. Marriage was exalted as an antidote to the problem of the disorderly or scandalous woman—in other words, the unattached, independent (and feasibly feared by men) woman.[9] Legal prostitution formed an integral part of the social scheme, serving to limit and constrain not only the socially and generically subversive possibilities represented by clandestine [*libres*] prostitutes but also the threat of what were perceived to be even more abominable vices.[10] In that regard, early modern Spanish theologians (as evidenced by the epigraph that opens this chapter) and legislators generally echoed the opinions of Saint Augustine and Thomas Aquinas regarding the acceptance of prostitution as the lesser of two evils. It was thought that the availability of

brothels prevented men from corrupting women who were not prostitutes or, much worse, from engaging in sodomy. Sánchez Ortega quotes
Aquinas as follows:

> Y assí Aristoteles reprueba el parecer de Platon en esto, diziendo, que
> mejor es tratar con las mugeres carnalmente, que caer en otros vicios
> más viles. Por lo qual dize san Agustín, que las rameras son al mundo
> como la sentina en la nave, y como las secretas en un palacio que si
> las quitas dél, se vendrá a henchir de hediondez, y lo mismo en la
> nave, sino hubiesse en ella sentina, quita a las rameras del mundo, y
> hincharase de sodomía. Y por esta causa dize el mismo san Agustín,
> que la ciudad terrena hizo torpeza lícita el uso de las casas públicas.
> (Quoted in Sánchez Ortega 1995, 133)

> [And thus Aristotle rejects Plato's opinion on this, saying that it is
> better to have carnal relations with women than to fall into other
> worse vices. Because of this, Saint Augustine says that prostitutes are
> to the world as the bilge is to a ship. And like the privies in a palace;
> if you remove them, it will be filled with stench, as in the ship with-
> out a bilge. Remove whores from the world, and it will be filled with
> sodomy. And for this reason Saint Augustine says that the earthly city
> made the use of public brothels a licit evil.]

However, not all concurred with this acceptance of prostitution as a
lesser evil. For example, Fray Gabriel de Maqueda, following reasoning
adverse to that of Aquinas, in his 1622 *Invectiva en forma de discurso
contra el uso de las casas públicas,* rejects public brothels:

> El primer inconveniente es que con haber casas públicas, no sólo no
> se evitan pecados más graves de sensualidad; pero en ellas se enseñan,
> ejercitan y usan pecados de sodomía y contra natura; de manera que
> ellas son escuelas de esta nefanda maldad y sus rameras maestras de
> este torpe vicio. (Quoted in San Jerónimo and Valle de la Cerda
> 1991, 8)

> [The first problem is that by having public brothels not only are
> worse sins of sensuality not avoided but also sins of sodomy against
> nature are taught, practiced, and used there. Thus, they are schools

of this nefarious evil and their whores are mistresses of this ugly vice.][11]

As an itinerant courtesan, however, Esperanza operates outside the institution of the licensed brothel and thus independently of direct male (if not female) control; this makes the conclusion of the novel even more striking. Contrary to what would be expected in an exemplary novel, whether by Cervantes or another author of the period, this prostitute neither finds herself redeemed from her profession nor enters the convent. The author avoids such conventional and socially favored solutions for repentant prostitutes.[12] Esperanza is neither repentant (since she was forced into the profession) nor redeemed; she is exploited. After all, the narrator claims that Claudia "era tan mezquina y avara, y tan señora de lo que la sobrina ganaba y adquiría, que jamás le daba un solo real para comprar lo que extraordinariamente hubiese menester" (Cervantes 2001, 637) [was so mean and avaricious, and so controlled all her niece's earnings and belongings, that she never gave her a single *real* in order to buy what she needed]. However, to assert that, at the end, the protagonist merely submits to further exploitation (by her husband and father-in-law) would be to interpret the situation from an excessively contemporary perspective. Nevertheless, what remains clear is that at no time does this young woman act independently. She embraces the student who offers her his hand "*como señor* y marido" (648, my emphasis) [as master and husband]. For her, matrimony is by far the more attractive of her severely limited choices, and, in fact, the possibility exists of her obtaining certain satisfaction in the domestic sphere. The ending represents a sort of formulaic (and, again, ironic) authorial stance in which the greatest transgressor of characters is redeemed by the least transgressive of acts: marriage. In his recent treatment of the interlacing of love and the law in the works of Cervantes, Roberto González Echevarría speaks of the function of marriage as "the social contract that resolves conflicts by taming desire and directing it toward reproduction and restored social stability" (2005, xv). I would argue, however, that Cervantes was aware of the conventionality of such views. The fact that he chose a traditional resolution, one that forecloses a socially destabilizing element (clandestine prostitution) does not negate the representational boldness of the narrative that precedes the "happy" ending.[13]

Given Esperanza's imposed alternatives, I would maintain that we cannot apply to *La tía fingida* the second birth thesis posited by Luis Rosales regarding Cervantine characters: "la primera por la gracia de Dios; la segunda, por su propia elección" (1960, 1:358) [the first by the grace of God, the second by personal choice]. If *La tía fingida* is taken into consideration, then Antonio Rey Hazas's updated conclusion that Cervantine literary freedom is "siempre amplia, tolerante, defensora de las peculiaridades individuales, nunca cerrada, excepto, quizá, en eso mismo, en el mantenimiento a ultranza de la *libertad*" (1990, 379–80) [always broad, tolerant, supportive of individual peculiarities, never closed, except perhaps in the maintenance of freedom at all costs] must be attenuated by the problematics of gender constraints. Esperanza's case is not one of free choice but rather of following her own inclination within the param- eters permitted for women at the time. She is neither the archetypical prostitute with the heart of gold (this, in a certain way, will be Cer- vantes's Maritornes) nor the prostitute who is essentially virtuous and is therefore redeemed from her profession by a man who risks his reputa- tion to save her. In this regard, Esperanza does not fit into any of the various types of prostitutes depicted in literature, no matter what the taxonomy (see, e.g., Pierre L. Horn and Mary Beth Pringle's *The Image of the Prostitute in Modern Literature* [1984]). Even though her plight is presented sympathetically, she remains a dehumanized object, a barren symbol that exposes the patriarchal values of the moment. As a young courtesan who is consistently desired, manipulated, and exploited by others, she embodies the type of prostitute who "sums up all the forms of feminine slavery at once" (Beauvoir 1974, 619).

The novella's denouement textualizes the elimination of the social menace and financial loss represented by itinerant, freelance prostitu- tion: One of the women is jailed; the other is married. *La tía fingida* does not contest the view that unregulated prostitution is generally quite severely punished, as is seen in the genre in which it most often appears— the female picaresque novel. For example, the end suffered by the epony- mous protagonists of both Fernando de Rojas's *La Celestina* and Alonso Jerónimo de Salas Barbadillo's *Elena, la hija de la Celestina* is notoriously violent and public.[14] In the jailed woman's case, the punishment meted out in the narration clearly corresponds to laws against *alcahuetería* in force at the time. In Mallorca, for example, legislation dating from 1584 decreed the punishment of five years as a galley slave for male *alcahuetes;*

female pimping was castigated by public flogging and banishment from the island (Puig and Tuset 1986, 79). Most local authorities throughout Spain followed the laws promulgated by Philip II in the 1560s and 1570s to regulate prostitution. These decrees were designed to protect prostitutes from economic exploitation by the brothel administrators, to provide for medical care to prevent the spread of syphilis, to limit the rent that prostitutes could be charged for their *boticas* [rooms], and to encourage the conversion of prostitutes into penitents (Sánchez Ortega 1995, 135–36). Obviously, the reasoning behind such laws was based on containment and control, both financial and social, rather than on any affirmation of female autonomy or philogyny. The eagerly rationalizing discursive formations that controlled sexuality in Spain were not simply parts of speech; they were facts of life to which all deviations were susceptible.

Because clandestine prostitution was perceived to represent a threat to the existing social order, multiple attempts, as we have seen, were made to increase its regulation during the sixteenth and seventeenth centuries. It is worth reiterating that although the concerns underlying the legislation of prostitution and public brothels were framed in a discourse of public safety, health, religion, and a morality that encompassed all of them, they were largely economic. Laws attempted to curb the unwanted competition posed by unregulated urban prostitution in order to funnel the proceeds from the trade to local government and to the Crown. Again, in Mallorca steep fines were levied against men who visited the public brothel carrying arms, who harbored prostitutes who had fled the bordello, or who pimped privately. Funds derived from these fines were split between the Crown and the brothel administrators. Thus, instead of responding to issues of public morality, increased legislation tacitly served to condone and possibly expand prostitution. The laws, in fact, were most concerned with the protection of what was a lucrative source of income for the monarchy (Puig and Tuset 1986, 74–75). At the same time, some of the laws against freelance prostitution seemed to result from pressure exerted by brothel administrators who were losing money (Galán Sánchez and López Beltrán 1984, 165). In Seville, Valencia, Madrid, and other large cities, the public brothels were administered, licensed, inspected, and even maintained by the city government, based on royal ordinances; these ordinances also responded to socioeconomic circumstances and, of course, to the movement and negotiation of passions represented by writers such as Cervantes. It was the sort of control to which sewers and rats would eventually be subjected in European society, and, as such, it became pablum for writers. With respect to a contemporaneous period of control in England, Stallybrass and White posit:

> The creation of a sublimated public body without smells, without coarse laughter, without organs, separate from the Court and the Church on the one hand and the market square, alehouse, street and fairground on the other—this was the great labour of bourgeois culture, complementary to that *institutionalizing inventiveness* of the same period which Foucault has mapped in *Madness and Civilization* and *Discipline and Punish* (1986, 93–94).

In Spain the property that housed city-licensed bordellos was owned by municipal authorities and religious corporations such as cathedral chapters and convents. They would lease the brothels to private individuals, who then rented rooms to the prostitutes, and the income generated would be directed, in principle, toward charitable works. The city government also appointed the men who quite symbolically became *padres*—a polysemous term denoting both patriarchy and the church—or administrators of these city-licensed brothels. As a consequence, the connection between the church and prostitution was, to a certain extent, common knowledge during the period, and not only in Spain.[15] For example, London's main brothel area—the stews—was owned by the bishops of Winchester. Throughout the Middle Ages many bishoprics, abbeys, monasteries, and even the Papacy profited from leasing out their properties to brothel keepers (McCall 1991, 183). Given this state of affairs, it is perhaps surprising that the church and its representatives play no active, definable role in *La tía fingida*: first because it would seem a narrative *lacuna* (in terms of the author's providing a fuller picture) and second because the inclusion of a powerful ecclesiastical figure as a patron or direct overseer would have made Esperanza's transgressive behavior a true force for instability. However, the textual absence of the church serves precisely to underscore the moral and economic threat that Esperanza and Claudia represent. Not only do they circumvent conventional morality but they also siphon off income that, if Esperanza been been placed in a public brothel, would have gone (at least partially and indirectly) to the church.

The delicate economic and moral equilibrium between prostitution and the state is similar to the analogy between the body and the city posited by Stallybrass and White and, in an ampler sense, by Raymond Williams in *The Country and the City* (1973) before them. Class and gender relationships are inscribed in this comparison because the axis of the body is transcoded through the axis of the city, and "whilst the bodily low is 'forgotten', the city's low becomes a site of obsessive pre-occupation, a preoccupation which is itself intimately conceptualized in terms of discourses of the body" (Stallybrass and White 1986, 145). For this reason legislation to control prostitution and sexuality abounded in this period. Regulated prostitution was, in the final analysis, a practi-cal tool to preserve the existing social order by solidifying hierarchical class and gender relationships. Perry points out that this regulation re-inforced the authority of the ruling class over unmarried females and provided jobs to women who might otherwise have starved (1978, 211). In times of inflation, currency devaluation, underemployment, or unemployment, many women were (like *Don Quixote*'s Maritornes) forced into prostitution out of economic necessity. Others were sold into service by their fathers, brothers, boyfriends, or husbands for ten or twenty ducats. Some women were pawned into brothels by those to whom they owed a debt. This social practice was finally prohibited by a 1621 ordinance in Seville (Perry 1978, 201). Prostitution also demon-strated the authority of the city oligarchy to define and confine evil as it simultaneously controlled the profits to be made (211). Within these possibilities we might, of course, find a thematic contemporaneity in *La tía fingida,* were it not for Esperanza's pose and provocation as a woman whose asocial persona wears a faint halo of autism, sort of cast against type.

Cervantes, in fact, had a plethora of referents from which to draw for his novella, and—although all may seem predictable for present-day representation—when seen in their particular historical context, these referents serve to emphasize Cervantes's well-known ability to superim-pose his artistry on works that are presumably secondary in his canon. This skill is evident in the way the socially, if not generically, correct conclusion of the novella resolves the dilemma occasioned by the simultaneous existence of the fear of and the desire for the "low Other" upon which Stallybrass and White theorize. In the narrative, this fear is embodied by a woman who, by all appearances, escapes enclosure and masculine subjugation but who, in fact, has replaced one type of enclosure with another. The quandary evaporates when Esperanza is reintegrated into society and placed under male jurisdiction and its corresponding patterns of normative behavioral practices. Once married off (an unlikely solution in real life at this time), Esperanza is effectively eliminated as a threat to the social order. Removed from the public space that she had appropriated, Esperanza is now safely enclosed within the realm of the private, the sphere historically perceived as women's domain. This return to normalcy serves as proof that there is no disengaged point from which power can be exercised without implicating the female subject in the social forces from which she would escape. In a way Esperanza is a sister to Maritornes and an anti-Dulcinea, but with suitors who are perhaps more Quixotic than the model knight.

Once excluded from the public sphere, women like Esperanza are also barred from the realm in which public opinion can be formed.[16] Thus, they are not privy to the criticism, control, influence, and blindness or insight that they, as part of a public body, could practice over the state, as early modern as it may be. In *La tía fingida* the low is effectively brought under the control of the high, that which both defines the low and defines itself against the low. Esperanza's life, which had also begun as transgression, comes full circle. Stolen in infancy from a church doorstep by the apocryphal aunt, she might very well be an illegitimate daughter of the nobility. Her situation is not, of course, unique in early modern Spanish literature. We should remember that when Guzmán de Alfarache returns to Seville, he discovers that his aged mother has "adopted" an abandoned young girl and is prostituting her throughout the outlying districts and towns (Moreno Mengíbar and Vázquez García 1999, 99). In contrast, in Cervantes's novella *La gitanilla,* the old gypsy woman who stole the infant Preciosa (Constanza de Azevedo) from her parents does not prostitute her, preferring instead to exploit her talents as a singer and dancer.

The narrator's concluding words call attention to the anomalous ending presented in *La tía fingida.* Instead of dying miserable and destitute in a hospital bed, Esperanza enters accepted society for the first time. As the narrator tells us, acknowledging that the ending is quite unorthodox, she finds comfort and (for the society into which she has been admitted) a conventional final resting place:

> Y muy pocas Esperanzas habrá en la vida que, de tan mala como ella la vivía salgan al descanso y buen paradero que ella tuvo; porque las más de su trato pueblan las camas de los hospitales, y mueren en ellos miserables y desventuradas. (Cervantes 2001, 649)

> [And there will be very few Esperanzas who, after such a bad life as she led, will come to the rest and good end that she did, because the majority of miserable and unfortunate women like her fill hospital beds and die in them.]

In fact, Esperanza does not suffer the common end of those who transgress, and the narrator's contrived moralism stresses that fact. Transgression involves limits, origins, and complete trajectories, but the relationship between limit and transgression is never clear-cut. As Foucault summarizes the situation, "Their relationship takes the form of a spiral which no simple infraction can exhaust" (1977a, 35). Esperanza is what Gerald Prince (1988) calls "the disnarrated," because her character is used to evoke a purely desired world, to express broken dreams or unjustified beliefs, failures, miscalculations, and the like. As the disnarrated, Esperanza reveals herself in the passages, sentences, and terms that express events that do or did not happen, from both the perspective of the narrator and the narrative.

With respect to the high/low scheme that we have been following to decode transgression in this novella, some might ask whether we can speak only of the category of the low when there is no high to oppose it. The fact is that the high pole would be the societal forces that are only subliminally represented in this text. The traditional society of the period discussed is precisely an implicit presence that determines the conduct of the members of the low pole. Simply put, as in all binary constructs, the dialectic between the two poles is a given, without need for the physical and detailed presence of each. Just as prostitution would enslave Esperanza, so too would the institutions that distort the true political representation of people like her. If the power of premodern societies functioned essentially through signs and levies, the higher society that is textually invisible in *La tía fingida* has assumed not only its existence but also the control of imperceptible techniques of power that were quite palpable to the lower strata.

Given the foregoing, there is no doubt that *La tía fingida* is a transgressive work in its presentation of the "low" theme of prostitution, but not specifically or fully in its sociohistorical perspective nor in its depiction of gender relationships. Esperanza's marriage saves her from attempted rape by the first student and continued exploitation by the procuress aunt. Nevertheless, at no time is a third option presented to Esperanza, one that would allow for free choice. Such a "progressive" attitude would be difficult, if not impossible, for a (male or female) writer to textualize at the time. As a consequence, the ending is presented as a happy one, with Esperanza enthusiastically accepting the hand of the would-be rapist. At this moment, in fact, he is cast into the role of liberator, or white knight. Thus, the author of *La tía fingida* would seem to view marriage unironically as a possible means of salvation for the professional prostitute and, perhaps, as a response to contemporaneous theological debates surrounding prostitution. This attitude is not absent from other Cervantine texts, such as *El casamiento engañoso,* in which the protagonists' marriage, while it lasts, is a relatively happy one. This is not the case in other literary genres, specifically with the female picaresque. In *La pícara Justina,* to pick a canonical work, through the protagonist's three marriages, Francisco López de Ubeda "casts doubt on the effectiveness of marriage to reform the protagonist and, by implication, questions its power as a social institution to protect society fully from the moral weaknesses of all women" (A. Cruz 1989a, 151).[17] The distancing from and implicit questioning of the deterministic and negative worldview of the picaresque novel that we find in *La tía fingida* (e.g., women are whores, and all marriages are a sham) might be interpreted as another facet of Cervantine discourse in this novella. This is especially possible given the fact that marriage is a central, recurring theme in Cervantes's exemplary novels. Thus, within the discourse of this novella, Esperanza can be rewarded with a happy ending, since she has done little to threaten the hierarchically constructed society in which she lives.

By the same token, in the text this prostitute is not condemned for moral transgression. She is treated more as a minor and is held unaccountable, morally or otherwise, for her acts; the responsibility falls upon her guardian. This is possible because, unlike the *alcahueta* Claudia, who (like Celestina) is punished for assuming the position of a clandestine *putero,* Esperanza has usurped no power position. Indeed, *La tía fingida* castigates not the prostitute but the system of authority that imprisons her. In reality, Esperanza obtains a husband in exchange for her abundant physical attributes. Her beauty, her desirability, is the only dowry that she, as "low Other," brings to the marriage. Examined from this perspective, her marriage is revealed, at least to twenty-first-century readers, as a mere substitution of *cárcel de amor,* a simple exchange of authority figures, as Esperanza is delivered from the tutelage of the aunt to the custody of the husband. In effect, regarding Renaissance marriage, Romeo De Maio states, "Por lo común el matrimonio era para la mujer un cambio de prisión, de la patria potestad a la marital" (1988, 102). [For women marriage was usually a change of prison, from parental to marital authority.] Of course, there is ample room here to speculate about the inherent possibilities for transgression upon exchanging an abusive maternal figure for the uncertainty of a husband and father-in-law whose reasons for proceeding with the marriage are far from even loosely based on romantic expectations.

Esperanza, the Exemplary Prostitute

Finally, perhaps most strange to the contemporary reader of this story of prostitution is the surprising lack of sexuality and sensuality, the subtext of which I have tried to recover by juxtaposing it with power relationships.[18] This aspect of the narrative runs contrary to the notion of obscene erotic discourse that much existing criticism of this novella has attempted to reveal, if not condemn. Consider, for example, Vicente de la Fuente's condemnation of the novella as "altamente inmoral y justamente prohibida. . . . Podría ser una excelente novela, suprimidas las obscenidades impertinentes y de pésimo gusto con que la manchó" (1884–89, 2:419) [highly immoral and justly prohibited. . . . It could be an excellent novel if the impertinent obscenities with which he tarnished it in such poor taste were removed]. Even in more recent years, E. T. Aylward has stated that the work was so bawdy that Cervantes wisely chose to omit it from his collected exemplary novels (1982, 13). Interestingly enough, the scenarios of prostitution that pepper Cervantes's highly canonical novella *Rinconete y Cortadillo* have aroused little if any such moralistic controversy. Nonetheless, the female prostitutes that populate Monipodio's microcosm of the Sevillian underworld in that work are far more abject than Esperanza, ensnared as they are in the psychology of abuse inflicted by their pimps (see Cervantes 2001, 196–99).

In fact, Esperanza is never seen occupied in sexual commerce. Instead, her ironic protestation "bien limpia soy" (366) is mimetized by the text, which is as chaste as its protagonist. Any erotic elements that, given the theme of prostitution, we might expect to find (and will find in *Don Quixote*) are conspicuously absent. Indeed, in this case the prostitute's transgression is preterit, unassumed, and concealed (or even pretended). While outside their home, neither Esperanza nor Claudia displays the outward trappings of the urban prostitute. They dress in costly attire and are accompanied by a retinue of squires and *dueñas*. Neither wears the distinctive and requisite garb of the prostitute: the obligatory yellow headdress (*toca açafranada*) that served to distinguish (albeit quite unreliably) the courtesan from the honest lady.[19] Claudia does, however, sport the official literary symbol of hypocrisy: the large-beaded rosary, a familiar Renaissance self-fashioning.

Because Esperanza's history of prostitution is understood through allusions and narrative half-truths, a great disparity exists between *La tía fingida* and Rojas's *Celestina,* which Cervantes himself described as an "obra divina si encubriera más lo humano" [a divine work if it would conceal the human more].[20] Is, perhaps, *La tía fingida* precisely the work that conceals the human, thus providing an implicit corrective to the work of Rojas? Given the perspective of transgression, we can read this as an anomalous text in which a prostitute is seen in another light. A "low" woman, discrete and beautiful, she is ultimately attractive and, in a certain way, quite moving. And in terms of the narration, she is a virgin, just as the text that encloses her still is for most critics of Cervantes's fiction. In fact, as Jorge Luis Borges emphasizes in his essays "Pierre Menard, autor del *Quijote*" and "Magias parciales del *Quijote*" (Borges 1974), the author of *La tía fingida* reveals a modern sensitivity that is very similar to the type of metafictional consciousness-raising that Cervantes displays in other works.

I do not dismiss the many speculations about the composition of this novella raised by those who would disprove Cervantine authorship. Nevertheless, the stylistic evidence in favor of Cervantine authorship adduced by critics such as Julián Apráiz (1906), José Toribio Medina (see Cervantes 1919), and José Luis Madrigal (2003) is extremely compelling. Tangentially, Cervantes has featured prostitutes in other works, of course: la Gananciosa, la Escalanta, and Juliana la Cariharta from the previously mentioned *Rinconete y Cortadillo;* Repulida, Pizpita, and Mostrenca from *El rufián viudo;* and Maritornes and the itinerant whores at the first inn from *Don Quixote* (addressed shortly)—all of whom represent the lowest stratum of prostitution. Perhaps it is also worth remembering that Cervantes resided in Madrid on Calle de Francos (known as Calle de Cervantes today), in the heart of the city's theater district. At the time, one of the city's three bordellos was located on that street, the brothel that was frequented by distinguished clientele (Sánchez Ortega 1995, 136). That proximity, plus Cervantes's years spent on the road, might well have provided considerable material from which to create such characters. At the same time, the questionable comportment of the women in Cervantes's immediate family—his sisters Magdalena and Andrea de Cervantes; Andrea's illegitimate daughter, Constanza de Ovando; and his own daughter, Isabel de Saavedra (called "the Cervantas")—undoubtedly fostered his tolerant attitude toward such women in need.[21] However, in spite of the undeniable and perhaps overwhelmingly Cervantine discourse of this novella, it continues to be silenced. The same occurs with certain poems that Cervantists are unwilling to accept as his: Their perceived erotic, scatological, or vituperative nature makes them distasteful to those who would insist on imposing obligatory chasteness on canonical literary figures (see Martín 1991, 156–66).

Since it is highly doubtful that authorship of *La tía fingida* will ever be definitively proved, it might be argued that the very same notion of author is what leads critics, of various schools of thought and historical moments, to vary little in their reflections. For this reason, I prefer to accept the notion of author proposed by Foucault in his 1969 essay "Qu'est-ce qu'un auteur?" [What Is an Author?] (see Foucault 1977b). He defines an author not according to his or her relationship with the real writer or the fictitious narrator but rather as what denotes a structure, type of work or language, style, attitude toward the reader or even toward a collection of miscellaneous writings. In other words, the author is treated as a function of the discourse, as a matter of public perception via the reception of written texts. From that perspective, it is essential to consider the characteristics that support this discourse and determine how different it is from others.

Because *La tía fingida* is, at all levels, a history of pretense and transgression, which are hardly disparate elements, the conventional notion of what an author is must cede to anonymity. In concluding this discussion of the novella, I submit that it is precisely the condition of the death of the author, as proposed by Roland Barthes (2001), that permits the interpretative richness of the text. In this sense the reader's primary task is not to ascertain whether it is Cervantes's ego or narrative experience that controls the story; moreover, he cannot be the center of intention by means of which we can examine the text. This conclusion is to be construed neither as a facile hermeneutic relativism about Cervantes's reception across the centuries nor as a deconstructionist paradox about authority in texts. On the contrary, the many transgressions of *La tía fingida* are another aspect of the very evident contemporaneity of this *autor fingido* whose name could be—and probably is—Cervantes.

Maritornes and Rural Prostitution in Don Quixote

A Cervantine woman of dubious repute who is considerably better known than Esperanza occupies a quite different sphere of prostitution: Maritornes, the Asturian servant girl at Juan Palomeque's inn, is one of the most indelible characters in Cervantes's masterpiece *Don Quixote*. The narrator places her, along with the unnamed innkeeper's daughter, in the oxymoronic category of "semidoncellas" in one of the novel's greatest ludic-erotic moments. In chapter 43 of part 1 of the novel, the two young women play a trick on the knight, leaving him hanging by his hand through the opening in the hayloft. It is not necessary to elaborate on the very obvious erotic allusions to (1) penetration (*paja*, meaning both "hay" and "sexual relations") and (2) frustrations and sexual irritations and arousal [*enojos*], double entendres that are all commonplace in Golden Age erotic literature. It is also unnecessary to revisit the sensual description of the "hand" that the knight proffers to the ladies in order that the innkeeper's daughter might, as the Asturian tells him, "desahogar con ella el gran deseo que a este agujero la ha traído, tan a peligro de su honor" [so that with it she can ease the great desire that has brought her to this opening at such great risk to her honor].[22] Readers who have not been blinkered by a prudish Cervantine critical tradition cannot help but feel that the organ being presented by the knight is of a different and more sexual nature: "No os la doy para que la beséis, sino para que miréis la contestura de sus nervios, la trabazón de sus músculos, la anchura y espaciosidad de sus venas, de donde sacaréis qué tal debe de ser la fuerza del brazo que tal mano tiene" (pt. 1:43). ["I do not give it to thee so that thou mayest kiss it, but so that thou mayest gaze upon the composition of its sinews, the consistency of its muscles, the width and capacity of its veins, and from this conjecture the might of the arm to which such a hand belongeth" (Grossman, 380)].

Unlike the chaste role that Esperanza plays in *La tía fingida*, Maritornes's memorable appearances in *Don Quixote* are characterized by an outpouring of playful erotic wordplay and innuendo similar to the language in the quotation just cited. But in spite of this (or perhaps because of it), the young servant girl has left relatively little impression in Cervantes criticism, although the description of her physical delights is remarkably expressive and succinct: "ancha de cara, llana de cogote, de nariz roma, del un ojo tuerta y del otro no muy sana" (pt. 1:16) ["a broad face, a back of the head that was flat, a nose that was snubbed, and one eye that was blind, while the other was not in very good condition" (109)]. Because of these rather unfortunate features, which Cervantes narrates with such vividness and irony, Maritornes is banished from the roster of female beauties who increasingly dazzle the other characters in part 1 of the novel, from the imaginary Dulcinea to Marcela, through Dorotea and Luscinda, and culminating in the exotic Moor Zoraida.[23] Quite to the contrary, Maritornes appears on that other list—briefly mentioned on page 40—which is perhaps not as lengthy but deserves greater critical scrutiny: the catalogue of Cervantine women (like Esperanza) of loose virtue.

If, in the social reality of the time, prostitutes occupied a social space that was both liminal and central and to a certain extent both hidden and evident, as we have discussed, then Maritornes, as an occasional rural sex worker, would be doubly marginalized within the binary contradictions that are so peculiar to *Don Quixote*. Because she dwells on the bottom rung of society's ladder—or close to it—and is physically repugnant, Maritornes also falls into the category of "low Other." She shows us, the readers, and the other characters in the novel who we are not and therefore becomes an actor in the construction of the subjectivity of others. Curiously enough, however, she also functions as an object of fascination and even desire, as we shall see.

It is remarkable that prostitutes have appeared relatively infrequently in feminist criticism engaged in what Ruth El Saffar (1989) called the recovery of the feminine in Cervantes's novels.[24] Equally revealing is the fact that the theme of prostitution does not deserve an entry in César Vidal's *Enciclopedia del Quijote* (1999) or similar compilations, in spite of their inclusion of entries for Maritornes. Because of these lacunae, it is worthwhile to round out this chapter on prostitution in the works of Cervantes by examining the rustic context in which Maritornes operates without necessarily recurring to the spent formula according to which only three viable options existed for women in Golden Age Spain: wife, nun, or whore.

Unfortunately, when we try to reconstruct a referential context for Maritornes, an obstacle immediately emerges: Historical studies generally focus on prostitution as a strictly urban social phenomenon no matter where it occurs—in bordellos, official *mancebías,* whorehouses, bathhouses, private homes (Esperanza's modus operandi), or on street corners. Historians and sociologists both point out that since medieval times, when prostitution became institutionalized, it flourished in incipient urban centers.[25] Spanish brothel literature is situated mainly in such urban environments, and it centers on such unforgettable figures and prototypes as Celestina (Salamanca), Lozana (Córdoba/Rome), and Esperanza (Salamanca). A great number of working girls weave in and out of Cervantes's novels and dramatic works, from the more or less "honest" courtesans such as Estefanía de Caicedo from *El casamiento engañoso* and Hipólita from *Persiles y Sigismunda* to the common whores named earlier and La Colindres, who—together with her constable pimp—tricks and robs the unfortunate Breton in *El coloquio de los perros.* Prostitutes also figure more or less prominently in the play *El rufián dichoso,* and in the interludes *El rufián viudo* and *El vizcaíno fingido.* Indeed, this list is only representative of many other examples.

But the trade was not confined to the urban social environments inhabited by these characters; it frequently transpired in rural locations.

Consequently, Jacques Rossiaud opens his seminal study on medieval prostitution by stating, "The towns were not the only place in which venal amours could thrive. Fleeting allusions in urban documentation give us glimpses of a flourishing rural prostitution" (1988, 3).[26] Ángel Luis Molina Molina proposes a similar demarcation in a more recent study of European prostitution, and his analysis stresses the indispensable role of literature as a source of historical evidence. Although he studies the "horizontal profession" in Spain's large urban centers, Molina also confirms the existence of allusions to a prosperous rural prostitution in historical documents and literary texts (1998, 13). Evidently, when we abandon urban centers, we confront a world that is still submerged in darkness and whose workings are difficult to pinpoint.[27] Since prostitution conducted surreptitiously outside municipal brothels was even more clandestine than its municipally controlled counterpart, it escaped not only official control but also documentation in the historical archive.

Peasant prostitutes would ply their trade among shepherds, travelers, and day laborers, whom they would arrange to meet in back streets and corners, huts, taverns, and roadside inns (Moreno Mengíbar and Vázquez García 1999, 105). A perfect example of this type of sex provider is the woman in the Ínsula Barataria episodes of *Don Quixote* who appears before Sancho and accuses the pig farmer of rape. After ascertaining that her accusations are lies, the new governor expels her from the island under penalty of two hundred lashes (the usual punishment for prostitution at that time) and orders her client, "Andad con Dios a vuestro lugar con vuestro dinero, y de aquí adelante, si no le queréis perder, procured que no os venga en voluntad de yogar con nadie" (pt. 2:45). ["Go with God to your home with your money, and from now on, if you don't want to lose it, try to hold off your desire to lie with anybody" (752)]. In addition, at the end of the novel, Sancho alludes to the threat that shepherds' lust can represent for innocent country girls, insisting to his master, "Tan bien suelen andar los amores y los no buenos deseos por los campos como por las ciudades y por las pastorales chozas como por los reales palacios" (pt. 2:67). ["Love and unchaste desires are as likely in the countryside as in the cities, in shepherd's huts as in royal palaces" (901)]. Relating the foregoing to venal love, we should keep in mind that with respect to country prostitutes (1) the women who worked in municipal brothels were in a distinct minority and

(2) there exists a great deal less documentation on their activities than on the activities of city prostitutes (Moreno Mengíbar and Vázquez García 1999, 96–97).

Consequently, if we wish to amplify the history of rural prostitution during Spain's Golden Age, we must scrutinize precisely those fleeting allusions that can be found in literary texts such as those of Cervantes. As servant at an inn and rural prostitute, Maritornes functions not only as a verisimilar literary figure but also as a historical document. As the historian Teofilo Ruiz points out:

> Novels are not like archival records; nor do they have the proximity to actual events that primary sources, the necessary tools of monographic literature, have. Fictional works nonetheless render powerful insights into the mental world of a remote past. The vignettes and sketches that move the narrative are based on a grasp of real life that can seldom be obtained from standard historical sources. (2001, 244–45)

Seen from this perspective, rural prostitution is as revealing of a historical imaginary as any other aspect of Golden Age social life.

What, therefore, does Maritornes's story tell us about her *mundillo* and about the power relationships discussed in the first part of this chapter? To begin, since ancient times (and just as occurs today with Spain's so-called *puticlubes*), public brothels tended to cluster around inns and taverns. These were ideal places for prostitution to flourish, since they were frequented by traveling artisans and tradesmen, leather and grain industry workers, cattlemen, drovers, and, of course, ruffians and pimps (see Lacarra 1993, 41–42). María Eugenia Lacarra cites the traditional connection between prostitution and the inns and taverns in the city of Salamanca, which can be deduced from city ordinances that prohibited inn and tavern keepers from admitting "muger que gane con su persona ni publica ni secretamente, ni biua escandalosamente, ni la consientan, aunque digan que es para su servicio" (41–43) [women who did business with their body, either publicly or secretly, or lived scandalously: this should not be allowed, even if the women claim it is of benefit to them]. In addition, in the late Middle Ages in areas of the kingdom of Granada that lacked a brothel, inn and tavern keepers were permitted to admit prostitutes to their premises in exchange for payment of an annual fee to the authority in charge of the kingdom's brothels (Menjot 1994, 193 n. 9). Years before Maritornes's time, a series of historical contingencies provides perhaps another contour for Cervantes's thinking. In 1494 the Catholic Monarchs passed a law prohibiting inn and tavern keepers throughout their kingdoms from admitting public women, pimps, or other lowlifes for a period longer than half a day (Lacarra 1993, 43). In a similar manner and as a result of the establishment of municipal brothels, a great number of laws were promulgated to control inn and tavern keepers in several Castilian cities. In Malaga, after 1492, women were prohibited from eating in or spending longer than one night at taverns unless they were ill and unable to leave (43).

Given this empirical background on attempts by the Crown to regulate, benefit from, and contain the spread of prostitution, we can contextualize Maritornes's social and sexual functions as a *moza de venta* whose inn is located on a dusty back road of La Mancha. As such, our Asturian would be one of those young girls who, according to many Spanish proverbs, mature early as a result of overhandling: "Moza mesonera, más tentada que breva"; "Figa verdal i moza de ostal, palpandose madura" (quoted in Joly 1982, 410). This association between inn servants and prostitution, which is fully documented in historical archives, is not restricted to the Christian world. In a 1991 study, Mark Meyerson asserts that since the fifteenth century the *alfondech* or *funduq,* described in documentation as a *hospitium maurorum* and located within the *morerías,* functioned as an inn for Muslim travelers and merchants and almost invariably as a center for Muslim prostitution (154). He affirms that the majority of the *funduqs* were quasi bordellos (155), since Christian brothels were strictly reserved for members of that faith and fornication by a non-Christian with a prostitute was considered to be an abomination and punishable with death by burning (Menjot 1994, 197).

Moreno Mengíbar and Vázquez García note that scullery maids and servant girls constitute another type of clandestine prostitute known for the facility with which they could be "seduced." As a result, on numerous occasions the local Sevillian power structure prohibited so-called *casas de gula* [eating establishments] from providing lodging for their clients (Moreno Mengíbar and Vázquez García 1999, 98). Perhaps this explains in part why Juan Palomeque's inn lacked similar comforts. But literary representation had been established earlier; therefore, it is not surprising that inn whores abound in picaresque literature. One example is Lazarillo de Tormes's mother, Antoña Pérez, who is flogged and then becomes a servant in the mesón de la Solana, where, according to Lázaro, she suffers "mil importunidades." The servant girl Maritornes, together with her colleagues La Tolosa and La Molinera, inherits this tradition and demonstrates how the business operated.[28] But as with everything in Cervantes, we are dealing with an extraordinary literary re-elaboration of a daily reality. Nevertheless, in continuing to evaluate the relevance of such women in Cervantes's work, it is worth remembering that the first human beings with whom Alonso Quijano—recently transformed into Don Quijote—interacts, are precisely two transient whores. These two easy women are examples of a slice of life that is familiar to all and that the novel's literary elements (the Quixotic transformations and the chivalric substratum) do not manage to conceal.

Within this reality Tolosa and Molinera, as well as Maritornes, have been interpreted as tragic and unfortunate creatures. After all, it would seem that Maritornes keeps her appointment with the mule driver not out of desire but out of obligation. As the narrator tells us, the girl "presumía muy de hidalga, y no tenía por afrenta estar en aquel ejercicio de servir en la venta, porque decía ella que desgracias y malos sucesos la habían traído a aquel estado" (Cervantes 2004, pt. 1:16) ["prided herself on being very wellborn and did not consider it an affront to be a servant in the inn because, she said, misfortunes and bad luck had brought her to that state" (Grossman, 112)]. As an occasional prostitute, Maritornes definitely has a referent in real life, since women entered the occupation for many different reasons: pressure from interested parties (as in Esperanza's case), male sexual abuse, and (as in the majority of cases) financial necessity. Many prostitutes were orphans or widows with no means of support, victims of war, or unemployed outsiders or immigrants. In the case of minors, parents would function as intermediaries in procuring jobs for them as servants, and this domestic service could constitute the first step toward female prostitution (Menjot 1994, 200). Indeed, the persistence of prostitution at the time corroborates the reduced options available to impecunious women who lacked male support and protection in a man's world.

As a character, Maritornes might find herself in any of these unfortunate situations. For precisely this reason, her name, as "sonoro y significativo" as others in the novel, is a variant of María—like Marica, Marina, and Mariquita—which are emblematic of the inn servant (see Joly 1982, 418).[29] To return for a moment to the *rameras* from the first inn, a typical brothel custom—according to the Roman *valijero* who instructs Lozana in the various types of prostitutes—is that upon entering the bordello, the presumptuous ones "se mudan los nombres con cognombres altivos y de grand sonido, como son: la Esquivela, la Cesarina, la Imperia y doña Tal . . . y ansí discurren mostrando por sus apellidos el precio de su labor" (Delicado 1969, 104) [adopt high-sounding sobriquets, such as la Esquivela, la Cesarina, la Imperia, and doña Tal . . . thus revealing by their names the price of their labors"]. Of course, Cervantes's ongoing parody deflates the elevated nicknames of his itinerant whores to Tolosa and Molinera, the latter resonant with erotic overtones and emblematic of her profession. As daughter of a miller (*molinero*), she is inextricably related to the world of sex, sexuality, and prostitution.[30] Augustin Redondo (1983) has analyzed in great detail the function of the mill in early modern literature as a locus of erotic initiation and sexual dalliance, a locus related to both fertility rites and the underworld. In the erotic idiom, to mill [*moler*]—and anything connected with that action (flour, sifting, sieve)—denotes sexual intercourse.[31]

Colón Calderón has examined the social context within which La Tolosa and La Molinera operate, registering their humble social condition as, respectively, daughters of a shoemaker and a miller and for whom prostitution was most likely the only ticket out of poverty (2005, 313). These young women are probably not plying their trade at the inn, in spite of their presence at its door, and their relationship with their mule driver traveling companions is ambiguous.[32] Colón Calderón proposes that they might be heading for Seville precisely because that large metropolis was known as a center for high-paying prostitution, where a working girl might earn up to 4,000 ducats a year (316).

It does not pay, however, to dramatize these fictional beings excessively. Readers should avoid adhering too closely to Miguel de Unamuno's overly tragic (or perhaps spiritual) sense of life that produces this exclamation in reference to Cervantes's prostitutes: "¡Pobres mujeres que sencillamente, sin ostentación cínica, doblan la cerviz a la necesidad del vicio y a la brutalidad del hombre, y para ganarse el pan se resignan a la infamia!" (1988, 178). [Unfortunate women who simply, without cynical ostentation, bow their heads to the needs of vice and the brutality of men, and resign themselves to infamy in order to earn their daily bread!] We should consider, instead, that (very different from Esperanza in *La tía fingida*) everything related to Maritornes, above all her assignation with the mule driver, occurs within the farcical realm of theatrical interludes: the absolute darkness and confusion, the silence interrupted by shouts and struggles, the collapsed bed, the constable's fortuitous arrival, and Juan Palomeque's resounding oath "¿Adónde estás, puta?" (Cervantes 2004, pt. 1:16). ["Where are you, you whore?" (Grossman, 114)]. Within this historical context and burlesque literary frame, it is to be expected that Maritornes would feel neither guilt nor shame for the life that she lives and would not attempt to curb the demands of her profession. The question, of course, will be put into perspective by the Mexican baroque poet Sor Juana Inés de la Cruz, when she writes this in her famous *redondilla* "Hombres necios que acusáis":"¿O cuál es más de culpar, / aunque cualquiera mal haga: / la que peca por la paga, / o el que paga por pecar" (1985, 405). [Who is more to blame, / although anyone can do wrong: / she who sins for payment / or he who pays to sin?] Centuries later, in his *Vida de Don Quijote y Sancho,* Unamuno seems to perceive Maritornes as a woman who is capable of performing miracles in spite of the fact that she is not a virgin and concludes, "No peca Maritornes ni por ociosidad y codicia, ni por lujuria; es decir, apenas peca. Ni trata de vivir sin trabajar ni trata de seducir a los hombres. Hay un fondo de pureza en su grosera impureza" (1988, 240). [Maritornes does not sin out of sloth, greed or lust; that is to say, she hardly sins at all. She neither tries to live without working nor attempts to seduce men. There is a reserve of purity in her gross impurity.] Whether or not we are willing to accept this sanitized and morally unblemished version of Maritornes, the fact is that if historically or in terms of fiction we can never determine the morality or ethics of prostitution and its mercantile function in the relationships between the sexes, the literary focus serves to bring this "low" topic to the fore, for better or worse.

In fact, in his study on the relationship between economics and ethics in Cervantes, Steven Hutchinson examines the modalities of debts and payments that construct value in human relationships: promises, penitence, revenge, punishments, and marriage. Although the ethics of venal love does not enter into his taxonomy, Hutchinson examines in detail the notion of promises. *Don Quixote,* he notes, contains promises that are explicit and implicit, conditional and unconditional, specific and ambiguous, sincere and deceitful, feasible and absurd (2001, 129). As a maidservant who keeps her promises and her word, Maritornes distinguishes herself among other characters—Don Fernando being the prime example—who have much higher social rank but less integrity. For this reason, the narrator assures the reader:

> Había el arriero concertado con ella que aquella noche se refocilarían juntos, y ella le había dado su palabra de que, en estando sosegados los huéspedes y durmiendo sus amos, le iría a buscar y satisfacerle el gusto en cuanto le mandase. Y cuéntase desta buena moza que jamás dio semejantes palabras que no las cumpliese, aunque las diese en un monte y sin testigo alguno. (Cervantes 2004, pt. 1:16)

> [The muledriver had arranged with Maritornes that they would take their pleasure that night, and she had given her word that when all the guests were quiet and her master and mistress asleep, she would come to him and satisfy his desire in any way he asked. It was said of this good servant that she never gave her word without keeping it, even if she gave it on a mountain with no witnesses.] (Grossman, 111–12)

Equally reliable and businesslike is Estefanía de Caicedo from Cervantes's *El casamiento engañoso,* who offers herself in matrimony to Alférez Campuzano in all frankness, telling him, "Simplicidad sería si yo quisiese venderme a vuesa merced por santa. Pecadora he sido y aún ahora lo soy" (2001, 525). [It would be foolish if I wished to sell myself to you as a saint. I have been and still am a sinner.] Hutchinson notes with respect to Estefanía's liberal marriage proposal that no male family members enter into this transaction and that she negotiates and closes the deal herself (175). I refer readers interested in the notion of women as merchandise to Hutchinson's study, but rather than ponder whether Estefanía can be considered a prostitute because she sells herself, I prefer to see in her initiative another demonstration of the type of self-knowledge and free will that characterizes Cervantes's female characters.

Ultimately, there is no need to overstate either the venal mercantile reality or the ethics of prostitution, within which we can contextualize Maritornes, the inn, and Juan Palomeque's daughter and for that mat-

ter Esperanza. Although these remarkable characters illustrate the functioning of power between men and women who sell sex in early modern
Spain, what really matters here is their literary re-creation, done by a
hand that is expert at honing and accommodating reality to the pen. In
Don Quixote, Cervantes's genius lies precisely in capturing the details of
a rustic environment, with its inn as human and social crossroads, and
creating great literature from it. The contemporary reader would have
recognized the scenario with no problem whatsoever: the squalid inn;
the roguish innkeeper, Juan Palomeque, and the world he connotes; the
innkeeper's daughter of doubtful virtue; and Maritornes—the last two a
pair of *semidoncellas* who appear to be quite well versed in erotic love.[33]
For this reason, and if we endorse our suppositions with the history
of sexuality without having to return to Foucault, none of the sexual
activities of Maritornes and her cohort are presented as abnormal, or
even as reprehensible, but as natural, acceptable, and accepted. They are
described openly, as they were or are, and from a comic angle in keeping
with the humorous spirit of the novel. Unlike Esperanza, a young girl as
unattractive as Maritornes would find it difficult to survive the competition in a city brothel or high-class private house of ill repute. Her lack
of physical charms would force her to exercise her trade sporadically
with people of very low social rank and even fewer expectations, such as
the mule driver. To involve ourselves in such considerations, however,
means to enter into the slippery world of perceptions of beauty, of the
personal tastes of the clients, and of the cultural codes of the epoch.
Therefore, it is not necessary to explore in greater depth the fact that
prostitution creates its own hierarchies and demands, a pyramid that
attests to its own self-sufficiency as an institution.

After having contextualized our protagonist within her professional
sisterhood, it is time to consider her nocturnal encounter with Don Quijote, which is so parodically punitive for him. Curiously, up to this moment in the novel, Maritornes is the only woman who inspires lascivious
thoughts in the imagination of the aging bachelor-cum-adventurer. The
beleaguered knight fantasizes that the chatelain's daughter will come to
lie with him, at which thought "se comenzó a cuitar y a pensar en el
peligroso trance en que su honestidad se había de ver, y propuso en su
corazón de no cometer alevosía a su señora Dulcinea del Toboso" (pt.
1:16) ["he became distressed as he began to think of the dangerous
predicament in which his virtue would find itself, and he resolved in

his heart not to betray his lady Dulcinea of Toboso" (113)]. Given the history of his attraction to Aldonza Lorenzo from afar, the moment in which Alonso Quijano/Don Quijote grasps Maritornes to him and fingers her chemise is probably the only moment in the life of this geriatric and celibate *hidalgo* that he enters into erotic physical contact with a woman.[34] And he notes—filtering his desire through the chivalric linguistic code—that if his vowed faithfulness to Dulcinea did not present an impossible obstacle, "no fuera yo tan sandio caballero, que dejara pasar en blanco la venturosa ocasión en que vuestra gran bondad me ha puesto" (pt. 1:16) ["I would not be so foolish a knight as to turn away from so gladsome an opportunity as this that thy great kindness affords me" (114)]. In this comic and totally farcical scene, Maritornes's primitive and mercenary, although seemingly naïve, sexuality clashes with Don Quijote's scrupulously repressed desires.[35] The knight gives himself up totally to his erotic fantasies, and after the beating that crowns the episode and after asking Sancho to guard the secret until after his death, he relates to his squire his version of what happened:

> Poco ha que a mí vino la hija del señor deste Castillo, que es la más apuesta y fermosa doncella que en gran parte de la tierra se puede hallar. ¿Qué te podría decir del adorno de su persona? ¿Qué de su gallardo entendimiento? ¿Qué de otras cosas ocultas, que, por guardar la fe que debo a mi señora Dulcinea del Toboso, dejaré pasar intactas y en silencio? (pt. 1:17)

> ["A short while ago the daughter of the lord of this castle came to me, and she is one of the most elegant and beauteous damsels to be found anywhere on earth. What can I say of the grace of her person, the nobility of her understanding, the other hidden things which, in order to keep the faith I owe to my lady Dulcinea of Toboso, I shall keep inviolate and pass over in silence?"] (117)

His words demonstrate not only male boasting but also a type of wistful and wishful thinking of an elderly gentleman. And in order to excuse his impotence, he explains:

> Al tiempo que yo estaba con ella en dulcísimos y amorosísimos coloquios, sin que yo la viese ni supiese por dónde venía vino una mano

pegada a algún brazo de algún descomunal gigante y asentome una
puñalada en las quijadas, tal, que las tengo todas bañadas en san-
gre. . . . Por donde conjeturo que el tesoro de la hermosura desta
doncella le debe de guardar algún encantado moro, y no debe de ser
para mí. (pt 1:17)

["As I was engaged in sweet and amorous conversation with her,
without my seeing or knowing whence it came, a hand attached to
the arm of some monstrous giant came down and struck me so hard
a blow on the jaws that they were bathed in blood. . . . And from this
I conjecture that the treasure of this maiden's beauty must be guarded
by some enchanted Moor and is not intended for me."] (117)

Don Quijote's perspective on what happened at the inn differs from
that presented by the narrator and received by the reader, since what
was an intense if frustrated erotic encounter for the knight is enter-
tainment and laughter for the rest. For this reason, if Don Quijote
provides a grotesquely parodic and pathetic version of the impetuous,
virile knight errant—an evident re-creation of the widely studied carni-
valesque upside-down world—Maritornes produces the same with the
beautiful and worldly courtesan, who has been downgraded here to a
lowly inn whore.

The episodes with Maritornes are firmly anchored in the supremely
human world of Juan Palomeque's inn. According to José Emilio
González, Maritornes is mainly a grotesque caricature and shares something in common with Diego Velázquez's dwarfs and monsters (1993,
116).[36] Álvaro Bautista has written that Cervantes is not treating Maritornes ironically but is providing a situation through which Don Quijote can mock the Asturian's nocturnal adventures and through which
she, in turn, can mock the knight's epic ideals. But in the end, everyone
returns to the realm of the human, and the author ends by comprehend-
ing rather than sanctioning his characters, and he involves the reader in
a community that finally happily accepts those who have fallen into
ridicule (1997, 417).

In several Golden Age literary works, desire takes a position of power
against the rigid morality of church and state and its sociojuridical po-
licing of sex. In many senses, we see the coexistence of two distinct
worlds, as in *Don Quixote* and *La tía fingida*: One—bound by the codes

of honor and shame, by theological formulations and government or-dinances—struggled to contain sexuality; the other tested the official limits placed on sexual practices and human desire (T. Ruiz 2001, 263). The latter would harbor Celestina, Lozana, and other women like them. Cervantes opposes his ironic, burlesque, although in the long run tol-erant view to the unrestrained sexuality that the inspectors of public morality tried to channel toward abstinence or the public brothel. It seems that, to Cervantes, prostitution—which was a source of moral and socioeconomic anxiety and debate up to and during the writing of *Don Quixote*—was simply one more fact of life, a function and result of economic need, highly visible and relevant, and therefore ripe for trans-formation into literature.[37] Consequently, the episodes with Maritornes and the mule driver, Don Quijote's dubbing by prostitutes, and the erotic trick that the girls play on the knight in the hayloft in chapter 43 of part 1 are all steeped in an atmosphere so redolent of familiarity that the purely literary elements cannot eradicate it.

In sum, the world of the inn that Cervantes represented had es-tablished certain systems of control that would have an effect that, if not clear in legal terms, would at least be present in the attitudes held with respect to Maritornes's occupation. Based on this indeterminacy, specification can be made of the interpretative world that has been constructed up to now around Esperanza, Maritornes, and other Cer-vantine characters who work in the skin trade. Whatever might have been the specific historical conditions in which these women made their living, we can never really know how a prostitute felt when she sur-rendered her body to anyone willing to pay. The fact is that, even in the best circumstances, sexual relations are marked by different drives. Thus, it is difficult to assign meaning to or make sense of sex that is bought and sold. How can we perform a microscopic investigation of fictional intimacy and sexual attraction? Eroticism in Cervantes would seem to more closely approximate the raw and passionate pleasure, the festivals of instinct that according to the novelist Mario Vargas Llosa describe a Pietro Aretino or a Giovanni Boccaccio, but not a Georges Bataille (1989), who feels that the pleasure men extract from vice is macabre and mental (see Vargas Llosa 1986). Consequently, Cervantes's erotic worlds—at least in the two works examined in this chapter—are distant from those sordid environments inhabited by the social outcasts who embody the prostitute-protagonists of the female picaresque novel.

Thus, his often virtuous unvirtuous women can be seen not only as one more Cervantine response to the prevailing economic conditions that led women into prostitution against their wishes, but also as a genial literary alternative to the overwhelmingly antifeminist and negative female picaresque.

Therefore, Esperanza's welcome escape into marriage and Maritornes's erotic stratagems might be pure means of survival, a way of converting their realities into another without prostituting themselves totally. Esperanza, as we saw earlier, eagerly grasps fortune's lock, exchanging a cruel future of repeated hymen repairs for the possibility of the soft marriage bed. For her part, and just like Alonso Quijano, Maritornes enjoys a mental, perhaps spiritual, and most definitely erotic refashioning by losing herself in the fantasy world—possibly, in her mind, living it—provided by the romances of chivalry. Don Quijote reroutes his libido into a fantasy adventure; Maritornes does the same with the rough trade inherent in her occupation. For this reason the servant girl's chivalric "readings" linger on the knights' sensual adventures when the books "cuentan que se está la otra señora debajo de unos naranjos abrazada con su caballero, y que les está una dueña haciéndoles la guarda, muerta de envidia y con mucho sobresalto" (pt. 1:32) ["tell about a lady under some orange trees in the arms of her knight, and a duenna's their lookout, and she's dying of envy and scared to death" (268)]. For this charitable and sensual *moza de venta,* "todo esto es cosa de mieles" (pt. 1:32) ["all that's as sweet as honey" (268)]. Through Maritornes's seemingly innocent allusion to a food of the gods—one that was believed to be an aphrodisiac and to promote virility and fertility—as well as to the sweetness inherent in chivalric love scenes, Cervantes grants his improbable character access into the honeyed world of all that is delicious and pleasurable in the realm of sensual desire.

CHAPTER TWO

Homosexuality and Satire

Qui fuer preso en sodomítico pecado, quemarlo.
    Fuero de Béjar

[Whoever is caught committing the sodomitical sin, burn him.]
    Law code of Béjar

Jean-Paul Sartre once commented that "the ass is the secret femininity of males, their passivity" (quoted in Bredbeck 1991, 31).[1] His juxtaposition of femininity and masculinity, of activity and passivity, and the specification of the anus as marker and magnet for homosexual desire—although not new for the present state of early modern sexuality studies—are concerns that are central to the topic of this chapter. Before we address them, however, it is important to point out the range of these assertions. The late rock composer and singer Frank Zappa—an existentialist who is more contemporary to us and less inclined to dialectical poles—made the following spirited comment with respect to human sexuality: "My attitude toward anybody's sexual persuasion is this: without deviation from the norm, progress is not possible" (quoted in Bredbeck 1991, 31). Less prosaic than Sartre's and Zappa's statements could be, and closer to the Spanish context of this book, is the philosophy of the late twentieth-century Spanish poet Luis Cernuda. In a poem entitled "No decía palabras," from the collection *Los placeres prohibidos*, he includes the verse, "El deseo es una pregunta cuya respuesta no existe" (2005, 178). [Desire is a question whose answer does not exist.] Since the poem focuses on homosexual love, it is not simply a matter of poeticizing a love that cannot speak its name; rather, the poet addresses the issue of how we deal with desire. For Cernuda, only the poet can intuit poetic-erotic rapture, because the various types of desire cannot be explained rationally. Precisely because the triggers of desire are out of control for most of us, the task of Cernuda's poetic voice is to normalize homosexuality for readers by linking it to the naturalness of sexual desires, as inexplicable as these may be.

Satire and the Poetics of Sodomy

Other literary venues exist to communicate the complexities of and attitudes toward homosexual desire; one common to the early modern period is satire. In this regard, the humorous vein that underlies Sartre's and Zappa's twentieth-century positioning of sexual otherness falls neatly within the purview of contemporary theorists of satire. Gilbert Highet (1962), Arthur Pollard (1970), Alastair Fowler (1982), and Margaret Rose (1993), to cite a canonical progression in discussing this mode, are at pains to specify the textual functioning of satire. However, they and the authors of most critical handbooks and dictionaries agree that in the discourse of satire all is permitted and the unmentionable is mentioned freely, often without the buffer of euphemism or reticence and always from a polemical or critical perspective. Such freedom of expression also prevailed in the early modern period. For this reason sodomy—the so-called *peccatum mutum* [silent sin], the crime that could not be named among Christians—was, in fact, textualized quite readily in satirical poetic discourse of the Spanish baroque. If this comes as a surprise to literary historians or cultured readers, it is most likely because until the advent of gender studies and queer theory in the final decades of the twentieth century, such poetry was rarely anthologized and was even more infrequently included as a topic worthy of academic scrutiny. Since 1990, with the publication of such foundational critical texts as Eve Kosofsky Sedgwick's *Epistemology of the Closet* and Judith Butler's *Gender Trouble,* it is a commonplace that queer theory challenges sexual orthodoxy by revealing the conceptual and discursive biases on which conventional categories of sexuality are based. In so doing, such theories ultimately question the "naturalization" of all sexualities and the resultant heteronormativity within Western society, often from a position of gay activism and advocacy.

Those theoretical lucubrations have led to the exploration of writers' sexual orientation and the manner in which it allegedly marks their work. Thus, several critics and/or biographers have attempted to "out" that most canonical of Golden Age figures, Miguel de Cervantes (see the discussion in Martín 1998). Nonetheless, in hispanism the representation of sexual "deviation" in literature has traditionally been silenced, and in many interpretative communities the outing of revered canonical authors is still considered distasteful or at best speculative. The reasoning behind such censorship can no longer be sustained, however, and in the past few years several books and essays have broached the topic of sexual otherness—particularly homosexuality—with respect to pre- and early modern Spanish texts.[2]

This chapter is not, however, an attempt to reconstruct the social reality that framed homosexuality in Golden Age Spain (a daunting if not impossible endeavor, given the still incipient state of historical and cultural studies on the topic).[3] It is, instead, an exploration of the uniqueness to which Randolph Trumbach (1977) refers (see the Trumbach passage quoted in the Preface) by elucidating the symbolic universe that surrounds the representation of sodomy in Spanish Golden Age poetic satire—what Cameron McFarlane has called the "complex signifying system" formed by the modes of representing the sodomite (1997, 33). By examining how the discourse of homosexuality functioned both literally and figuratively, this chapter explores the particular sociocultural conditions that explain the attitudes that determine and control the reception of homosexuality and assign to it categories of deviance. To address these issues here involves a double hermeneutic quest: (1) a study of the pursuit and repression of sodomy conducted in Spain by the Inquisition, by the civil courts, and by society at large and (2) my own textual-based search for images of sodomy in Golden Age literature that might modify or at least expand literary history. By exploring how writers mark sexual otherness and how the presumed audience receives their texts, it becomes clear that "deviance" is an expression of conflicts, desires, expectations, and inner impulses that can produce a social chain reaction.

It seems that in the Renaissance "anxiety over sexual behavior led to an outpouring of sodomy laws. Assumptions about male sexual desire in tandem with the social norm of late marriage not only kept courts occupied with trials of *stuprum* and *defloratio* but also led to the institutionalization and elaborate regulation of prostitution. In turn, prostitution institutionalized misogyny" (Schwartz and Finucci 1994, 5). Not surprisingly, concomitant with this growing social anxiety over what were considered to be non-normative sexual practices was an increased presence of antisodomite satire.

In keeping with the expectations and increasingly recorded reactions of seventeenth-century Spain's social audience, this satire typically presents the sodomitical subject framed by the notion of misfortune. This is the much repeated concept of *desgracia,* which in the discourse of sodomy is intimately related to the anus. In *Gracias y desgracias del ojo del culo,* commonly acknowledged as the *enfant terrible* of all the prose works by Francisco de Quevedo, the author links the two in the most graphic way. Here this most ardently scatological of Golden Age satirists lists and explains the fortunes and misfortunes of this least poetic part of human anatomy, ending (as it were) as follows:

> Finalmente, tan desgraciado es el culo que siendo así que todos los miembros del cuerpo se han holgado y huelgan muchas veces, los ojos de la cara gozando de lo hermoso, las narices de los buenos olores, la boca de lo bien sazonado y besando lo que ama, la lengua retozando entre los dientes, deleitándose con el reír, conversar y con ser pródiga y una vez que quiso holgar el pobre culo le quemaron. (Quevedo 1991, 37)

> [Finally, the ass is so unfortunate that even though all the body's members have amused and do amuse themselves many times—the eyes with beauty, the nose with pleasant aromas, the mouth with well-seasoned food and the beloved's kiss, the tongue frolicking between the teeth and delighting with laughter, conversation, and extravagance—on the one occasion that the ass wanted to amuse itself, it was burned.]

Quevedo's concluding allusion to the conventional locus of male homoerotic activity and to the punishment suffered by accused sodomites transports the text from the realm of comic anal epistemology and sensual synesthesia to that of homosexual, or sodomitical, cultural discourse, teetering perilously close to the edge of farce. Tangentially, I recognize not only that to employ the term *homosexual* with respect to premodern times might be considered anachronistic but also—because here I focus mainly on male subjects—that "sexual difference cannot determine sexual desire, because desire originates in the unconscious and the unconscious knows nothing of sexual difference" (Dean 2000, 87–88). In the introduction to his much debated *History of Sexuality* (first published in 1978), Michel Foucault contends that homosexuality (as a social category) was born in the nineteenth century, with the appearance in psychiatry, jurisprudence, and literature of a whole series of discourses on homosexuality that demanded that its legitimacy be acknowledged (1990a, 101). Although some of his claims and chronology have been questioned as arbitrary and blind to an evident earlier homosexual reality,[4] his book redirected the history of sexuality, divorcing it from the physical and biological sciences and linking it to sociology, anthropology, and philosophy, which ultimately posited it as a "cultural production."[5]

Thus, Foucault maintains, the early modern sinner who engaged in deviant acts (the sodomite) becomes the nineteenth-century "homosexual"—someone whose identity is inextricably linked to and determined by choice of sexual partner. This hermeneutic shift sets the stage for what theorists of sexuality call constructionism—the notion that sexual identities are not "given" by nature but are culturally constituted or produced—and its corresponding debate with essentialism, whose proponents feel that there is an atemporal or "natural" basis for sexual meaning. Both positions are discussed in Weeks 1986 and Halperin 1990; the most convincing defense of essentialism is found in Norton 1997. My own view is that both positions are intellectually rigid and not necessarily mutually exclusive. Sexuality, I believe, is an essential, timeless, and (to some still unknown extent) biologically determined facet of human life. Homosexuals, understood as individuals who are sexually attracted to members of the same sex, clearly have always existed and most often, but not always, have been deemed incongruent with the heterosexual norm. As a consequence, their customs and behavior have been viewed and judged in different ways.

However, homosexuality (or any sexuality) is not monolithic; like heterosexuality, homosexuality is composed of a diversity and range of desires, experiences, behaviors, and identities. Indeed, there are numerous varieties of sexualities, and they cannot nor should they be pigeon-holed into the labels hetero-, bi- or homosexuality. At the same time, as the following pages on images of homosexuality in satire explore, the change in attitudes toward homosexuality and homosexuals across time and cultures has constructed categories of sexuality. As David F. Greenberg's encyclopedic survey, *The Construction of Homosexuality* (1988), has shown, "Homoerotic desire and behavior are transhistorical and transcultural phenomena documented in every conceivable kind of society; what varies are the meanings that they are accorded from era to era and place to place" (quoted in Summers 1992, 3). There-fore, while historians continue to piece together the hidden history of homosexuality, its complex "nature" and roots remain to a great ex-tent an enigma. Nonetheless, it bears repeating that the study of his-torical attitudes toward sexuality and homosexuality as represented in literature can be extremely revealing in terms of sexual, cultural, and literary norms and in explorations of the nature of eroticism. Repre-sentations of sexuality and eroticism in literature are not, of course, necessarily positive. Not all exaltations of sensuality, of bodily pleasures and the joys of sex are represented as commendable or even desirable; sometimes they are, instead, ridiculed or abhorred.[6] Viewed from our twenty-first-century perspective, certain Golden Age manifestations of eroticism (especially what we would call homosexual activity) can be patently misogynistic, homophobic, or even pornographic. This should come as no surprise.

To return to the history of homosexuality, the fact that early mod-ern Spain acknowledged only the *pecado nefando* [nefarious sin]—sodomy—does not preclude the existence of what we would now call a homosexual subculture in that country. Such was the case for the six-teenth-century English court of James I, notorious for its homosexual alliances and the king's attachment to his favorite, the duke of Bucking-ham (see Lockyer 1981 and Bergeron 1991). In this regard, Trumbach has affirmed that underground homosexual communities flourished in the large urban centers of eighteenth-century Europe. He notes that these communities shared not only behavioral patterns and modes of recognition but also a distinct lexicon. By extension, it would be absurd to conclude that the sex represented by that lexicon was predictably sneaky, guilt ridden, or inexpert and exaggerated. Distinct linguistic registers are, of course, typical of many secret and persecuted societies.

In the seventeenth and eighteenth centuries, London's so-called molly houses were, in fact, gathering places frequented by cross-dressed men (Halperin 1990, 8–9). With respect to Renaissance Spain, in the only book-length study to date on the repression of homosexuality by the Inquisition, the historian Rafael Carrasco (1985, 134–37) also confirms the existence of what he calls a homosexual ghetto in sixteenth- through eighteenth-century Valencia.[7] He bases his assertions on the testimony of accused sodomites who appeared before the Inquisition and testified regarding where homosexuals congregated, who their partners were, what their demeanor was, and which secret signs they used to recognize and communicate with each other.[8]

In addition, in his highly influential study on male erotics in ancient Greece, David Halperin reaffirms that homosexuality and heterosexuality, as we currently understand them, are decidedly modern, Western, bourgeois productions. Nevertheless, he adds that beginning in the high Middle Ages certain kinds of sexual acts became identified with people of certain specific sexualities. A "sodomite" begins to name not merely the person who commits an act of sodomy but also the person who is distinguished by a particular type of sexual subjectivity, which is assumed to incline such a person to commit this act. Such inclinations notwithstanding, during this period, sodomy remains, in the eyes of society, a sinful act that any person, given sufficient temptation, can be induced to commit (Halperin 1990, 8).

The sin and subsequent punishment were extended even to those who claimed to have sodomized another. For example, the Fuero [law code] of Zorita de los Canes in the Spanish province of Guadalajara included the following stipulation: "Otroquesi, tod aquel que dixiere a otro: Yo te fodi por el culo; si pudiere seer prouado que assi es uerdat, amos deuen seer quemados. Si non, que sea quemado qui tan gran nemiga dixiere" (Cela 1988, vol. 1, s.v. "culo"). [Moreover, whoever should say to another: I fucked you in the ass; if it can be proved that this is true, both should be burned. If not, let he who said such a vile thing be burned.] This stipulation reveals the grave social and legal implications of a public accusation (whether or not it was true) of passive sodomy. By the same token, and for the same historical period, Francis Bezler finds that Spanish books of penance provided a woman the option of seeking a divorce if her husband was found guilty of what at that time passed for homosexuality (1994, 214–15).

When such personal and institutional mediations are transplanted to poetry, the literary images evidence the recognition of at least certain aspects of homosexuality, including the purported nature of sodomitical lust (but not love). Again, since sodomitical desire was inevitably linked to the anus (Mikhail Bakhtin's lower bodily stratum), the imagery associated with it, although ingenious, is probably the most vulgar of Spanish literature. This is, after all, the lyric province in which Quevedo (in his sonnet "La voz del ojo, que llamamos pedo") will refer to farts as "ruiseñor de los putos" (1990, 578–79) [nightingale of sodomites].

During the Christian Renaissance, "sodomy" was a general signifier encompassing all the so-called sins against nature: masturbation, incest, anal intercourse between men or between a man and a woman, bestiality, and any sort of nonprocreative sexual behavior. According to Christian belief, and as Thomas Aquinas admonished in his *Summa Theologica,* sex was created *by nature* exclusively for procreation. Therefore, any act that avoided conception or misspent the male seed was considered to be *against nature.* The Spanish legal historian Francisco Tomás y Valiente quotes the mid-sixteenth-century Castilian jurist Antonio Gómez in this regard:

> "Si quis habet accesum ad quamlibet aliam speciem vel materiam non aptam nec determinatam a natura ad coitum et generationem secundum propriam speciem, committit delictum et crimen contra naturam". Es decir, "si alguien realiza un acceso carnal que no está ordenado al coito natural y a la generación dentro de su especie, comete delito y crimen contra natura". Este es el concepto amplio del pecado o delito contra natura, más amplio que la pura relación sexual entre personas del mismo sexo. (Tomás y Valiente 1990, 38)

> [That is to say, "if someone performs a carnal act that is not for the purpose of coitus or procreation of the species, he or she is committing a crime against nature." This is the broad concept of sin or crime against nature, broader than carnal relations between persons of the same sex.]

As we have seen, any sexual activity that did not lead to fecundation was considered a "pecado de Sodoma" [sodomitical sin]. Consequently, an anonymous *letrilla* ("Di, hija, ¿por qué te matas") collected in the

Pierre Alzieu, Robert Jammes, and Yvan Lissorgues edition of *Poesía
erótica del Siglo de Oro* (henceforth referred to herein as *PESO*), advises
women against lovemaking with eunuchs, since the act cannot be pleasurable, considering the castrated lover's mechanical insufficiencies, and
also involves an unpardonable sin:

> Tan gran cargo de conciencia
> jamás le absuelven en Roma,
> que es pecado de Sodoma,
> porque les falta potencia;
> son nubes sin poluencia,
> rato sin conversación,
> *que tienen grandes las patas*
> *y chiquito el espolón.*
>   (1984, 188)

[Such great remorse will never be pardoned in Rome, since it is a
sin of Sodom. Because they lack potency, they are clouds without a
storm, an interval without conversation; *they have big feet but a little
spur.*]

Because the eunuch is impotent, to engage in sexual activity with a
eunuch cannot be productive; therefore, according to religious logic, its
only purpose is the pursuit of pleasure. However, according to conventional attitudes, even pleasure cannot result, since the sine qua non for
female sexual pleasure is an erect penis.[9]

In a similar vein, and notwithstanding official proscriptions against
such sodomitical activities, Luis de Góngora's *letrilla* "Ya que rompí
las cadenas" satirizes not only male and female homosexuality but also
the practice of heterosexual anal sex as a means of conserving female
virginity:

> De doncella con maleta,
> ordinario y estafeta,
> que quiere contra derecho
> pasando por el estrecho
> llegar entera a Colibre,
> *Dios me libre.*

Y del galán perfumado,
para holocaustos guardado,
que hace cara a los afeites
para dar a sus deleites
espaldas, como cobarde,
     Dios me guarde.
. . . .
De doncella que entra en casa
porque guisa y porque amasa,
y hace mejor un guisado
con la mujer del honrado
que con clavos y gengibre,
     Dios me libre.
          (1967, 426–27)

[God save me from the maiden with suitcase and post who wants, against what is right, to arrive intact to Collioure by passing through the strait. And God save me from the perfumed lover reserved for holocausts, who turns his face to cosmetics in order to turn his back to his pleasures like a coward. . . . And God save me from the maiden who enters the house to cook and knead and makes a better stew with the cuckold's wife than with cloves and ginger.]

Góngora's poem, which is dated circa 1590, is structured around the alternation of women and men who engage in a series of sexual misbehaviors or deviances, from whom the poetic voice begs that God distance and free him (*"Dios me libre/Dios me guarde"*). In the first strophe quoted, the verses, on the surface, allude to the difficulty of crossing the pirate-ridden Mediterranean to arrive safely at Collioure in the eastern Pyrenees of southern France. This important harbor, which was annexed to the kingdom of Aragon from the twelfth to the seventeenth centuries, was Spanish territory at that time. At the same time, the expression "pasando por el estrecho" unmistakably alludes to the use of anal sex in order to keep the female partner's hymen intact ("entera"). Immediately following is the "galán perfumado," whose effeminacy the poet links with sodomy and who is therefore destined to be consumed by the Inquisitorial flames ("para holocaustos guardado"). This man displays the emblematic traits attributed to homosexuals in early modern texts, especially in satire: effeminacy, cowardice, and debauchery. It is not irrelevant for my overall argument that Cervantes uses such features to characterize the effeminate *galán* Cornelio in his novella *El amante liberal* (see Martín 1999). In Góngora's poem the man indulges in excessive personal grooming ("afeites") and turns his back—both to flee as a coward and to assume the position of the passive partner in the sodomitical acts that are his pleasures ("sus deleites").

However, these acts were not the exclusive province of male characters. In the last strophe the poet describes the young serving girl who cuckolds her master (*honrado* is often used in satire to mean cuckold) by engaging in lesbian sexual relations with his wife. Here the joke lies in the wordplay with "guisa" and "guisado." Using the word *guisado*, which means "stew" in conventional usage but "brothel" in thieves' slang, the poet describes the girl as someone who cooks and bakes for the family ("guisa y amasa") but who makes a spicier "stew" with her mistress than with cloves and ginger. The implicit reference here to baking and bread—*pan*—through the act of kneading is an allusion, commonly found in erotic literature, to the vagina and sex. Louise Vasvári (1983), Francisco Márquez Villanueva (1987), and José Ramón Fernández de Cano y Martín (1990) have all analyzed the erotically charged, polysemous nature of the word. In burlesque literature, because the female baker—the *panadera*—sold her "bread" [body, vagina], she was associated with procuring and prostitution. Therein lies the humorous significance of the ballad "Cruz cruzada, panadera" from Juan Ruiz's *Libro de buen amor* (1988). Vasvári documents the multiple sexual connotations of *pan* in her meticulous study of the erotic language used in that poem. In his drama *Los españoles en Flandes,* Lope de Vega constructed an entire play around the image of bread, signifying female genitalia (López-Baralt and Márquez Villanueva 1995a, 12–13).

Finally, the circumstance textualized in this poem reflects a proverb collected in Correas 2000: "La mala casada tratos tiene con su criada" [the bad wife has dealings with her maid], and it is similar to the situation poeticized in greater detail in Fray Melchor de la Serna's verse novella *Sueño de la viuda,* published in 1976 (see the discussion in Chapter Three). However, in Golden Age texts the sexual dalliances of mistresses are not limited to relationships with female servants. For example, in the *letrilla* "Allá darás, rayo" Góngora ironically points to another erotic pairing common to burlesque and satirical literature:

> Con su lacayo en Castilla
> se acomodó una casada;
> no se le dió al señor nada,
> porque no es gran maravilla
> que el amo deje la silla,
> y que la ocupe el lacayo.
>   (1967, 319)

[A wife from Castile took up with her servant, and her husband was not surprised, because it is no marvel that when the master dismounts, the servant climbs into the saddle.]

This poem's debasement of women to the level of a beast that is to be ridden by master and servant is quite in keeping with the phallocentric, if not misogynistic, tenor of much Golden Age erotic and satirical poetry. This tone can be observed, for example, in Melchor de la Serna's *Jardín de Venus,* probably the best-known collection of Spanish erotic poetry from this period.[10] The patent misogyny of such verse is inescapable (although the phallus clearly does not escape ridicule either), and its role in determining the history of Golden Age erotic literature cannot be underemphasized. It is obvious that allusions, puns, conceits, double entendres, and other related types of metatextual poetic utterances serve to highlight the cryptic nature that readers may generally expect of this type of poetry. These textual procedures make the dissemination of this body of works that much more compelling.

As the foregoing examples suggest, in early modern Europe the concept underlying the term *sodomy* was not specifically what we would now call homosexuality; it was the more general notion of sexual debauchery, to which all people were, in principle, subject. Gregory Bredbeck—echoing Foucault, who declares sodomy to be "that utterly confused category" (1990a, 101)—has pointed out in this regard that up to the seventeenth century, the specification of sodomy in English literature was a way to encompass a multitude of sins with a minimum of signs (Bredbeck 1991, 13). Nevertheless, the unifying injunction against such literary representations is against the spilling of the male seed into an inappropriate vessel. As a consequence, within the broad realm of nonreproductive sexuality in early modern Europe, anal sex— whether performed by homosexual or heterosexual couples—was by far the most serious crime. Contemporary Spanish handbooks of penance reveal that no other forbidden sexual act was punished as harshly. In his *Avisos históricos,* for example, José Pellicer reports two cases of sodomy punished by death: In October 1640 a man and his young partner were burned at the stake for the *pecado nefando.* In November 1644 a wife accused her husband of performing anal sex with her; he was burned to death two weeks later (1962, 88, 258–59). In *Grandeza y miseria en Andalucía,* Pedro de León (1981) lists the names and execution dates for numerous men accused in Andalucía. With respect to sodomy and the Inquisition, Carrasco exhaustively confirms that of all the crimes of the flesh, the *pecado nefando* was the most shameful and the most severely punished (1985, 7–8). Finally, whereas Carrasco limits his scope to Valencia, Mary Elizabeth Perry (1989) has written on the "nefarious sin" with respect to Seville. Their research also provides ample evidence that such transgressions were not limited to the large cities of the period.

In order to analyze how the social attitudes that I have contextualized are played out in literary terms, I have selected for discussion several poems that are representative of the characterization of homosexuals in the one literary genre in which they appear quite frequently and in a manner that is usually free of subtlety or disguise. The homosexual is mentioned often in Spanish burlesque and satirical verse; I concentrate, however, on the poems in which the homosexual appears as protagonist or subject. I should add that in terms of interpretive possibilities and the study of early modern mentalities, it seems just as productive to seek out the general representation of homosexuality in poetry as to examine the poetry of specifically homosexual love. The latter is, of course, much more difficult to discern in the poetry of the period. Claude Summers has analyzed how the classical literature of homosexuality provided Renaissance writers with "a set of references by which homosexual desire could be encoded into their own literature and by which they could interpret their own experience" (1992, 8). However, in response to social, religious, and legal prohibitions, male homosexuality was Christianized and spiritualized (for example by neoplatonists), and the sources of representations of passionate love between men were either discreetly de-eroticized or heterosexualized. Summers concludes that "representations of homosexuality then as now were subject to containment, suppression, and denial" (8). This is certainly true for most early modern Spanish literature, where images of male/male erotic love are a rarity.

As far as I have been able to ascertain, there are no extant Golden Age Spanish texts equivalent to William Shakespeare's or Michelangelo's homosexual love poems (see Saslow 1988), at least none have been discovered to date.[11] This is not the case for Christian and especially Arabic and Hebrew poetry written in medieval Spain, in which the theme of "boy-love" is common.[12]

These exceptions notwithstanding, the lack of Golden Age homosexual texts is understandable, since at the time the Inquisition in the kingdom of Aragon and the civil courts in Castile actively pursued homosexuals. Thus, "prudent individuals rarely left any record of this aspect of their lives" (A. Gilbert 1980–81, 57). As we will see, this apparent absence of Spanish texts might also reflect the naïve or willful misinterpretation of extant works, due to readers' misplaced prudery. Among texts that invite renewed, possibly psychoanalytical approaches (since we are dealing with imaginary orders, sublimations, and symptoms that distance themselves from the purely symbolic) are several poems that the early seventeenth-century nun Sor Violante del Cielo devotes to another woman.[13] Such verse facilitates a deeper understanding of the complexities and varieties of early modern Spanish desire and sexual practices. It also shows that in the early modern period, as now, reality constantly irrupts in texts that conventional interpretations perceive as having purely internal dimensions and no external referents.

Quevedo and the Bujarrón

The first poem examined, a sonnet by Quevedo, serves to exemplify the textual dynamics that surround the sociohistorical and literary constraints of homosexual discourse in Golden Age Spain. In "Por no comer la carne sodomita," his satirical epitaph to a fictional procuress/witch named Madre Muñatones de la Sierra, the poet reveals that baroque verse did not simply cover up or chastise homosexuality within its poetics of wit. Rather, by broadening the semiotics of passions, it related or psychologically projected its transgressive character onto other marginalized persons of that period, a mode of thought and behavior that typified the Counter Reformation. The first two strophes of the sonnet read as follows:

Por no comer la carne sodomita
destos malditos miembros luteranos,
se morirán de hambre los gusanos,
que aborrecen vianda tan maldita.
No hay que tratar de cruz y agua bendita;
eso se gaste en almas de cristianos.
Pasen sobre ella, brujos, los gitanos;
vengan coroza y tronchos, risa y grita.
    (1969–81, 2:57)

[Since they will not eat the sodomitical flesh of these damned Lutherans, the maggots will die of hunger because they despise such damned meat. A cross and holy water should not be used; let those be saved for Christian souls. May the gypsy sorcerers pass over them; bring on the conical caps, the laughter and shouting.]

Quite clearly, the initial level of identification lies in the formula "sodomite equals Lutheran;" hence this sodomitic, damned flesh is rejected even by maggots and is undeserving of the last rites as symbolized by the crucifix and holy water, which is properly reserved for Christians. The *coroza,* a conical paper hat that delinquents were obliged to wear as a visible symbol of public shaming, was probably the least of the punishments that the poetic voice recommends. However, the first tercet of the sonnet expounds further on the marginal status of those remains:

Estos los güesos son de aquella vieja
que dio a los hombres en la bolsa guerra,
y paz a los cabrones en el rabo.
    (1969–81, 2:57)

[These are the bones of that old crone who gave men battle in their purse and the kiss of peace on the tail to he-goats.][14]

The final verse refers to the reputed practice of witches whereby they would kiss the devil's anus. Thus, in one person a triple marginality is conflated—sodomite, Lutheran, and witch—and Quevedo's poem manages to configure emotions allied to suspicion, contempt, fear, hatred, and phobia, to say nothing of distrust, worry, and zeal. The three crimes condensed in the poem, which were punishable by death, were, in reality, constituents of the worst sin of all: religious heresy contrary to the holy Catholic faith.[15] Lutherans were heretics by nature, sodomites were heretics because they contravened church doctrine by performing the act or by maintaining that such an act was not a sin, and witches were heretics because they reputedly engaged in sexual commerce with demons and the devil. Given what present scholarship about them reveals, it is not surprising that heresy, witchcraft, and sexuality are tightly interwoven in the early modern European mind and that sexual and religious deviants commonly transgress together. Thus, behind the accusation of sodomy typically lurks that of heresy and most often by extension in Spain, the *converso* [Jewish convert]. It is worth remembering that the worst possible insult in Counter Reformation Spain was *puto judío* [Jew faggot, or male whore], a slur of no small consequence for the insulted, since it melded what were perceived to be the two worst threats to social and political stability.

Given the prevalence of the unholy pair sodomite/heretic in seventeenth-century Spain, it is also not surprising that it appears in much earlier periods in peninsular satire. In fact, it is perhaps the most common accusation hurled against the members of Henry IV's Castilian court in the infamous *Coplas del Provincial.* This milestone of political invective, composed between 1465 and 1466, is a 596-verse allegory, written in octosyllabic quatrains, that narrates the fictional visit to a convent made by the ecclesiastical provincial.[16] The real and/ or imagined personal vices of the fifteenth-century Castilian oligarchy are denounced in these *coplas,* most often through the most rabid ad hominem attacks. The noblemen are accused of being, among other things, Jewish sodomites, debauchers, Moriscos, mulattos, effeminates, cuckolds, and consenting husbands. The noblewomen, in turn, are characterized as whores, witches, Jews, and at the very least adulteresses. Because the anonymous author or authors name names, both the Inquisition and the families accused in the poem tried to destroy all existing copies of the *Coplas*—but to no avail (Rodríguez Puértolas 1984, 234).

An infamous target of the *Coplas* is Henry IV's favorite, Beltrán de la Cueva ("conde Cascorvillo" in the poem). Cueva was commonly believed to be Queen Juana's lover and the father of the royal princess, nicknamed Juana la Beltraneja. The poem denounces Cueva's adulterous coupling with the queen but also accuses him of maintaining a homosexual relationship with the king. It even suggests that he was awarded the title of count of Ledesma by the king for deviant sexual "services rendered" ("que te dieron Ledesma / por labrar en Val Hondillo"):

A ti, conde Cascorvillo
renegador en cuaresma,
que te dieron Ledesma
por labrar en Val Hondillo,
y es pública voz y fama
que odiste personas tres:
a tu amo y a tu ama
y a la hija del marqués
    (quoted in Rodríguez Puértolas 1984, 239)

[Count Cascorvillo, apostate in Lent, they awarded you the title of Ledesma for digging in Val Hondillo, and it is public knowledge that you fucked all three: your master, your mistress, and the daughter of the marquise.]

Highet's notion that satire deals with "real" persons is applicable to the poem in that Cueva's third sexual partner, "la hija del marqués," is his wife, Mencía de Mendoza, daughter of the second marqués de Santillana. The fact that other favorites of the king are treated with equal venom shows that these poets had converted the Renaissance value and practice of ethos and pathos (when addressing a particular audience) into poetic technique. For example, Álvaro Pérez Orozco embodies the despised combination of Jewish convert and sodomite. In this instance, the Jewish nose and the sodomitical anus, two common images in early Spanish satire, are fused into one infernal figure:

A ti, fraile bujarrón,
Álvaro Pérez Orozco,
por ser de los de Faraón
en la nariz te conozco,
y es tan grande que me asombra,
y a los diablos del infierno,

que haze en el verano sombra
y rabos hace en invierno.
    (quoted in Rodríguez Puértolas 1984, 241)

[Friar bugger, Álvaro Pérez Orozco, I can tell by your nose that you belong to the race of the Pharaohs; it is so big that it amazes me and the devils of hell, since it casts a shadow in summer and turns tail in winter.]

Similar assaults and accusations of Jewish sodomite (quoted in Rodríguez Puértolas 1984) are suffered by the king's *converso* accountant, Diego Arias ("puto / que eres y fuiste judío" [245] [faggot Jew that you were and are]) and the *converso* Pedro Méndez ("que el un cuarto es de marrano / y los tres de sodomía" [252] [who is one-quarter Marrano and three-quarters sodomite]).

Such personal attacks on figures of power via accusations of deviant sexual practices were subsequently favored by Quevedo, as evidenced in one of at least two other epitaphs that he dedicated to alleged homosexuals. The epigraph of one poem—"Epitafio a un italiano llamado Julio"—might refer to the owner of the Imprenta Real during the early 1600s.[17] It also provides a revealing social frame for homosexual satire, since in Quevedo's time Italians were stereotyped as effeminate and, in the semiotics of the time, homosexual.[18] For example, in his *Vejamen . . .* (Biblioteca Nacional de Madrid manuscript 3941, folio 20), Anastasio Pantaleón de Ribera affirms this in his reference to the Italian José Camerino: "Es demas desto visioso y Mujeriego, si bien es en esto virtud, por auer nacido en Pais donde los mas son Hombreriegos" (quoted in Carrasco 1985, 218). [Besides this he is a vice-ridden womanizer, although this is a virtue, since he was born in a country where most are manizers.]

Returning to Quevedo and Italians, men of this nation, who were severely repressed by the Spanish Inquisition, composed 13.5% of the total number of men prosecuted in Valencia during the period between 1566 and 1775 (a percentage equal to the number of clergy prosecuted). The majority of these men were impecunious soldiers, sailors, and vagabonds from Naples and Sicily whom the Spaniards viewed with great suspicion (Carrasco 1985, 217). Interestingly, the connection between homosexuality and Italians is made even in Italy at the time. In an essay on Burchiello's "nonsense verse," Alan Smith studies the nexus of poetry, politics, and sodomy in quattrocento Florence, whose inhabitants were reckoned to be notorious sodomites. English Protestants popularized the figure of the popish sodomite, and Catholics hurled similar slurs at Protestants (see Schleiner 1994). In this respect, Alan Bray has pointed out that the Protestant party was simply adapting to its own use the identification of religious deviation with sexual deviation that the Catholic church had already constructed during the twelfth century (1982, 19).

Quevedo's first epitaph textualizes such historicized suppositions regarding nationality and perversion quite graphically, since ultimately his choice of language subsumes contemporary attitudes toward sexual otherness. In this case rhyming does not militate against the singularity of the language chosen, and the poet proceeds to show and tell directly, with little oblique restraint or lack of force:

Epitafio a un italiano llamado Julio

Yace en aqueste llano
Julio el italïano,
que a marzo parecía
en el volver de rabo cada día.
Tú, que caminas la campaña rasa,
cósete el culo, viandante, y pasa.
Murióse el triste mozo malogrado
de enfermedad de mula de alquileres,
que es decir que murió de cabalgado.
Con palma le enterraron las mujeres;
y si el caso se advierte,
como es hembra la Muerte,
celosa y ofendida,
siempre a los putos deja corta vida.
Luego que le enterraron,
del cuerpo corrompido
gusanos se criaron
a él tan parecidos,
que en diversos montones
eran, unos con otros, bujarrones.
(1969–81, 2:110)

[Epitaph to an Italian named Julio. Here lies Julio the Italian, who was like March because he turned his back every day. You who walk the open country, sew up your ass and keep walking. The poor boy died before his time of a rented mule's ailment, that is, he was ridden to death. The women buried him a virgin. And his case shows that since Death is a woman, when jealous and offended, she always gives buggers a short life. After he was buried, maggots fed on his rotting body and were so like him that they buggered one another in heaps.]

This *silva* reveals the same anal obsession found in much of Quevedo's work.[19] The first strophe speaks of Julio's similarity to the month of March, which in many Spanish proverbs turns its back [*vuelve el rabo*] and is windy [*ventoso*]. In satire the latter description most often means "flatulent." In this poem the allusion is to Julio's daily practice of turning his back to assume the position for passive anal sex—hence the poem's subsequent exhortation to the passerby (and to the reader) to protect his or her rear, so to speak, which is the sine qua non of burlesque and satirical poetry that deals with male homosexuality. In this epitaph the reader then learns that young Julio was, in fact, "ridden to death," like a rental mule. His demise is celebrated ("con palma") by all women, including Death herself, who—out of female jealousy—typically grants short lives to *putos*. Since, according to the *Diccionario de la Real Academia Española*, *enterrar con palma* also refers to burying a person "en estado de virginidad," Julio, with respect to women, indeed dies a virgin and thus is gleefully buried by them in verse ten.[20] Finally, following Julio's example, the writhing heaps of maggots that feed on his remains position themselves like *bujarrones* (buggers).

The bodily preoccupations and anal obsession evident in this poem reflect the commonly held early modern fears associated with the anus, which satire attempts to exorcise. Arthur Gilbert has traced the anal sex taboo in Western Europe to the origins of Christianity, which completely separated body and spirit. St. Paul and others referred to the human body as a temple, a holy vessel. Sexual acts that involved the anal passage were regarded as the ultimate form of evil, a pact with the devil, a violation of the upwardly striving Christian attempt to find salvation. Fear of anal sex was certainly as powerful a force in the Western imagination as fear of homosexual relations (A. Gilbert 1980–81, 65–66). If we are to believe the poetic traditions inscribed in the literary histories of more contemporary periods, to this day self/world dualism remains defined by such fears.

There is a parallel to this profound dread of anal penetration in the Arabic world that, given the racial and cultural composition of medieval and early modern Spain, is quite pertinent here. In a study based on historical documents, legal tracts, medical treatises, and literature, Everett Rowson (1991) points out that in the medieval Arabic world, passive male homosexuality (known as *ubna* or *bigha* and characterized by a desire to be penetrated) was uniformly considered sick, perverted, and shameful.[21] Women's sexual pleasure was assumed (by men of the period) to be linked correspondingly to their sense of generalized subordination.

Probably for this reason, if we are to believe what we read in satirical and/or erotic poetry of this period, heterosexual anal intercourse was viewed (once again, by heterosexual men) to be somewhat pleasurable (if not as pleasurable as vaginal intercourse) for women, since they were perceived as naturally subordinate. These assumed pleasures of anal sex for women are perhaps best illustrated in Pietro Aretino's *Sonetti lussuriosi,* a series of sixteen erotic sonnets that he wrote to accompany Marcantonio Raimondi's notorious engravings of heterosexual intercourse called "I modi."[22] In sonnet 8 the woman responds to her partner, who desires anal sex, as follows:

Fottimi, e fa di me cio, che tu voi,
Et in potta in cul, che me ne curo poco,
Dove, che tu ti faccia i fatti tuoi;
Ch'io per me ne la potta, et in cul ho'l foco
Et quanti cazzi han muli, asini, e buoi,
Non scemariano a la mia foia un poco;
Poi saresti un da poco
A farme'l ne la potta a usanza antica;
Che s'un huomo foss'io non vorrei fica.

[Fuck me and do with me what you will both in my pussy and my behind; it matters little to me where you go about your business. Because I, for my part, am aflame in both places; and all of the pizzles of mules, asses, and oxen would not diminish my lust even a little.

Then you would be a no-count fellow to do it to me in my snatch,
in accordance with ancient ways. If I were a man, I wouldn't want
pussy.] (Quoted and translated in Talvacchia 1999, 209)

In contrast to Aretino's graphic representation of female desire, for a
man to seek penetration (i.e., sexual submission to the great phallus)
was inexplicable and could be attributed only to various pathologies
based on libidinal economies that were not the norm. As a result of
this phallocentric view of sexuality, the active male partner in anal sex
is generally feared and the passive partner ridiculed in satire, whereas
the woman who desires anal penetration is a recurring sexual fantasy in
Golden Age erotic poetry.

In Quevedo's and other poems of the period, the lexicon serves as
an archcode and reading protocol that cues the listener or reader to
the homosexual subject matter. The crime referred to is the *pecado de
Sodoma* and its corrupt perpetrator is predictably signified as *sodomita,
sodomético, somético, puto, marica, marión,* or *bujarrón* (referring most
exactly to an active as opposed to a passive homosexual). *Marión* is a
term used frequently at the time, as in the interludes "El marión" by
Quevedo and "Los mariones" by Luis Quiñones de Benavente. James
Saslow has noted with respect to homosexual discourse that beyond this
vocabulary, there was also an extensive terminology for male homosexual activity and individuals who engaged in it, suggesting that some
rudimentary notion existed of their distinctive psychological nature.
Unlike modern constructs, however, this conception was not inclusive
of both parties: The terms used by Baldassarre Castiglione, Pietro Aretino, and other sixteenth-century authors distinguished between an active and passive partner (Saslow 1988, 82). Quevedo's anal-sodomitical
vocabulary (terms such as *cola, culo, rabo, cabalgar, ojo,* and their derivatives) expands further the nomenclature of homoeroticism following
the norms of baroque discursive plurality and what certain traditionalist
criticism dismissively called the corruption of good taste and style by
baroque authors.

Another poetic epitaph by Quevedo, which has the simple epigraph
"A un bujarrón," is worth reproducing in its entirety for its overwhelming signifiers:

Aquí yace Misser de la Florida,
y dicen que le hizo buen provecho
a Satanás su vida.
Ningún coño le vio jamás arrecho.
De Herodes fue enemigo y de sus gentes,
no porque degolló los inocentes,
mas porque, siendo niños y tan bellos,
los mandó degollar y no jodellos.
Pues tanto amó los niños y de suerte
(inmenso bujarrón hasta la muerte),
que si él en Babilonia se hallara,
por los tres niños en el horno entrara.
¡Oh, tú, cualquiera cosa que te seas,
pues por su sepultura te paseas,
o niño o sabandija,
o perro o lagartija,
o mico o gallo o mulo,
o sierpe o animal que tengas cosa
que de mil leguas se parezca a culo:
Guárdate del varón que aquí reposa,
que tras un rabo, bujarrón profundo,
si le dejan, vendrá del otro mundo!
No en tormentos eternos
condenaron su alma a los infiernos;
mas los infiernos fueron condenados
a que tengan su alma y sus pecados.
Pero si honrar pretendes su memoria,
di que goce de mierda y no de gloria;
y pues tanta lisonja se le hace,
di: "Requiescat in culo, mas no in pace."
    (1969–81, 2:111)

[Here lies Misser de la Florida, and they say his life was of great benefit to Satan. No cunt ever saw him horny. He was an enemy of Herod and his people, not because he beheaded innocent boys but because they were young and beautiful and he ordered them to be beheaded rather than fucked. He loved boys so much (immense bugger right up to his death) that if he were in Babylon, he would

go into the oven after the three boys. Hey you! since you are passing by his grave, whatever you may be, boy or vermin, dog or lizard,
monkey, cock or mule, snake or animal that has anything that from
a thousand leagues looks like an ass: Keep away from the man who
lies here because bugger that he is, if they let him, he will come back
from the other world after an ass. They did not condemn his soul
to Hell in eternal torments, but Hell was condemned to house his
soul and sins. But if you intend to honor his memory, say that he
should enjoy shit and not glory, and since he is being flattered, say:
"Requiescat in ass, but not in pace."]

In this text the formula that equates Italians with homosexuality appears
once again with the Italianism "Misser" in the first verse. The poem satirizes the dead person's fondness for little boys (another commonplace
was to identify Italians, especially Sicilians, as pedophiles) and affirms
the absence of attraction to females and their genitalia ("Ningún coño
le vio jamás arrecho"). Again, the primordial role of language in this
type of poetry can be underscored by an excursus on "arrecho." The
term does not appear in Sebastián de Covarrubias's *Tesoro de la lengua castellana o española* (1611), yet it is frequently employed today in
Spanish America with the meaning "lustful," or "sexually aroused" that
Quevedo (and others) ascribes to it.[23] Suffice it to say that the American
English "horny" or British "randy" are successful translations, the former at least being as vulgar as the original Spanish. It can also be said,
in passing, that the 1992 edition of the *Diccionario de la Real Academia
Española* provides "tieso" and "erguido" as primary definitions, which
also work well for what is semanticized in Quevedo's poem.

Misser's pedophilic proclivities (according to Bezler 1994 [191–92],
the children involved were also subject to penance under the rubric
"De ludis puerilibus") are further articulated by the biblical references
in the text. First he is presented as an enemy of Herod, the king of
Judea who ordered all male children to be beheaded in the hope that
the child Jesus would be among them. The poet explains that Misser
would have preferred that the beautiful young innocents be sodomized
rather than beheaded. Quevedo adds that if Misser were in Babylon, he
would jump into the fire after the three Jews Shadrach, Meshach, and
Abed-nego (transformed into children in the poem) who King Nebu-
chadnezzar had cast into a furnace for refusing to worship a golden

image (see Daniel 1994, iii). And, once again, the poetic voice exhorts whoever and whatever pass by the grave to watch their backsides. The concluding witticism suggests a new and more appropriate epitaph for Misser, and it is an overwhelmingly transgressive act against the formulas associated with Christianity's last wish for the soul—that it rest in peace.

Within this context of social marginality, other figures often associated with homosexuality are members of the non-European races. For example, although prosecutions for sodomy were very rare in Renaissance England, Alan Bray (1982) cites the case of Domingo Cassedon Drago, a black man (Negro, in the original) from one of the Spanish colonies.[24] He notes that in England homosexuals functioned as scapegoats in times of social upheaval, when fear crystallized around customary figures of evil. The Spanish context was not very different, since the period of the poems included here was one of political and Counter Reformation religious upheaval. In Quevedo's poem to a mulatto hermit—"A un ermitaño mulato"—the man is accused of bestiality and masturbation, crimes of nonprocreation, which fall under the blanket designation of sodomy, as we have seen. The poet expands upon the conventional figure within satire of the sinful hermit and closes the poem with the indispensable warning—this time bracketed clearly by the wordplay on "abrir el ojo," meaning both "to be observant" ("to watch one's step") and "to adopt the position for anal penetration":[25]

A un ermitaño mulato

¿Ermitaño tú? ¡El mulato,
oh pasajero, habita
en esta soledad la pobre ermita!
Si no eres me[n]tecato,
pon en reca[u]do el culo y arrodea
primero que te güela u que te vea;
que cabalgando reses del ganado,
entre pastores hizo el noviciado.
Y haciendo la puñeta,
estuvo amancebado con su mano,
seis años retirado en una isleta,
y después fue hortelano,

donde llevó su honra a dos mastines.
Graduó sus cojones de bacines.
Mas si acaso no quieres
arrodear, y por la ermita fueres
llevado de tu antojo,
alerta y abre el ojo.
Mas no le abras, antes has tapialle:
que abrirle, para él será brindalle.
　　　(1969–81, 2:110–11)

[To a mulatto hermit. You, a hermit? Oh passerby, a mulatto dwells in the poor hermitage in this solitude. If you are not a fool, safeguard your ass and go around before he smells you or sees you, because he spent his novitiate riding cattle among shepherds. He retired to an island and slept with his hand for six years; afterward he became a gardener and gave his manhood to two mastiffs. He measured his balls with chamber pots. But if perhaps you don't want to go around and you pass by the hermitage on a whim, be alert and keep an open eye. But no, don't open it; you should cover it up instead, because an open eye will be an invitation to him.]

Golden Age authors commonly made a fairly predictable connection between mulattos, Moors, and sodomy when citing the double epistemological error of the followers of Islam. These were people who were purported not only to venerate a false prophet but also to violate natural law by being incestuous, bestial, and great sodomites (Carrasco 1985, 212).[26] This is akin to the later Kantian view of sexuality analyzed by Michael Ruse, in which homosexuality was also equated with masturbation and bestiality. This *crimina carnis contra naturam* was contrary to sound reason, as opposed to *crimina carnis,* which was abuse of one's sexuality. But the real dilemma, which Ruse traces to modern times, is this: "Mention the vices and you draw people's attention to them; fail to mention them and you do not warn people of them" (1995, 113). It bears repeating that in Quevedo's poem about the mulatto cited previously, as in early modern society, all crimes against nature are ultimately reduced to one, that of *delito nefando.* However repetitive it may be as literature, the concept is perfectly in accordance with popular sentiment toward the homosexual—the sodomite—as the sum of all vices.[27] The concept also reveals the tension that comes from the tripartite para-dox of poetry—that language is social, poetry is language, yet poetry is not defined by the sociological outlook it most resembles (Ward 1981, 202).

Góngora, from Sodom to Fuenterrabía

As we have seen, Góngora, no less canonical than Quevedo, was also partial to peppering his burlesque and satirical verse with references to homosexuality.[28] In one sonnet, "Contra ciertos hombres, a quienes moteja de afeminados," the poet's pen turns to Castile, where sustained wordplay identifies as homosexuals three young men named Carrión, Olivares, and Tordesillas (which, of course, are also place names).[29] This erotic triangle certainly serves to clarify the presentism of theories such as those developed by Sedgwick in *Between Men* (1985). Sedgwick pres-ents the notion that in any male-dominated society there is a special relationship between male homosocial (including homosexual) desire and the structures for maintaining and transmitting patriarchal power:

> Hay entre Carrión y Tordesillas,
> en Castilla la Vieja, dos lugares
> de dos vecinos tan particulares,
> que en su particular tienen cosquillas.
> Todas son arrabales estas Villas,
> y su término todo es Olivares;
> sus campos escarchados, que a millares
> producen oro, y plata a maravillas.
> Ser quiere alcalde de una y otra aldea
> Gil Rabadán; pero reprocha alguno
> que aprieta a los rabeles el cerrojo.
> Por justo y por rebelde es bien lo sea,
> porque les dé lo suyo a cada uno,
> y les mete la vara por el ojo.
>   (Góngora 1967, 555)

[There are two places in Old Castile, between Carrión and Tordesi-llas, where two neighbors are so particular that their particular place is ticklish. All these towns are in the outskirts, and their terminus is Olivares; their frosty fields produce a marvelous abundance of gold and silver. Gil Rabadán wants to be mayor of both villages, but he is reproached by some for forcing locks. Because he is just and a rebel, it is good that he be mayor, so that he may give to each his own and stick his staff in their eye.]

The first strophe allows, of course, for an erotic reading involving male genitalia. But more pertinent to the discussion that I have been developing is that in this poem much of the wordplay that surrounds male homosexuality is based on variations or polyvalent and allusive derivations of the words *culo, rabo, arrabales,* and *rabel*—all of which signify "tail" or "anus" but are more directly and fittingly translated for this context as "asshole." Here the young men's *particular* or *parte cular* is ticklish and obviously anal. As for the towns, and the three men, "todas son arrabales" (from *rabo*). Carrión (Carrión de los Condes) is located north, and Tordesillas south of Valladolid in the heart of Old Castile. This geographical positioning discloses the poem's function as another *burla castellana* related to the anti-Madrid and anti-Valladolid satire written by the Andalusian poet. This mocking often centered on the rivers of the two Castilian capitals: the Manzanares and the Esgueva, which Góngora ridiculed for their insignificant flow and filth in such intensely scatological poems as "Duélete de esa puente, Manzanares," "¿Qué lleva el señor Esgueva?" and "¿Vos sois Valladolid? ¿Vos sois el valle." In the poem under analysis here, there is a double ghettoization of social formations that are already marginal: The town is outside, and its sodomitical inhabitants even farther away from any possible center. Their only centers are the parts of the body that societal traditions generally sublimate.

The name Gil Rabadán is clearly another reference to *rabo,* or to the homophonous phrase *por el rabo le dan* [he gets it from behind]. Moreover, this aspiring town mayor is identified as a sodomite: "que aprieta a los rabeles el cerrojo" [who squeezes or forces assholes]. With respect to this verse, it appears that Juan and Isabel Millé y Giménez substituted the word *cerrojo* for *terrojo*; the latter appears on almost all the codices and in Biruté Ciplijauskaité's (1975) edition of Góngora's sonnets. The emendation would seem to make sense, given the context of the poem and the fact that the meaning of *terrojo* has been considered doubtful by most critics. However, in his *Diccionario del erotismo,* Camilo José Cela lists *terre* with the meaning *culo* and cites the following Castilian proverb from Francisco Rodríguez Marín's collection: "En los meses que no tienen *erre,* no te arrimes al terre" [In the months that don't have an "r," don't get close to the rear] with the accompanying gloss, "El vulgo sevillano suele llamar *terre* a las nalgas" [Sevillians usually call the buttocks "terre"] (Cela 1988, vol. 2, s.v. "terre"). The Andalusian connection supports the legitimacy of *terrojo* (*terre-ojo*), meaning "asshole." "Que aprieta a los rabeles el terrojo [or 'cerrojo']" obviously means "who sodomizes another"; this is a perfect example of the ambivalent and virtual significance of sexual language. Any object, or any repeated rhythmic action, can have a virtual sexual significance, most especially in erotic poetry and its passional syntax. Here the eye of the lock is penetrated by the young would-be mayor. To continue, "les dé lo suyo" means copulation, and the dilogies "vara" and "ojo" in the last verse—"y les mete la vara por el ojo"—are clear within the sexual context of the poem and any possible subtext. The *vara* not only represents the mayoral staff of office; it is also a familiar metaphor for the penis. In fact, one of the more memorable literary uses of *vara* with this meaning occurs when Preciosa, the protagonist of Cervantes's novella "La gitanilla," tells doña Clara's fortune by reading her palm. In her ambiguous but highly obscene *buenaventura,* she describes the *tinienta's* fornicating husband as follows: "Que es juguetón el tiniente, / y quiere arrimar la vara" (2001, 48). [The deputy is playful and wants to stick his staff in.] It is worth remembering, if only for the sake of literary history, that Góngora's poem and other similar poems, although markedly homophobic and often misogynistic, manage to capture an essential part of the late Renaissance spirit: a sensuous flow of the erotic and, by extension, the dialectic between sensitization and moralization.

Góngora's poem might also have a pointed political significance, given the tantalizing presence of the name Olivares. Gaspar de Guzmán, conde duque de Olivares, was Philip IV's favorite during the last five years of Góngora's life. It is likely that Góngora's status as an outsider residing in the Castilian courts nurtured his penchant for the "menosprecio de corte" theme. The count-duke was an Andalusian aristocrat who had tremendous power, access to the Crown as *privado,* and a questionable sexual reputation, given the sodomitical circle that surrounded the king. All these facts point to the count-duke as possible referent and empirical model for the Olivares in the sonnet.

The lexical archcode mentioned previously with respect to the terms *rabo, ojo,* and *cola* and the wordplay that they engender is rampant in satirical verse, as is the constant and perhaps obvious opposition of *adelante* and *atrás*. All of these dialectics are evident and quite confrontational in the anonymous but admittedly very Gongorine poem "A un puto," whose discursive building blocks are the satirical references to *ojo, Fuenterrabía, rabel, cola,* and *rabo*—in other words, to the anus and anality:

> A un puto, sin más ni más,
> prendieron por delincuente,
> no por culpas de presente,
> sino por culpas de atrás.
> Juzga su prisión antojo
> y que está sin culpa preso,
> pero yo sé que el proceso
> está que le llena el ojo.
> El juzga que es niñería
> y que el Rey le ha de librar,
> porque supo pelear
> en lo de Fuenterrabía.
> A ratos, cuando quiere él
> mostrar sus habilidades,
> se ve que en sus mocedades
> fue muy diestro en el rabel.
> No tiene esta gracia sola,
> Que en guitarra es eminente,
> y, por si salta la puente,
> anda siempre con la cola.
> Si el juez le quisiere librar,
> no hay razón por do no pueda,
> puesto que ya no le queda
> el rabo por desollar.
>   (*PESO,* 250–51)

[A bugger was arrested as a delinquent, not for present crimes but for ones from behind. He thinks that his imprisonment is a whim and that he is innocent, but I know that the trial makes him very happy. He believes that the case is trivial and that the king will free him because he fought in Fuenterrabía. At times, when he wants to display his abilities, it is obvious that in his youth he was skillful on the rebec. But this is not his only talent, because he is eminent on the guitar, and he always carries glue in case the bridge pops off. If the judge wants to, there is no reason not to set him free, since the difficult part is already done.]

As this poem illustrates, in satirical verse that deals with male homosexuality, the anus is the site and marker of sexual deviation. At the same time, the poem epitomizes the complex nature of virtual erotic discourse, whose humorous wordplay, perhaps more than any other, seems untranslatable.

Humor and Homophobia

The foregoing samples of homosexual verse illustrate that satirical and burlesque poetic forms were very much in accord with the homophobia prevalent at all levels of Golden Age society. As a "supplement," the portrayal of a different sexuality was vicarious and expendable, a textual refuge that literary history treated as ready refuse. As John Boswell asserts, hostility to homosexuals of the type found in the literary history invoked here provides singularly revealing examples of the confusion of religious beliefs with popular prejudice (1980, 5–6). In Spain the satirical response to gender bending pointed to what was ultimately perceived as a social danger: By abolishing the difference between the sexes, sodomy presented a challenge to the established male social hierarchy. In other words, this type of literature depicts and cautions against a disorder in sexual relations that might occur anywhere and become a force for social destabilization. Perhaps for this reason physiological explanations of homosexual behavior were omitted from early medical treatises in favor of ethical considerations. Danielle Jacquart and Claude Thomasset have found that in France physicians believed the origin of homosexual behavior to be a corruption of the soul and to bear no relationship to the physical body (1989, 162).

I reiterate that those most often prosecuted for sodomy in Spain were members of the marginal classes, often people of color: soldiers, slaves, foreigners, beggars, vagabonds, gypsies, Moriscos. The corpus of satirical verse discussed in this chapter reconfirms these distinctions and their textualizations. The full weight of the law would fall on such outcasts while well-known aristocrats and the clergy were often protected and spared the humiliation of public scrutiny. One example is the case of the actor Cosme Pérez, the most famous seventeenth-century *gracioso de entremeses*. Creator of the theatrical effeminate Juan Rana, Pérez's own identity was inextricably linked with Rana's (see P. Thompson 2006). The actor was accused of sodomy but was incarcerated for only a brief time. A 1636 notice reproduced in Serralta 1990 states:

> En cuanto al negocio de los que están presos por el pecado nefando, no se usa del rigor que se esperaba, o sea esto porque el ruido ha sido mayor que las nueces, o sea que verdaderamente el poder y el dinero alcanzan lo que quieren. A don Nicolás, el paje del Conde de Castrillo, vemos que anda por la calle, y a Juan Rana, famoso representante, han soltado. (82)

> [With respect to the business of those men who were imprisoned for the nefarious sin, the type of rigor that one would expect is not used, either because it was much ado about nothing or because money and power can achieve anything. We see Don Nicolás, the Count of Castrillo's page, out walking the streets and the famous actor Juan Rana has been released.]

Another prominent suspected homosexual in literary and courtly circles was Juan de Tassis, conde de Villamediana. The count was an aspirant to *privanza* at the court of Philip IV, a king who was notorious for his sexual excess.

The preceding prosecutory prejudice is further complicated by the role of religion, then a true "ideological state apparatus," in Louis Althusser's (1976) terms. The issue of homosexuality among the clergy was acknowledged quite publicly at the time, and clerics were by no means exempt from penances (Bezler 1994, 193–200), although they were often protected from prosecution.[30] In his 1619 *Compendio* (a heterogeneous report of his missionary work in Andalusia between 1578 and 1616), the Jesuit reformer Pedro de León, who spent his life ministering to criminals and prostitutes, reports that sodomy was a serious problem among both the religious and secular clergy.[31] Probably inadvertently, the priest actually points to cover-ups to protect the clergy who were involved in what at the time were crimes of *pecado nefando.* He reports that he persuaded defendants not to incriminate other clergymen in their testimonies and used his influence with judges to dissuade them from conducting public proceedings against members of the clergy (encouraging the judges to allow the accused clergy members' superiors to mete out punishments instead). For these acts of mercy, his superiors and other principal members of the cloth were grateful (P. de León 1981, 436–38). Carrasco also speaks of the huge number of clergy prosecuted for sodomy by the Inquisition in Valencia (1985, 174–87). The majority of the condemned were friars accused of solicitation, or what would today be called child abuse, often of the young novitiates in their charge.

Despite the overwhelming historical evidence regarding sodomy among men of the cloth, it appears that the subject was somewhat silenced in satire.[32] Since the topic is by nature the most scandalous and therefore taboo, this type of verse would, of necessity, be semiclandestine and anonymous. Although I have come across no poems whose protagonists are homosexual friars, existing fragments indicate that the topic was probably fairly common. A likely source for as yet undiscovered texts is the anticlerical satire collected in unpublished and unstudied extant *cancioneros* and manuscripts of erotic poetry. One example of the subject is found in a misogynist, anticlerical *letrilla* attributed to Góngora. Its final strophe, advising a certain Brás against placing his love in *beatas,* warns against even more unpleasant torments to be administered by the priest and sacristan:

Y sin haçer testamento,
si regalarlas procuras,
tendrás capillas seguras
donde haçer tu enterramiento,
y por darte más tormento
el cura y el sacristán

alegras encajarán
çirios en tu candelero.
   (see Carreira 1994, 210)

[And without needing a will, if you pursue them, you will secure a
chapel for your burial, and to torment you even more, the priest and
sacristan will happily stick candles in your candlestick.]

The use of *çirios* and *candeleros* points to the elusive and allusive nature
of sexual language. As I have noted, in poetry such as this, common
terms and repeated actions—here the insertion of an elongated object
into a holder—obtain a virtual sexual significance.[33]

Another brief text involving a man of religion is a *décima* by Fray
Damián Cornejo, "Don Juan, no tengo por bueno."[34] In this poem a
jealous *dama* complains to her *galán* (a suitor of questionable sexual
preferences, since she refers to him as "lindo") because he is being pursued by an Italian friar. The poem concludes in a tone and language
similar to others examined previously: "Que al fin le llenaste el ojo, / y
temo que te le llene" (*PESO*, 253). [Finally you caught (filled) his eye,
and I am afraid that he will catch yours.] Once again, the play on the
word *ojo* foregrounds the anus as iconic signifier of the sodomite.

It is fairly evident, then, that the male homosexual was intimately
and ultimately linked to the notion of alterity that played into the public
phobias fanned by a Counter Reformation atmosphere of social repression and control. And as Peter Stallybrass and Allon White (1986) have
argued, a fascination with the excluded "other" is not so much a sign of
sickness in a society as it is a necessary element in the attempt by society
to define itself by opposing itself to what it is not. Thus, the sodomite
becomes the foil against which "natural," heterosexual orthodoxy, both
religious and social, fashions itself at a time when any form of heterodoxy is extremely dangerous.[35] In this way, the homosexual becomes the
scapegoat about whom René Girard has theorized in his article "Mime-
sis and Violence": the subject of collective action by a community that
purifies itself through the sacrificial immolation of a victim (2000, 11).
Such a ritual purging serves to symbolically cleanse society of its ills and
internal violence, whether these are rooted in sexual, racial, or any other
"difference."

As part of a preliminary conclusion for this chapter, it must be allowed that even though the poetics of sodomy teaches us a great deal about the intricacies of Renaissance mentalities, it is also important to remember that we are dealing with a *literary* genre based on humor.[36] The poems discussed here are, in fact, jokes (whether or not the individual reader finds them in bad taste) at the expense of others. As such, they are "far more likely to depend for their effectiveness on implicit, or indeed explicit, hostility, and may reveal just where societal attitudes are most uncompromising" (Rowson 1991, 53). To understand how uncompromising these attitudes were in early modern Spain, we need only read in León's *Grandeza y miseria en Andalucía* the chilling list of men who were executed for sodomy ("quemado por el pecado nefando"). However, to fail to recognize the significance and the complexities of the comic nature of this verse (and consequently to dismiss it as simple homophobia) is to err through presentism—that is, through a reading process that takes *now* as the only source of moral and literary authority. Accordingly, it is more productive to confront a posteriori readings for what they are and to engage with the *différance* clearly inscribed in the past.

Descriptions of male sodomy in lyric poetry are, in the final analysis and beyond social scapegoating, part of an alternative and antagonistic literary stance toward such serious poetic movements as Petrarchism. These images represent the irruption into verse of the love that cannot speak its name, albeit as an *ejemplo vitando* or in the case of female/female sexuality as titillation for men and women (see the discussion in Chapter Three). Thus, satire embraces both the historically unthinkable (homosexuality) and the poetically unspeakable (the obscene language that inscribes it).[37] In a very full sense, this is a transgressive challenge to literary history and the canons that make it so normative. Within a literary system, especially after formalist accountings of it, the distinction between aesthetic and extra-aesthetic function is the differentiation between the communicative and the artistic functions of language. But as John Frow reminds us, and this type of satirical poetry affirms, this division "still does not fully clarify the way in which the poetic sign manages to signify simultaneously in two different ways" (1986, 95). In this regard, it is necessary to observe that if we fail to take into account what these signs offer in Spanish satirical poetry with a deviant theme, many phenomena become incomprehensible.

Finally, it is evident that only through an understanding of the cultured poetic traditions operative in the seventeenth century can we see clearly that, in the texts examined here, the conventional notions and terminology of love are significantly absent in order to accommodate those of vice. The discourse of satire cannot, in fact, accommodate the notion of male "homosexual love." This expression itself is an impossible oxymoron, since the language of Renaissance desire is, exclusively and by nature, that of heterosexual love. In this regard, Joseph Cady (1993) discusses the fact that in the English Renaissance, although both homosexuality and heterosexuality are recognized as real categories of experience, "love" and its associated terminology are the de facto language for heterosexuality. As Chapter One argues in the discussion of *La tía fingida,* social action does not always arise out of desire. Perhaps because or even in spite of this implausibility, the rich vein of satirical poetry that deals with homosexuality and its economies can do much to illuminate the critical sphere of Spanish Golden Age studies. The center of these poems is paradoxically both outside society and part of it. It would be a mistake to try to follow them as a point-by-point satire or simply as representative of the fastidious connoisseurship of the unmentionable. Because these poems rely on the violation of tradition, it is useless to try to find the deterministic code that may rule them without exception. Resistant readers, in their disgust, make moral judgments, whereas (at most) they should admit to aesthetic judgments (Ruse 1995, 123). It does serve a purpose, however, to explore the criteria that they follow and to study how each poem is related to them. To admit such works into our canon permits us to elucidate further not only a peculiar strand of the transgressive poetics of satire but also the sociology of early modern sexuality and deviance as they were both experienced and textualized in Spain.

CHAPTER THREE

Lesbianism
as Dream and Myth

Oh, what will be the end of me, whom a love possesses
that no one ever heard of, a strange and monstrous love?
　　Ovid, *Metamorphoses*

In *The Renaissance of Lesbianism in Early Modern England* (2002), Valerie Traub argues that in English history women's homoerotic desire seems to have fallen into a great vacuum of silence and invisibility. It is not simply that female subordination was aggravated by the confinement of women to nonliterary spaces, as current criticism continues to argue. The answer lies in the gaps of literary history and the gaps of the history of sexuality, which are gradually being filled in recent years with the empirical findings noted throughout this book. Although the historical void that Traub mentions has been narrowed by Terry Castle's 2003 anthology, *The Literature of Lesbianism,* early modern Spain and its literature continue to be excluded from such compilations.[1] In Spain, although the depiction of female homoeroticism is much rarer and quite different from the highly critical images of male homosexuality discussed in Chapter Two, it is by no means invisible and it is often clearly sensual. Nonetheless, it would seem that lesbian sexual preferences in early modern Spain, as in England, "were considered improbable, impossible, implausible, insignificant. . . . On the other hand, such desires were culturally practiced and represented in a variety of ways, although often according to a governing logic that attempted to reinscribe their impossibility" (Traub 2002, 6). This is certainly true of Golden Age Spanish texts, which exploited the titillation of female-female desire while at the same time disavowing it as impossible.

It is useful, therefore, to review the historical context of lesbian sexuality in early modern society. The term *lesbian,* like the term *homosexuality,* was not commonly used until the nineteenth century, and even then it tended to designate certain acts rather than a distinct sexual identity and social group. It appears that sixteenth-century European men found it difficult to accept the notion that women could be sensually attracted to other women, since the prevailing phallocentric view of human sexuality made it doubtful that a woman could sustain the sexual desires of another. Because of this, in law, medicine, and the public mind, sexual relations between women, although acknowledged, were in general ignored (Brown 1986, 6).

As the most hushed aspect of the silent sin, or *peccatum mutum,* female homosexuality was virtually imperceptible, although not to the extent previously thought.[2] Erotic intimacy between women was certainly not unknown during the time of the writers discussed in this chapter; however, transgressors were not allowed to indulge their desires freely. For example, in his *Relación de la cárcel de Sevilla* (1983), written during the last years of the sixteenth century, Cristóbal de Chaves states that "many women" engaged in sexual relations with each other in the royal prison in Seville.[3] In effect, although female sodomy was recognized as a crime against nature by Gregorio López in his gloss to *Las siete partidas* (Crompton 1980–8, 18–19; see also *Las siete partidas* [Sanponts y Barba, Martí de Eixalá, and Ferrer y Subirana 1843–44, 4:330–31]), very few of the hundreds, if not thousands, of cases of sodomy prosecuted by civil and ecclesiastical courts in early modern Europe involved women. Moreover, at least when they did not use an instrument for vaginal penetration, women accused of sodomy generally received lighter sentences than burning at the stake (the usual punishment for men).[4]

However, Thomas Laqueur discusses the condemnation of the tribade, the woman who performed the "man's role" in lesbian relations, as the partner who was perceived as a threat to the social order, since she played out, literally embodied, "radical, culturally unacceptable reversals of power and prestige" (1990, 53). Traub explores the fact that in the early modern period the clitoris and the tribade were given their first sustained articulation as objects of anatomical inquiry, leading to their inevitable linking in cultural history (2002, 190). In the early seventeenth century, in her *Razón y forma de la Galera y Casa Real* (1608), the women's prison administrator Magdalena de San Jerónimo strove to establish a penitentiary regimen that equaled women with men in terms of the imposition of punishments and the method of carrying them out.[5]

Although the same relative silence observed in the historical record occurs to a significant degree in early modern literature, we must allow that at times this silence confirms what history conceals or prohibits. Nevertheless, when homosexuality is mentioned in literature, its protagonists are generally men, and, as we have seen, their conduct is often veiled by reticence or disavowed in satire. Meanwhile, female homosexual desire is not only generally mute but also scarcely visible (or at least is disguised) in literature. Significant exceptions exist, of course, as with the burlesque erotic poetry and other texts discussed here and the numerous examples from other literatures compiled in Castle 2003.

Rather than condemn lesbian practices as unnatural vice (as occurs with male homosexuality), Spanish Golden Age literature seems to depict—and often dismiss—such behavior as harmless sexual play, as an inconsequential pastime that occurs when males are unavailable, as a supplement, as an apprenticeship for "real" sex with men, as a dream, or as myth. Rarely, if ever, is female homoeroticism—as titillating as it might be—presented as an emotionally valid or sexually complete relationship. Instead, early modern texts (and at times their exegetes) tend to transform and refocus the impossible proposition of female-female emotional attachment and sexual practice in order to force fit them, consciously or not, into a male-centered view of sexuality. For this reason what we would now call "lesbian literature," literature that depicts female homoeroticism, paradoxically can be just as phallocentric as any other Golden Age erotic writing.

Prosthetic Pleasures

Given this early modern condition, it is not surprising that in burlesque and satirical poetry female-female sexuality is generally defined and activated, as it were, by the male substitute or prosthetic penis, often called a *baldrés*. *Baldrés*, an early form of the word *baldés*, meaning a type of dildo, is a soft sheepskin that the *Diccionario de la Real Academia Española* (1992) still defines as "una piel de oveja curtida, suave y endeble, que sirve para guantes *y otras cosas*" (my emphasis) [a soft, delicate sheepskin that is used for gloves *and other things*].[6] This sex toy, made out of leather, horn, or wood and at times covered with velvet, is described in Chaves's *Relación;* the "other things" for which the *baldrés* is employed are specified there as follows: "Y habiendo muchas mujeres que queriendo más ser hombres que lo que naturaleza les dió, se han castigado muchas que en la cárcel se han hecho gallos con un valdrés hecho en forma de natura de hombre, que atado con sus cintas se lo ponian; y han llevado por esto docientos azotes" (1983, 25–26). [Many women in prison were punished who, wanting to be more of a man than nature allowed them, turned themselves into cocks with a false penis, which they tied on themselves with ribbon. This earned them two hundred lashes.]

An early mention of the *baldrés* as phallic substitute appears in the "Coplas del Provincial," cited in the discussion of the sodomite/heretic pairing in Chapter Two. Verses 413–16 denounce an unnamed marquise who replaces her absent husband with a *baldrés*:

> Decid, la dama sin nombre
> por no ofender al marqués,
> ¿a cómo vale el valdrés
> por falta de cuerpo de hombre?
>   (In Rodríguez Puértolas 1984, 255)

> [Tell me, nameless lady, so as not to offend the marquis, when you lack a man's body, how much is a dildo worth?]

Probably even earlier than the foregoing "Coplas," the use of a prosthetic penis is mentioned in a fifteenth-century Catalonian medical treatise on coitus and sexual hygiene, *Speculum al foderi* [*The Mirror of Coitus*]. There the *baldrés* (or *gedoma*) is described as a means by which women might satisfy desires unmet by men:

> E sapiats que a les fembres que los ve lo talent molt calt, que no se avénen ab elles los hòmens, e per aquesta rahó [h]a y fembres d'aquestes que usen de gedoma; si que és fet de cuyr lent e de cotó

confeccionat de dins a forma de vit; e usen ab ell e meten-lo en lo cony entró són fartas e perden lo desig. (Quoted in Solomon 1990, 80)

[You should know that ardent women who enjoy orgasm, but who have no man with whom to lie, use a dildo, which is made of soft leather and cotton, and formed in the shape of a penis; they insert this into their vagina until their desire is satiated.] (36)[7]

The most graphic and detailed early modern reference to dildos, however, is surely the one that appears in Pietro Aretino's *Ragionamenti*. In the first dialogue on the life of nuns, Nanna describes to Antonia the convent orgies, during which the nuns are served glass fruits designed to hold warm water and made in Murano "to look like a prick, except that these had two large dangling bells that would have done honor to a tambourine. . . . And blessed, not just lucky, was the woman who grabbed the biggest, thickest fruit, nor did a single one of them forget to kiss hers, saying as she did: 'These little things abate the temptations of the flesh'" (1994, 22). Nanna later relates very graphically how she put the glass cocks to use.

Such references attest to the fact that although lesbianism as a sexual/social identifier was probably not recognized at the time, awareness of female homoeroticism existed. For this reason the category of sodomite was applicable to both women and men, as we saw in Chapter Two with the witch protagonist in "Por no comer la carne sodomita." However, as noted, the imposition of legal strictures differed for the sexes, and in Spain the punishment for sodomy was generally less severe for women than for men. Similarly, Guido Ruggiero asserts that lesbianism was not prosecuted in Renaissance Venice probably because it did not threaten the structure of the family with the birth of illegitimate children. He also surmises that lack of respect for women's bodies may have played a role (1985, 189–90 n. 21). As we have seen, although López's 1565 gloss to the thirteenth-century legal code *Las siete partidas* stipulated the death penalty for crimes against nature committed by both sexes, unless they used some sort of device for penetration, women were rarely prosecuted for sodomy in Spain (see López 1829–31). Francisco Tomás y Valiente discusses López's gloss in his essay "El crimen y pecado contra natura." He explains that López believed that the death penalty should be withheld in cases of female sodomy because although he viewed it as a criminal act, he considered it less serious than male sodomy, since coitus involving the spilling of male semen is not possible between women, which eliminates the possibility that the male seed can be misspent. Instead, whipping and incarceration were to be applied, "pena que deberá agravarse cuando mediante 'aliquo instrumento virginitas violetur'" (quoted in Tomás y Valiente 1990, 46) [a punishment that should be graver when the crime is committed using an instrument that violates the hymen].

With respect to this last issue, Tomás y Valiente provides a chilling quotation in which Antonio Gómez, another early modern jurist, addresses the issue of putting nuns to death for using an instrument for penetration: "*quod iste casu jam contingit de facto in quibus monialibus quae fuerunt combustae*" (48). It would appear that these nuns provide viable proof that if women were convicted of using a phallic substitute, they might be burned at the stake for sodomy.[8] The use of such a tool linked the crime of sodomy to appropriation of the position and function of men, a much more serious matter in terms of social and gender hierarchies. Female homoeroticism *ut sodomitico more* is typically documented in trial records in terms of one woman attempting to behave as a man with another woman. Thus, the emphasis (legal documents, like literature, have a written narrative and subjectivity) is placed on what was perceived to be the real aberration: inversion of sex and gender roles through prosthetic supplementation. In such instances, crime was possible only if penetration occurred. Thus, once a woman assumed the sexual, social, and cultural attributes of masculinity, thereby abolishing the difference between the sexes, she was immediately punished (Carrasco 1985, 36).

Although, to date, no recorded cases of female sodomy actually punished by death in Spain have been brought to light, much evidence exists of public whippings (hence Chaves's reference to the two hundred lashes meted out in the Seville jail). This was not the case beyond the Pyrenees, however. Lorraine Daston and Katharine Park assert that despite the assumption that most persons brought to trial for sodomy were men, female sodomy was the object of strenuous prosecution in Renaissance France (1985, 8–9).[9] The aforementioned notwithstanding, in the verse examined in Chapter Two and in this section of the present chapter, satirical responses are created to usurp the textual space of "serious" poetry. Therefore, in spite of stern contemporary social and legal proscriptions against what we would now conventionally call lesbianism, erotic humor tends to prevail in satirical and burlesque verse. For example, the sonnet "Hallándose dos damas en faldeta" from Fray Melchor de la Serna's *Jardín de Venus* depicts a scene of female homoerotics in a tone best described as lighthearted:[10]

> Hallándose dos damas en faldeta
> tratando del amor con mucha risa,
> se quitaron las faldetas y camisa
> por hacer más gustosa la burleta.
> La una con la otra recio aprieta,
> mas dales pena ver la carne lisa.
> Entonces llegó Amor, con mucha prisa,
> y puso entre las dos una saeta.
> La una se apartó muy consolada
> por haber ya labrado su provecho,
> la otra se quedó con la agujeta.
> Y como se miró, viéndose armada,
> por el daño que el dómine había hecho
> le puso por prisión una bragueta.
>   (*PESO,* 46)

[Two ladies, while laughing and chatting about love, took off their skirts and chemises to make the game more enjoyable. They clutched each other tightly but were saddened to see smooth flesh. Then Love arrived very quickly and placed an arrow between them. One moved away greatly consoled after having satisfied herself; the other remained with the stiff prick. And when she looked down and saw herself armed, because of the damage that master had caused, she imprisoned him in a codpiece.]

What typifies this sonnet and at the same time surpasses its satirical tenor is the overwhelming erotic phallocentrism that it reflects. Indeed, the attitude that prevails in this poem, which was dominant in early modern society (at least among males), was that, by nature, all sex had to involve a male partner or at least a male substitute. To signify at all, penetration had to occur. As we have seen, this is the attitude that underlies the legal discussions and prohibitions surrounding female sodomy. As a result, in the masculinist perception, one of the partners would have to adopt and adapt the male role in order for sex between women to be possible and to have any meaning. Cupid's arrow, a borrowing from conventional love poetry, here becomes the eroticized signifying instrument, the supplement that enables sexual satisfaction. And the woman who is literally armed with the false phallus immediately becomes the male, covering her/himself with a codpiece and thus upsetting all horizons of expectation.[11]

Another noticeable characteristic of "Hallándose dos damas en faldeta" is that the poem inscribes sex between women in terms of play. For example, the expressions "tratando del amor con mucha risa" and "burleta" (and the "eta" rhyme of the two quatrains) establish the poem's ludic tone and present the women's lovemaking as a racy anecdote to be retold by men—and perhaps women—in private camaraderie, which was probably one of the main (if not only) societal functions for poems such as these. Consequently, female sodomy is presented in a less scandalous way, and the mode of female sexuality that it represents is integrated into the universe of (masculine) erotic fantasy and is presented as playful fun. Again, what brings female sexuality into existence here, what takes it from play to sex, is the richness of its supplement, its surplus value in a society for which women had lesser value. As Jacques Derrida observes in *La dissémination* (1972), it is impossible to think about the logic of supplement without thinking about the logic of *différance* and play at the same time. Yet what is ultimately revealed about this period, in its Spanish specificity, is the lack of knowledge and understanding of, and a lack of concern with, female eroticism in male discourse—what Traub has called the (in)significance of women's erotic desire for each other. At the same time, however, we should note that the phallus is reduced to an easily appropriated and replaceable (by any of a number of available and inventive substitutes) sex tool operated as much by women as by men.

The sexual supplement, or substitute, is the theme of other anonymous poems, such as the ballad "Fue Teresa a su majuelo," included in *PESO* (277–80). In this poem the young peasant Teresa experiences an unexpected erotic and onanistic interlude with a turnip while inspecting her vines. This composition belongs to the erotic lyric tradition common to the *romancero nuevo,* in which the country garden and vegetables are the scene and symbol or instrument of rustic sex. By the same token and since the ballads in principle reflect practically every phase of Spanish life, this could well add to the literary history of the *romancero* tradition. In this same vein, Lope de Vega registers the erotic possibilities of certain vegetables and plants of distinctive shapes and properties in his ballads on Belardo el Hortelano.[12] In "Fue Teresa a su majuelo," the protagonist happily accommodates a sprouting turnip and two suggestive chickpeas into her "pot" (*puchero*), ludically converting them into a sexual cure-all. This poem is a good example of how an imaginative erotic poet can transform practically any round or elongated object into a metaphor for testicle or penis.

An anonymous sonnet on the same theme and within the same tradition illustrates how a widow ingeniously substitutes for the absent male partner whatever is at hand, as it were. In this case a "compassionate radish" performs the sexual functions (the only ones that the widow seems to miss) of her dead husband:

> Tú, rábano piadoso, en este día
> visopija serás en mi trabajo;
> serás lugarteniente de un carajo,
> mi marido serás, legumbre mía.
> (*PESO,* 226–27)

[You, compassionate radish, today you will be a cock in my labors, a deputy cock; you will be my husband, vegetable of mine.]

It is obvious that while, in principle, burlesque erotic poems such as those discussed herein play with notions of female desire and sexuality, they actually serve to textualize and foreground the phallus, either to aggrandize it in the tradition of the *Priapea* of Roman antiquity and the Renaissance or to subvert its supposed superiority in a playful way.[13] Whether it is present, absent, or replaced, the phallus is central to the male-authored lyric of female desire. At the same time, the permissive and jocose tone of this poetry can lead us safely to suppose that sixteenth- and seventeenth-century Western European culture at times permitted (or at least acknowledged) female autoeroticism and what we now know as lesbianism (the latter at least in theory) because it was believed (by men) that sex between women was a prelude to or inconsequential simulacrum for heterosexual sex. Lillian Faderman has pointed out in this regard that in the erotic literature of the French libertines lesbianism was considered to be a mere apprenticeship for sex with men, serving when men were unavailable and losing its appeal when they were not (1981, 24).

Dreams and Transformations: "El sueño de la viuda de Aragón"

The mental context described forms the background for an unusual narrative poem composed by Fray Melchor de la Serna, "El sueño de la viuda de Aragón."[14] At the beginning of this tale of transformation, we learn that a widow shares a bed with her two young, beautiful, and virginal maids, Teodora (described as "varonil" or manly) and Medulina ("menor, más delicada y femenina") (see Martín and Díez Fernández 2003, 84, vv. 23–24) [younger, more delicate and feminine]. The widow longs for her late husband and remembers with nostalgia old times spent in bed. As the poetic voice tells us, "De aquellas dulces noches se acordaba / que con su buen marido ella dormía" (85, vv. 51–52). [She recalled those sweet nights when she used to sleep with her good husband.]

The stanzas that follow reveal with great frankness the desire that consumes the widow as she reminisces and dreams about her husband: "Y muchas—creo yo—que ella soñaba / que entre sus blancas piernas le tenía / y quisiera durara el sueño un año / por hurtarle la vuelta al desengaño" (85, vv. 53–56). [And many more nights, I believe, she dreamed that she had him between her white legs and wished that the dream would last a year in order to forestall her disappointment.] At this point, while her yearnings are firmly rooted in heterosexual desire, the narrator introduces the theme of erotic dream. The poet expresses the protagonist's ardor through a series of highly charged erotic similes that reproduce the various stages of lovemaking between a *dama* and a *galán* that Petrarchan love lyric so chastely circumvents. In her dream the husband instructs his wife to climb on top of him so that the couple might share the sexual tasks. Since he is not available, she mounts Teodora, who is lying next to her asleep and feels nothing. The widow gropes for the male organ as she used to do with her husband but obviously does not find it on Teodora. At this moment a miraculous development occurs with the materialization of the phallic supplement. This narrative and literal deus ex machina will allow the widow to satisfy her desire:

> Mas ahora su fortuna le ayudase,
> o tal planeta entonces confluyese,
> o la fuerza del sueño lo causase,
> o la imaginación lo permitiese,
> como a Teodora el vientre le atentase
> y más bajo la mano le pusiese,
> natura hubo por bien de mejorarse
> y de nueva figura disfrazarse.
> De la concavidad que antes tuviera
> produjo un tal pimpollo tan lozano,
> que ninguna mujer, por más matrera,
> podrá con los halagos de su mano.
> En todo lo demás cual antes era,
> excepto esta señal del sexo humano,
> quedó Teodora, que ni fue barbada
> ni se le enronqueció la voz delgada.
>   (85–86, vv. 81–96)

[But now whether fortune helped her or a planet influenced it, or the force of her desire caused it, or her imagination allowed it, when she touched Teodora's belly and placed her hand farther down, nature decided to improve Teodora and dress her in a new figure. From the previous hollowness emerged such a vigorous sprout that no woman, no matter how clever, could handle it. In everything else she remained as before—except for this sign of human sex—she neither grew a beard nor did her voice deepen.]

In other words, that strange protrusion, whether a product of fate, of the stars, of the dream, or of the widow's own keen imagination, allows Teodora to function sexually as a man, without totally transforming her into one. In this sense Serna's tale varies from the fable of gender transformation that probably inspired it, Ovid's story of Iphis and Ianthe in book 9, vv. 666–797 of *Metamorphoses* (see Ovid 1984, 2:50–61). In this tale a husband instructs his pregnant wife to kill their unborn child if it is a girl. To save her daughter, the mother dresses her as a boy. Once Iphis reaches adolescence, she is betrothed to Ianthe, whom she loves passionately. The anomalous nature of such a love is an enigma to Iphis, who wonders how a woman could possibly love another, since such a passion is impossible in nature:

> "Oh, what will be the end of me," she said, "whom a love possesses that no one ever heard of, a strange and monstrous love? . . . Cows do not love cows, nor mares, mares; but the ram desires the sheep, and his own doe follows the stag. So also birds mate, and in the whole animal world there is no female smitten with love for female! (Ovid 1984, 55–57)

Isis resolves the erotic impasse—the impossibility of same-sex passion—by transforming Iphis into a man, and the marriage is happily consummated. In the widow of Aragon's tale, Serna emulates the manner in which Ovid narrates the metamorphosis:

> Her face seemed of a darker hue, her strength seemed greater, her very features sharper, and her locks, all unadorned, were shorter than before. She seemed more vigorous than was her girlish wont. In fact, you who but lately were a girl are now a boy! (Ovid 1984, 59–61)

Serna parodies this unlikely female-to-male conversion by refraining from transforming Teodora into a man: "En todo lo demás, cual antes era / excepto esta señal del sexo humano, / quedó Teodora, que ni fue barbada / ni se le enronqueció la voz delgada" (86, vv. 93–96).[15] Instead of transforming her, Serna chooses to supplement her by tacking on the male sex organ that she lacks. By focusing on the even more unlikely spontaneous generation of a penis, Serna textualizes what Ovid leaves unsaid. By doing so and by emulating the ancient poet's ironic sense of humor, Serna parodies the notion of metamorphosis performed by and upon the Olympian gods. The poet also dedicates a considerable number of strophes to elaborate on the women's intimacy with sexually charged similes, detailed descriptions of copulation, and an insistence on the women's passionate abandon while under the guise of dreaming. In fact, the story reads very much like a presumed heterosexual male fantasy of lesbian lovemaking.

Beyond considerations of Ovidian literary models, however, and according to Laqueur (1990), the one-sex/two-gender model dominated thinking about sexual difference during this period. In other words, a woman's body was observed by anatomists to be like a man's in form but inferior. The female genitalia were seen as an inverted, thus imperfect, penis.[16] Therefore, perhaps what is represented in this poem is simply an extension of nature, a handy enlargement of the female sex organs as they were at the time perceived to be, in order to facilitate genital sex with another woman.

In this regard, Traub points out that early seventeenth-century French and English gynecological texts refer repeatedly to clitoral hypertrophy (2002, 194). Both Ambroise Paré's *Des monstres et prodiges* (1573) and subsequently Helkiah Crooke's *Microcosmographia* (1615) relate an enlarged clitoris to "unnatural" lesbian desires:

> Sometimes [the clitoris] groweth to such a length that it hangeth without the cleft like a mans member, especially when it is fretted with the touch of the cloaths, and so strutteth and groweth to a rigiditie as doth the yarde [penis] of a man. And this part it is which those wicked women doe abuse called *Tribades* (often mentioned by many authors, and in some states worthily punished) to their mutual and unnatural lusts. (Crooke quoted in Traub 2002, 194)

At the same time, it was believed in many circles that the excessive indulgence in genital self-stimulation that was believed to cause clitoral enlargement was owed to women's "natural" hypersexuality.

Another extraliterary possibility might be that Serna's text of gender transmutation reflects the growing interest during the seventeenth century in cases of women who spontaneously changed sex. Jacobo Sanz Hermida has addressed this social phenomenon, noting that such transformations garnered the attention of doctors, moralists, and writers, and writers echoed citizens' concerns regarding the possibility of such gender mutations (1996, 518). These transformations frequently included the late eruption of a penis and were signaled by the sprouting of a beard and the deepening of the woman's voice. This, however, does not happen to Teodora. The cases of gender mutation probably reflect the medical and social confusion caused by people of ambiguous genitalia, who were (at a time when these individuals were not surgically "reassigned" to a specific sex at birth, as has been the controversial practice in modern times) frequently classified as hermaphrodites.[17]

Obviously, Fray Melchor was aware of commonly held ideas regarding the power of the imagination to modify the body and even bring about sex change. During his time people believed that a pregnant woman's imagination, for example, could modify her own body or the body of her fetus (Fisher 2006, 14). Teodora's spontaneous generation of a penis, then, is not particularly remarkable within this sociohistorical context, especially since sexual transformations were also thought to be prompted by sexual play (Fisher 2006, 8).

This poem's early modern medical context certainly tended to reinforce and reserve sexual relations for heterosexual couples. In a penetrating analysis of Renaissance erotic pathology, Roger Bartra affirms, "Es interesante notar que, desde antiguo, uno de los remedios contra la melancolía erótica que recomendaban los médicos fue el coito, que permitía expulsar los humores excedentes, eliminar ideas fijas y, según Rufus de Éfeso, 'disolver el amor'" (2001, 92). [It is interesting to note that since ancient times, one of the cures recommended by doctors for erotic melancholy was coitus, which permitted the expulsion of excess humors, the elimination of obsessions, and, according to Rufus of Ephesus, 'the dissolution of love.'"] In this atmosphere, both Teodora and Serna's other female protagonists can be viewed as superfluous, or part of an excess masculinity, because certain perceptions governed that mentality. Bartra describes these perceptions as follows: "Como señala Mary Wack, el coito terapéutico no parece haber planteado demasiados dilemas éticos, porque las relaciones sexuales de los hombres fuera del matrimonio, especialmente con prostitutas, no amenazaban el orden familiar ni la pureza de la descendencia; además, el fácil acceso a prostitutas en muchas ciudades permite suponer que el coito como remedio no ofrecía muchas dificultades prácticas" (93). [As Mary Wack has pointed out, therapeutic coitus does not seem to have presented too many ethical dilemmas, because men's extramarital sexual relations, especially with prostitutes, did not threaten the family or lineage; moreover, the easy access to prostitutes in many cities allows us to suppose that coitus as a cure did not present many practical difficulties.] Consequently, it is not too far-fetched to propose that in the final analysis and beyond his strictly "literary" messages, Serna is portraying the sexual "cures" available during his time.

Sanz Hermida presents Serna's description of Teodora's transformation as evidence that the poet was familiar with the contributing factors commonly held responsible for gender mutations: planetary influences or the power of dream or the imagination (1996, 519). I believe that Serna's sources and concerns are far more literary than scientific, since he was, after all, a humanist and an Ovidian scholar. Be that as it may, the paradoxical result is that we are reading the textualization of a heterosexual act, despite the fact that it occurs between two women. That is to say, the sex act in which these two women engage, supposedly in their sleep, is depicted as a simulacrum of heterosexual lovemaking. Thus, it is a result of the "true" desire that a woman "unquestionably" feels for a man. The author effectively disallows the possibility that any erotic activities that do not involve a penis substitute might be satisfying to women.

The ladies fall asleep, and two hours later they awake astonished to find themselves in each other's arms. The confused widow lovingly says to Teodora, "Yo no sé si eres él o si eres ella. / Respóndeme, que soy muy cuidadosa / porque de la mujer tienes el nombre / y tus hechos no son sino de hombre" (Martín and Díez Fernández 2003, 86, vv. 117–20). [I don't know if you are a he or a she. Answer me, because I am very worried, since you have a woman's name but your actions are those of a man.] Teodora, perturbed, responds that she cannot understand her own metamorphosis either:

> "Señora, yo no sé qué responderme.
> Estoy de mi figura tan mudada
> que no puedo a mí misma conocerme.
> De lo que ahora soy, yo no sé nada,
> ni quién barón de hembra pudo hacerme,
> verdad es que después de ser dormida
> soñé que era en hombre convertida."
>
> (87, vv. 122–28)

[Mistress, I don't know what to answer. My figure is so changed that I cannot even recognize myself. I know nothing of what I am now or who could change me from a female into a male. The truth is that after I fell asleep, I dreamed that I was transformed into a man.]

In this way the poet reminds us that both women have been dreaming and that, strangely and happily, their dreams coincide with Teodora's sexual conversion (in her dream) into a "mancebo muy apuesto" (87, v. 138) [a very handsome young man] who has pursued and made love to the widow. Consequently, women's sexual desires and lives are but a dream, a fact not mitigated by the literary use that is made of them.

For an age (today) concerned with tracing the history of unconventional sexualities and the literature in which they appear, Serna would seem to provide fertile ground. However, both the desire expressed in this novella and the manner of its satisfaction are firmly anchored in a rather conventional and normative heterosexuality. As well as functioning as a sexual facilitator, the miraculous phallus conducts the reader or listener to the symbolic center of the novella. This is the burlesque encomium to the phallus that appears between verses 153 and 216 and that commences when the delighted widow grasps Teodora's miraculous organ:

Tomábale después entre las manos
el miembro genital recién nacido,
al cual daba loores soberanos
poniéndole continuo este apellido:
"¡O padre universal de los humanos
de quien tantas naciones han salido!
¡Tú solo das contento a las mujeres
y en ti se cifran todos sus placeres!
                    (87–88, vv. 153–60)

[Afterward she took the newborn member in her hands and praised it supremely, giving it this name: Oh universal human father, from whom so many nations have emerged! You alone make women happy and are the center of all their pleasures!]

The sixty-verse homage is ingenious but conventional within the parameters of priapic literature, with its many echoes of Aretino. The poet tells us that no women—from maidens, married women, widows, and *beatas* to orphans, queens, and slaves—can resist the pleasures to be found in the phallus. The final verses confirm that feminine physical charms cannot be the source of women's desire; only the phallus can provide true pleasure. As if to certify the truth of the widow's speech, and perhaps to coddle the vanity of male readers and listeners, the widow and Teodora fall into each other's arms once again to make love with great abandon. In the remainder of this narrative poem, the widow's desire grows continually as she makes love to Teodora all night and every night. Medulina, the other maid, still shares their bed, but—no ménages à trois here—they discretely delay their lovemaking until she has fallen asleep. In all this the older woman corresponds to the literary convention of the insatiably lusty widow so popular in the erotic tradition.

Eventually, Teodora tires of sex with only one partner, an older woman at that ("mujer en días entrada" [91, v. 300]) and falls in love with Medulina. Her companion is confused but captivated by Teodora's new body part, and the two become lovers. Finally, Teodora invents a trick to dispense with the widow. Medulina goes to the older woman's bed posing in the dark as Teodora.[18] A comic and eminently visual scene follows in which the widow grabs at Medulina, thinking that she is the well-endowed Teodora, desperately trying to find her penis:

> ¡Qué es esto! ¿Estoy despierta? ¡Sí, por cierto!
> ¿Siento qué toco? ¡Sí, muy bien lo siento!
> ¿Acierto, sí o no? ¡Muy bien acierto!
> ¿Yo tiento carnes? ¡Sí, carnes atiento!
> ¿Hay algo aquí? ¡No, todo está desierto!
> ¿Es éste su lugar? ¡Sí, este es su asunto!
> ¿Pues qué es de ello? Que aquesto que aquí toco
> no es lo que busco, no; ni esto tampoco.
>   (97, vv. 505–12)

[What is this! Am I awake? Yes, indeed. Do I feel what I am touching? Yes, I feel it very well. Am I right, yes or no? I am very right!

Am I not touching flesh? Yes, I am! Is there something here? No, everything is dead! Is this the place? Yes, this is her thing. But what happened to the other thing? What I'm touching here isn't what I'm looking for, no, nor is this.]

A very similar situation of women desperately seeking the phallus occurs in Cristóbal de Villalón's satirical but sober *El Crótalon* (1990), discussed later in this chapter. In Serna's tale Medulina pretends to be Teodora, who has supposedly awakened transformed back into a woman. The novella ends quickly with the sad and penitent widow returning to attend to her affairs, leaving the two young women to theirs. Medulina ends up mysteriously pregnant; the poetic voice does not say by whom, although it would seem that the miraculous phallus has recovered its original procreative function as "universal father." The tale concludes with the following verses: "Y despertemos ya de tan gran sueño / no digan que es más grande que su dueño" (99, vv. 575–76). [And let us awaken now from such a great dream, lest they say it is greater than the one who is having it.]

Obviously, the narrative frame of a dream excludes from any claim of legitimacy the lesbian lovemaking that has been depicted in such sensual detail, thus neutralizing its potentially transgressive charge. These final verses, where the readers or listeners are urged to awaken from their dream, clearly link this novella to the *sueño erótico* poetry that has been anthologized by Antonio Alatorre (2003) and analyzed by Christopher Maurer (1990). Maurer observes that Golden Age erotic dream sonnets are characterized by reticence; in other words, the poet uses chaste euphemisms to allude to the sexual delights attained in the dream instead of describing them directly. As I have argued, that is to be expected of the time; moreover, in Spain the more explicitly a poem describes sexual pleasure, the more closely it approximates burlesque or pornographic verse.

As a consequence, the burlesque aspects of "El sueño de la viuda" are of fundamental significance. In effect, by using humor, by relegating female homoeroticism to the status of harmless play in the absence of a "real" sex partner, this poem implicitly affirms that sex without a phallus is neither conceivable nor truly sex. Indeed, in the very structure of the poem, whereby sex between women leads directly to Priapus, an obvious conclusion is that within the androcentric erotics of the poem no space exists for female agency. As we have seen, lesbian eros is at best a dream and does not matter, since any risks that it might pose to the masculine ego and sexual power structure by usurping the male are placed in checkmate. At the same time, however, the effortless excision and splicing of the phallus onto an otherwise unchanged female body encourages readers to question the locus and determinants of masculinity. Therefore, the overarching burlesque tone of the poem, plus the inherent irony in the rather redundant homage to the phallus, vacates the poem of any serious misogynistic intent as it foregrounds female sexuality. This verse novella should be read within the humorous humanistic context of Serna's poetic output.

Nevertheless, it is evident that even in, or perhaps especially in, erotic poetry, libidinal currents rarely flow against the heterosexual current or are conceived outside it, particularly in texts that are written by men and are designed in great part to entertain and titillate a masculine (although by no means exclusively so) public. In fact, Dutch historians have suggested that in Holland women were not prosecuted on same-sex charges until the end of the eighteenth century because female-female sexual activities were considered to be a source of erotic attraction for men (van der Meer 1992, 202). In this regard, the motivation behind the explicit depiction of lesbian sex in "El sueño de la viuda" is to shock, entice, amuse, entertain, and arouse the reader, whether male or female. I include female, since for early modern lesbians sexually explicit texts that headlined female-female erotics, even when phallicly mediated, would have been a good read. But as Maria Grazia Profeti has pointed out with respect to erotic poetry in general, another motivation is the pure pleasure of naming the unmentionable and thus transgressing the taboos of discourse (1992, 63).

Nonetheless, the depiction of female homoerotics in literature is as generically determined as are other themes. For this reason the genre that showcases the theme of lesbian attraction determines, to a great extent, the presentation, interpretation, tone, and significance of the topic. This is why when we examine the depiction of early modern lesbianism, the tale of Julio and Julieta from Villalón's *El Crótalon de Cristóforo Gnofoso,* although it is similar to "El sueño de la viuda," brings different issues to bear.

Twins and Trickery: El Crótalon

Although it belongs to a different genre and was potentially written for a different audience, the Julio-Julieta tale shares certain affinities with Serna's novella. Antonio Rodríguez Moñino first pointed out this similarity (although he mistakenly attributes Serna's work to Cristóbal de Tamariz) in his 1959 *Relieves de erudición* (Villalón 1990, 254 n. 28).[19] The authors of these very different works were both humanist scholars and academicians (Serna at Salamanca and Villalón at Valladolid). Villalón also held university degrees in art (from Salamanca) and theology (from Valladolid) (Villalón 1990, 21). In addition, both were skilled humorists who burlesqued certain aspects of religious life, although the critique is more serious in *El Crótalon*.[20]

The Julio-Julieta episode is a tale within a misogynistic cautionary tale (that of Alberto de Cleph and Arnao Guillén) on the theme of betrayed friendship, which involves a love triangle not dissimilar to the one formed by Anselmo, Lotario, and Camila in Miguel de Cervantes's tale of impertinent curiosity from part 1 of *Don Quijote de la Mancha*.[21] In *El Crótalon,* however, the story revolves around a spouse who is consumed with desire for her husband's friend. This frame situation allows for the telling of the story of two fraternal twins, Julio and Julieta, who enjoy dressing in each other's clothes to entertain and play tricks on their parents. One day Julieta sails off in masculine dress in a brigantine and is shipwrecked off the English coast. She is rescued by the royal princess Melisa, who immediately falls in love with the person she believes to be a chivalric knight. In order to gracefully rebuff Melisa's amorous advances and avoid being taken for an effeminate noble, Julieta confesses to her real sex. Instead of being extinguished by the "impossibility" of such a love, Melisa's passion and accompanying frustration grow and she curses her bad luck, since any other love, even a dishonest one, could be consummated. She importunes Love, "Hasme herido de llaga muy contra natural, pues nunca una dama de otra se enamoró, ni entre los animales. . . . Para mi locura no habría Dédalo que injeniasse dar algún remedio contra lo que naturaleza tan firmemente apartó" (252).[22] [You have wounded me unnaturally, since a lady has never fallen in love with another, not even among animals. . . . There will be no Dedalus to invent a cure for my madness, which nature so firmly separated.] The Ovidian reminiscences here are evident, as Iphis says of her love for

Ianthe that such love is impossible in the natural world: "In the whole animal world, there is no female smitten with love for female!" (Ovid 1984, 55, 57).

Impossibilities aside, Julieta and Melisa sleep in the same bed and in a sensual display of lesbian erotics, Melisa is consumed by desire for her sleeping companion. At this point the episode echoes Serna, albeit without the humor that characterizes "El sueño de la viuda de Aragón":

> Y luego [Melisa] sueña que el çielo la ha conçedido que Julieta sea vuelta varón, y como aconteçe a algún enfermo si de una gran calentura cobdiçioso de agua se ha dormido con gran sed, en aquel poquito de sueño se le pareçen cuantas fuentes en su vida vido, ansí estando el spíritu de Melisa deseoso páreciale que vía lo que sueña; y ansí despertando no se confía hasta que tienta con la mano y ve ser vanidad su sueño. (Villalón 1990, 254)

> [And then (Melisa) dreams that the heavens have turned Julieta into a male, and just as a person who is sick with fever falls asleep with a great thirst and in that brief sleep all the fountains that he has seen in his entire life appear to him, Melisa's spirit, filled with desire, thought the dream was real; thus, when Melisa awoke, she was not sure until she felt with her hand and realized that her illusion was a dream.]

Once again the expression of overwhelming sexual desire is enabled through dream. As a result, lesbian erotics are safely contained within these parameters. However, this interesting anecdote does not end here, since Julieta eventually returns home and relates her experiences with the lovely Melisa to her brother. Julio sets off for England, disguised as Julieta and determined to enjoy what she could not, since, in the narrator's view, she lacks the proper equipment. Once there, he explains to Melisa that his grandmother has transformed him into a man in order for them to be able to consummate their love, which they do with great passion and mutual satisfaction. These encounters between Melisa and the twins are tremendously sensual, whether she is with Julio or Julieta. However, at all times the text insists on the natural impossibility of genital sex between women. Once again, female-female desire is presented as *amor impossibilis,* and sex without a phallus cannot be satisfactorily consummated. Moreover, the phallus must be real; thus, Julio urges Melisa to look at and touch his as proof. Not without certain irony, the text reads, "Aunque ve, toca y tienta lo que tanto desea, no lo cree hasta que lo prueba; y ansí dezía: "Si éste es sueño haga Dios que nunca yo despierte" (259). [Even though she sees and touches what she desires so much, she does not believe it until she tries it out, saying, "If this is a dream, I pray God never to wake me."] This brief episode reveals that if Villalón does not negate the possibility of same-sex desire, he nevertheless suggests that it cannot be brought to a "natural" conclusion without the mediation of a male. At the same time, the underlying misogyny points to women as sexual predators, whether their desire is hetero- or homosexual.

The Myth of Lesbian Desire in Jorge de Montemayor's Diana

The modeling of female homoeroticism in other Golden Age literary genres differs from the modeling that we have seen in poetic and prose satire. Although in pastoral romance, for example, lesbian desire is also carefully harnessed, a different process safely rechannels it toward heteronormativity. Before we pursue this idea, however, it is helpful to revisit the notion of desire (which existed, of course, long before Sigmund Freud, Carl Jung, Jacques Lacan, Julia Kristeva, and company attempted to fixate it theoretically as the means by which knowledge has been mastered and controlled in the Western imaginary). Even though for many humanistic disciplines desire motivates and controls human endeavors, until fairly recently that very human drive has been quite absent from Golden Age literary studies. As a result of this conceptual lack, the axes of this consideration of lesbian desire as myth may be deceptive or ambiguous to readers in at least two ways.

Again, it may be considered problematic to employ the term *homosexual* (understood as an identity based on the perceived sexual orientation of an individual or group) to articulate the subtexts of Spanish literature from the early modern period. It is even more problematic, perhaps, to employ the term *lesbianism*. As I have noted, however, in recent years various scholars of sexuality have contested Michel Foucault's view of the emergence of the homosexual as "species" in the nineteenth century by pointing out the existence of early modern subcultures that they term homosexual. James Saslow, for example, has emphasized correctly that the lack of our modern terms *heterosexual* and *homosexual* did not prevent Renaissance theorists from clearly differentiating between two kinds of love based on the gender of the lover and the love object (1988, 81). This fact is of no little importance in the interpretation of a significant episode in Montemayor's eminently canonical sixteenth-century pastoral novel, *Los siete libros de la Diana*.

The other ambiguity of the axes that I have chosen is privileging the term *myth*. I use the term neither to mean "a parable or allegory" nor according to the exclusively formal, causal, historical, or psychological aspects that guide its relationship with literature. Instead, I employ the term *myth* in the well-known Barthesian sense: as a word, a message, a semiotic system, and a language of connotation, with all the contradictions that these usages contain. Homer used the word *muthos* to refer to narration and conversation rather than to a fiction. Plato, in turn, employed the word *muthoi* to denote something that was not totally true but mainly fictional. Ultimately, in literature, myth becomes an unfounded and unstable notion, something having only an imaginary or unverifiable existence. However, I recognize the emotional and ideological negotiation that Bruno Damiani and Joan Cammarata detail for the concept of myth in *La Diana* when, for example, the mythical world appears as a necessary component of the pastoral world (1994, 34). Nonetheless, I attempt to show here that what is imaginary and unverifiable as discourse in *La Diana* is precisely lesbian desire.

My analysis centers on a homoerotic interlude that occurs early in the novel between the Portuguese shepherdess, Selvagia, and Ysmenia. Selvagia makes her entrance at the beginning of the first book, when she relates her story of "endiablada pasión" [diabolical passion] to Sireno and Sylvano. The episode that she narrates occurs within the context of the feast of Minerva, a time when shepherdesses and nymphs dress in their finery to visit and pass the night in the goddess's temple. The shepherds who accompany the women briefly pay their respects and then immediately exit the temple "porque las pastoras y ninfas quedasen solas, y sin ocasión de entender en otra cosa, sino celebrar la fiesta regocijándose unas con otras" (Montemayor 1991, 140) [in order that the shepherdesses and nymphs might be alone and unconcerned with

anything other than celebrating the feast and enjoying themselves to-
gether].[23] Therefore, the temple provides the locus of an exclusively female and celebratory sphere from which males are excluded and within
which a tale of female passion will be played out. The desire examined
here is what gives the commonplace of women grouped together in a
closed community particular significance in Montemayor's work.

Selvagia relates how another group of shepherdesses enters the
temple, one of whom sits next to her. The newcomer's face is discreetly
veiled, and she enters into a coquettish exchange of glances, arousing
the interest and soon the passion of Selvagia. We should remember,
with respect to this and initially, that in Agnolo Firenzuola's *Discorsi
delle bellezze delle donne,* to which I refer later (see Firenzuola 1992),
the homonymous character Selvagia (one of four women with whom
Celso dialogues) represents, as her name indicates, summer, heat and
choler, and strong character. She does so in opposition to the other
Renaissance humors that Firenzuola assigns to the other three women.
With this in mind, let us see by which paths desire leads Selvagia to
the unknown woman Ysmenia, whose beautiful eyes and hands quickly
enamor her:

> Y todavía todas las veces que yo me descuidaba la pastora no quitaba
> los ojos de mí, y tanto que mil veces estuve por hablalla, enamorada
> de unos hermosos ojos que solamente tenía descubiertos. Pues es-
> tando yo con toda la atención posible, sacó la más hermosa y delicada
> mano que yo después acá he visto, y tomándome la mía, me la estuvo
> mirando un poco. Yo que estaba más enamorada della de lo que po-
> dría decir, le dije: "Hermosa y graciosa pastora, no es sola esa mano
> la que está aparejada para serviros, mas también lo está el corazón y
> el pensamiento de cuya ella es." (Montemayor 1991, 140–41)

> [And whenever I let my thoughts wander, the shepherdess never took
> her eyes off me, so much so that I was on the point of speaking to
> her a thousand times, enamored of her beautiful eyes, which were
> the only part of her face uncovered. I was paying the greatest atten-
> tion to her when she took out the most beautiful and delicate hand
> that I have ever seen since, and taking mine in hers, she gazed at it
> for a while. I was stricken with a greater love than I could ever say
> and said to her: "Fair and gracious shepherdess, it is not only that

hand that wants to serve you but also the heart and thoughts of her to whom it belongs."]

It is impossible, given such a declaration, that the lover's discourse fail to engender desire in the beloved. As a consequence, and according to Selvagia, Ysmenia responds sotto voce:

Graciosa pastora, soy tan vuestra que como tal me atreví a hacer lo que hice, suplícoos que no os escandalicéis porque en viendo vuestro hermoso rostro no tuve más poder en mí. (141)

[Graceful shepherdess, because I am so much yours, I dared to do what I did, and I pray that you are not offended by me, for as soon as I saw your beautiful face, I lost power over myself.]

Selvagia reacts to Ysmenia's declaration as follows:

Yo entonces muy contenta me llegué más a ella, y le dije medio riendo: "¿Cómo puede ser pastora que siendo vos tan hermosa os enamoréis de otra que tanto le falta para serlo, y más siendo mujer como vos?" (141)

[I was so happy that I came closer and said to her with a smile: "How can it be, shepherdess, being as fair as you are, that you fall in love with another who is so far from being beautiful, especially being a woman as I am?"]

The two women then fall into each other's arms in a suggestive scene that contemporary queer critique would safely surmise as lesbian, although not genital:

Y después de esto los abrazos fueron tantos, los amores que la una a la otra nos decíamos, y de mi parte tan verdaderos, que ni teníamos cuenta con los cantares de las pastoras, ni mirábamos las danzas de las ninfas, ni otros regocijos que en el templo se hacían. (141–42)

[After this our embraces and our loving words to one another (on my part so true) were so many that we paid no regard to the shep-

herdesses' songs, and we beheld neither the nymphs' dances nor any
of the festivities that took place in the temple.]

Since desire is a game of deflection and concentration, Selvagia begs
Ysmenia to unveil her face and identify herself. Ysmenia complies, but
at the same time she reveals a secret: She claims to be a man, Alanio,
dressed as a woman. Selvagia remarks that although Ysmenia's counte-
nance was somewhat manly, her beauty was so remarkable that it caused
wonder (142). Naturally, this history of desire becomes more complex;
it turns out that Ysmenia is, in fact, a woman, and she is in love with a
cousin named Alanio. The cousins are so alike that, as Selvagia puts it,
"si no fueran los dos de género diferente, no hubiera quien no juzgara el
uno por el otro" (144) [if they had not been of opposite sexes, nobody
could have judged one from the other]. This situation, of course, brings
to mind the twins Julio and Julieta from *El Crótalon,* who "como fueron
de un parto fueron los más semejantes que nunca criaturas nacieron"
(Villalón 1990, 248) [as twins were more alike than any two creatures
ever born]. By feigning love, Ysmenia claims to have played a cruel
practical joke on Selvagia, which she later recounts to Alanio. Alanio's
curiosity is piqued, he visits Selvagia, and the two fall in love. Ysmenia
subsequently falls in love with Montano, an enemy of Alanio's. Alanio,
jealous and angered by his enemy's good fortune, forgets Selvagia, and
his love for Ysmenia returns. A curious chain of unrequited love ensues wherein Selvagia loves Alanio, Alanio loves Ysmenia, Ysmenia loves
Montano, and Montano then falls in love with Selvagia.

The development of that complicated plot, to an extent conventional in all aspects of the pastoral genre, is the frame for what I aim to
develop regarding the episode previously quoted. Selvagia and Ysmenia's
suggestive interlude in Minerva's temple has generally been neglected
by *La Diana* critics. One notable exception is Marcelino Menéndez y
Pelayo, who indignantly denounced it as "extravagante y monstruosa
. . . y desagradable" (1961, 1:273) [extravagant, monstrous . . . and un-
pleasant].[24] What I explore here is the significance of the episode within
the context of this pastoral romance and the reason that, given its explicit (and not burlesque) homoerotic content, it raised few objections
in its own time. I find the scene profoundly provocative, which leads me
to disagree with Elizabeth Rhodes's statement (in an article on critical
reactions to eroticism in *La Diana*) that there are no provocative scenes

in pastoral romances (1987, 132). In addition to the Selvagia-Ysmenia episode, the episode in which Belisa is discovered asleep, "el blanco pie descalzo" (Montemayor 1991, 228) [her white foot unshod], is quite provocative, given the fact that the female foot was a fetishized object at the time.

As a corollary and by viewing this scene from the historical context developed earlier, my objective is to explain how this episode creates a myth of female-female desire that is safely assimilated, via Neoplatonist theory, into the heteronormative early modern view of love and desire. Considering the sociocultural binds detailed at the beginning of this chapter and their relationship with the hermeneutic tradition, the Selvagia-Ysmenia episode is quite unique.[25] According to Carroll Johnson, who has noted the dearth of studies on the encounter between these two women from the perspective of homosexuality, everything that happens to the female characters in *La Diana* is a deformation or deviation of the processes of sexual attraction considered to be normal (1995, 169). Johnson is correct, although it might not be easy for the reader to locate her- or himself totally and temporally in another of his assertions: "Lo que se establece en el lector, a fin de cuentas, es una tensión intrapsíquica, entre sus propios impulsos erótico/transgresivos y su adhesión a la ortodoxia social, tensión que tampoco desaparece del todo" (172). [Ultimately, what is established in the reader is an intrapsychic tension between the reader's own erotic/transgressive impulses and his or her adherence to social orthodoxy, a tension that does not disappear totally.] To respect certain borders between literature and life has perhaps been the wise ambiguity of the early modern epoch.

For these reasons, although women often fall in love with other women in early modern Spanish literature (the situation is, after all, a staple of Golden Age theater), this situation usually occurs because one of them has disguised herself as a man. This is the case with Celia in *La Diana*: She falls in love with Felismena, who is posing as a page. Selvagia, by contrast, clearly feels a homoerotic attraction for Ysmenia, who is most evidently a woman, with her captivating delicate hand and eyes. Her very conventional femininity is precisely what arouses Selvagia's desire.[26] It is unusual, therefore, that Johnson does not pursue the implications of the problem when he concludes, "Pero hay algo terriblemente inquietante aquí. Se trata de una mujer que se enamora de otra mujer, una transgresión si las hubo de las normas sociales y de las reglas del amor" (171). [But there is something terribly disquieting here. A woman falls in love with another woman, a transgression if ever there was one of social norms and the rules of love.] But does this episode really contradict the rules of love on which the pastoral is constructed?

Ernst Robert Curtius has pointed out that all varieties of erotic motifs form the thematic base of the pastoral (1973, 187), a perception that Rallo takes up in her edition of *Los siete libros de la Diana*. And since *La Diana* is generally read as a literaturization of Neoplatonic love theory, especially by León Hebreo (1953), Selvagia and Ysmenia's sudden passion represents one possible implication of that theory.[27] In the Neoplatonic tradition, love is inspired by the sight of beauty, which has no specific gender. Thus, Marsilio Ficino affirms in his *De amore* that all the ancient philosophers maintain the Platonic definition of love as the desire for beauty (see Ficino 1985). Following this theory, love joins together two souls, which, according to early modern belief, are also ungendered. Therefore, it would seem licit for two members of the same sex to love each other. Moreover, in his excellent study of Ficino's philosophy, Paul Oskar Kristeller explains that

> since love between two persons is conceived as a mutual love, although free from any sensual element, the difference between the two sexes, which actually determines erotic relations in the ordinary sense, loses its basic importance in Ficino's theory of love. Not only man and woman but also two men or two women may be united by a sentiment of love. (1964, 277)

In truth, Ficino's influence should not be underestimated, including for precursory works in defense of women, such as Firenzuola's 1548 *Discorsi delle bellezze delle donne,* mentioned earlier. For this dialogue, as for others in the Renaissance

> the proliferation of the Neoplatonic dialogues helped to disseminate and popularize the ideas developed by Ficino in his *Commentary on Plato's Symposium.* Although the Latin version of the *Commentary* had been published in 1484, the Italian translation was not printed until 1544. As a result, the popularization of Ficino's ideas about Platonic love was primarily the work of others, and especially of the authors of

dialogues written in Italian. These vernacular works were in the main responsible for transmitting the Neoplatonic philosophy of love to a wider and less-learned audience than that which had frequented the Florentine Academy. (Eisenbichler and Murray 1992, xxviii)

For this reason it is perfectly comprehensible that within the context of Renaissance humanism Ysmenia's beauty inspires Selvagia's love. Selvagia's sudden rapture is fundamentally a reflection of "good love," of "the Neoplatonist's love of beauty: to see beauty is to desire it, in a spiritual sense, wherever it may be found" (Solé-Leris 1980, 38–39). According to its scrutiny by Hebreo, instead of proceeding from sensual desire or appetite as does imperfect or false love, this perfect love

> es la que engendra el deseo de la persona amada, y no procede del deseo o apetito. Al contrario. Al amar primero perfectamente, la fuerza del amor hace desear la unión espiritual y corporal con la persona amada. Por consiguiente, así como el primer amor es hijo del deseo, éste le es padre y verdadero progenitor. (1953, 36)

> [is that which engenders the desire of the beloved and does not proceed from desire or appetite. To the contrary. Upon first loving perfectly, the force of love leads to the desire for spiritual and bodily union with the beloved. As a result, just as the first love is the child of desire, this is its father and true progenitor].

Based on what we know of Neoplatonism, there is sufficient textual evidence to suppose that if two men had experienced the rapture, the implications of Neoplatonic love theory would, at least in principle, function with equal force.[28] As I have argued, however, concerns about masculinity render male homoerotic "love" (as opposed to lust) an impossibility in Spanish Golden Age literature.

Since our fragment deals with two women, we should keep in mind that the rupture that can be verified in the erotic diction is directly proportional to the selection of addressee. In other words, as the consignee is broadened, the transgression diminishes.[29] In turn, Bryant Creel interprets the lack of importance given to homoerotic attraction in the episode as follows:

The love between Selvagia and Ysmenia establishes a second high social norm, this time in the realm of the sensuous: the two fell in love with such force that they did not take time even *to establish one another's sexual identities.* Yet the discovery of the situation causes no feeling of shame in either of them precisely because the sensuous (visual) appreciation of corporeal beauty that stimulated their mutual infatuation was alien to a self-seeking, narrowly gratifying sensual impulse (pure sexual instinct). *For that reason sexual differences are not important.* (1990, 5, my emphasis)

If love is blind, according to the implications of Creel's argument, it should not be gendered; moreover, the lover should not be ashamed to discover that she is the same sex as the beloved. This is precisely what happens in this episode, since there is no doubt in either lover's mind that they are both women, and Selvagia's question about how Ysmenia can love another woman is definitely a leading one. But love at first sight generally culminates in a more material relationship, something that admittedly does not occur in this episode (at least beyond embraces and words) because of the Neoplatonic philosophy with which Monte-mayor endorsed his romance. Nevertheless, it is reasonable to think that no matter how "pure" this love is, the problematic that I am pursuing enters the mind of the protagonists and the readers. In other words, the desire—even when filtered through myth—that is at the center of any amorous initiative is inescapable, as is ideology.

Desire in *La Diana* is not subdivided into homosexual and hetero-sexual. However, because Western society organizes desire based on masculine domination, it is all but futile to try to deal with the theme of female homosexuality within a masculinist frame and ideology.[30] Sexual labels, I repeat along with others, are social creations, and if we follow that tangent, it is not difficult to prove that desire and repression are at the root of (to mention only two aspects of society) politics and criti-cism itself.

Hebreo divides love into "good" and "false," and as he explains in his dialogues, true and perfect love is born of reason (1953, 36). Based on the foregoing, we should ask what false love (*falso amor*) would be for works similar in context, because the relationships between the different types of love extend beyond desire and the purely mythical to the ideo-logical. Even though he believes *La Diana* to be the foundational text for the pastoral novel, in his study on the philosophy of love in Spanish Golden Age literature Alexander Parker considers implicitly that the false love of this *Diana* is opposed to reason. He also proposes that this imperfect love does not seek spiritual union with the beloved (as does *buen amor*) because it emerges from the appetites of instinct and seeks physical satisfaction (1985, 130).

We would perhaps be erring through presentism if we were to affirm that this criterion denies the very real and historical role of desire in human beings. However, we should not diminish the paranoia of purity created in the Neoplatonic literary mentality of that time. Nurtured by the frustrations of the ancient elites and the Catholic petite bourgeoisie and other administrators of desire, the distinctions between good love and false, or bad, love becomes a dichotomy that is at times difficult to separate, omnipresent in the spirit of the time, and crystallized by the exclusivist norms of the historical moment. In this sense, Begoña Souviron López argues:

> La novela de Montemayor presenta la amplia casuística amorosa y en la variedad de personajes un análisis y descripción detallada del amor como proceso de conocimiento y una profundidad hasta entonces nunca alcanzada en la psicología de los personajes, concediendo especial atención a la mujer. (1997, 113)

> [Montemayor's novel presents in its broad love casuistry and variety of characters an analysis and detailed description of love as a process of knowing and a depth previously unknown in the psychology of the characters, granting special attention to women.]

Precisely given such observations, it is surprising that Souviron López, who admittedly embraces the revelations of more recent postmodern interdisciplinary criticism (1997, 9), does not discuss the implications of the "other" sexuality in the episode under discussion. For this reason it is pertinent to observe, as Parker adds, that love produced by desire differs little from love produced by reason:

> In either case, the nature of the resulting feeling is equally passionate and beyond the control of the lover's reason; love is a doom against which it is useless for the lover to struggle. Suffering is inseparable

from love and an ennobling aspect of it. *Fulfilment is therefore not desirable, since it would put an end to the exquisite, ennobling suffering of suspense.* (1985, 109, my emphasis)

Homosexual love in *La Diana* is not presented negatively as vice, that is, false love. *Amor vicioso* or *amor falso* is personified by the savages who attack the nymphs in the first book for the simple purpose of satisfying their base needs. As Bruce Wardropper has noted, "True love derives from reason, however unreasonable the effects of such a love may be; false love stems from 'un apetito baxo y deshonesto'" (1951, 135). According to Johnson, this reading is invoked in order to neutralize the Neoplatonic context of homosexuality (1995, 172). It is worth remembering that in his *Defence of Poesie*, Sir Philip Sidney—who was, according to several critics, influenced by Montemayor—reveals not only an extensive range of critical Renaissance attitudes similar to those of Wardropper but also two aspects that are pertinent to my argument.[31]

The first is the Neoplatonic idea that the poet betters appearances, and the second is that desire has not been dominated by reason. Rallo points out, in turn, that the concept of love that Montemayor wants to explain initiates from a premise of purity and approaches, as sublimation, an exclusively spiritual sentiment (see Montemayor 1991, 65). At the same time, because the pastoral depicts not only a pure but also a pagan world, one in which Christian scriptures do not apply, the Christian proscriptions against homosexuality can be disregarded.[32] Therefore, given the philosophical nature of the pastoral genre in which love occurs in the chaste abstract, homosexuality is not a threat but at best a myth. Moreover, since in the pastoral romance sensual desires must, by definition, be left unsatisfied and love is generally unrequited, it is a safe genre for the exploration of all facets of human love, even love between members of the same sex. This proves to be a new dilemma for the interpreter of Renaissance prose.

As I argue throughout, lawmakers and theologians sought to discipline sexual "deviants" in order to maintain social stability and the gendered status quo. It is for this reason that the sex crimes most pursued by the Inquisition were fornication, bigamy, marriage by priests or monks, homosexuality, and solicitation by confessors (Cardaillac and Jammes 1985, 185–89). The crimes most pursued, that is to say, were those committed by men, since, as Louis Cardaillac and Robert Jammes note, homosexuality was viewed exclusively as a male issue (188). We also know that the 1583 Gaspar de Quiroga index of banned books (based on the first Spanish inquisitorial index—the Fernando de Valdés index—which was published in the same year as *La Diana*) calls for the specific prohibition of not only Montemayor's novel but also *La Celestina* and, above all (and for well-known reasons), the chivalric romances.

In contrast, as we saw earlier, in the analysis of Serna's "El sueño de la viuda," lesbian sexuality was at times condoned (at least in theory or in the abstract and externally to the law), because it was viewed (by men) as light training for heterosexual lovemaking. As long as these practices were limited to mere erotic diversion when men were unavailable and as long as the women usurped no male privileges, lesbian lovemaking (at least in literature) could be tolerated. In a certain way, this is what happens to Selvagia in *La Diana*. Her sensual exchange with Ysmenia becomes a prologue to the deeper, "truer" love that she subsequently feels for Alanio. Moreover, since homosexual love could not lead to marriage, the natural culmination of love within Montemayor's purview, it could not progress to any sort of resolution.

Queer theorists have found something here to anchor their arguments, which maintain that the relationships between people of different sexes cannot be understood without understanding the relationships, sexual or otherwise, between people of the same sex. Kristeva says that desire is an index of heterogeneity and an objective that is given only in literature and in criticism, because writing changes for the signifier the formulation of desire into objective law (1980, 116–18). That is, literature and its interpretation illustrate how desire functions and how its mythification is always part of the human sphere as virtual object, without having a fixed content. *La Diana* demonstrates this in order to account for the wide range of desires contained in its episodes.[33]

In other words—and expanding on an idea suggested by Ruth El Saffar (1971, 184)—specifically because Montemayor's concept of love does not admit reciprocity between partners in a love situation, the suggestion of lesbianism can be allowed. If Selvagia's love for Ysmenia had been reciprocated and the male sex sidestepped, it would have presented an unacceptable challenge to masculine sexual hegemony and, concomitantly, to literary mores. It bears repeating here that homosexuality at the time (at least for the heterosexual majority) did not imply love or sentimental attachment; it implied only sodomitical acts. The province of love was considered to be heterosexual, and it is in this context that one can speak of the myth of lesbian desire.

In his seminal article on Montemayor's pastoral book, "The *Diana* of Montemayor: Revaluation and Interpretation," Wardropper noted:

> The shepherdesses in the *Diana* speak more than the shepherds. The novel, indeed, not only recognizes that the feminine point of view is different; it gives it its fullest expression in the Spanish Renaissance. . . . The great originality of the *Diana* was that it gave men and women an opportunity to exchange points of view. Men for the first time were able to see themselves as women saw them. (1951, 142)

Forty years later, Rhodes contextualized the issue within Catholic reformism, making basically the same point.[34] These perspicacious insights notwithstanding, it is nevertheless obvious that there is little understanding of female sexuality or desire, whether homosexual or heterosexual, in *La Diana*. The book gives no insight into female affectivity and erotic practices of the time and clearly neutralizes female homoerotics. However, sexuality is not at issue in the pastoral, even taking into account the difference between types and genders of readers (Johnson 1995, 176). According to my reading, what is at issue is a philosophy of love that allows for female homosexual desire based on the ungendered, or degendered, pursuit of beauty.[35] Because of the philosophical bases on which the narrative is structured, female homoeroticism and heterosexuality become, in fact, contiguous, thus complicating the mythology of desire.

Therefore, the episode under discussion here is ultimately nontransgressive, since no threat is posed to heterosexuality and the politics of gender difference. The episode does not signify erotically and thus is insignificant for author, reader, and critic. The possibility of women not needing men for love—intimated in Selvagia and Ysmenia's brief erotic interlude—becomes threatening only when homosexuality is viewed, as in Menéndez y Pelayo's time, as a sentimental and social possibility. Fortunately, today the possibility of seeing in the text a parallelism with the process of critical dialogue is greater. This may help us reclaim not only what is mythical in homosexuality and what is homosexual in myth but also the ideology that defines both considerations.

The examples of textualized lesbian eros analyzed in this chapter all sidestep the implacable social and legal system of repressive control to which non-normative erotic activity was subjected in Golden Age Spain. The authors engage in a literary skirmish whose methodology includes imposture, deflection, and contention—not to censure or erase but, instead, to explore the erotic possibilities of lesbian sexuality while simultaneously defusing the potential threat to the masculine order. As a result, and in contrast to works that textualize male homosexuality, lesbian texts such as these can be incorporated into the realm of the (homo)erotic, providing a sensual spectacle for readers of any sexual inclination.

CHAPTER FOUR

Wild Women and Warrior Maidens

Los hombres que han sido afeminados, han sido torpísimo
vituperio en el mundo. Las mujeres que han sido varoniles,
siempre fueron milagrosa aclamación de los siglos.
   Francisco de Quevedo, *Marco Bruto*

[Effeminate men have been reviled as an obscenity in the world.
Throughout the centuries, manly women were always acclaimed as
a miracle.]

Evidently, religious, societal, and even aesthetic injunctions have done
little to prevent non-normative sexual representations from seeping into
the fiber of early modern Spanish culture. In current times, with trans-
national, transhistorical, transgendered, and transideological figures
and themes being eagerly pursued, tales of young women who disguise
themselves as men to seek independence from institutions or individuals, to go to war, to uphold family honor or to redress their own honor,
to seek adventure, or to otherwise attain the freedom normally associated with the male sex are intensely appealing. Indeed, the motif of the
transvestite warrior maiden or female fighter has not only a particular
and lively intertextual relevance across centuries and national traditions
but also tremendous popular interest, as the commercial success of films
such as China's *Crouching Tiger, Hidden Dragon* attest.
   As cross-dressed women who successfully pass as men, warrior
maidens were (especially in the early modern period, with its fixed gen-

der expectations and norms) and are both sexually transgressive and often potently erotic to both sexes. In other cases, especially on the early modern stage, the adoption of male dress as a symbolic means of assuming masculine identity and identifying with the male value system serves paradoxically to intensify female beauty. This chapter explores the literature and the myth of the female fighter, focusing on several legendary figures: the *doncella guerrera* [warrior maiden] celebrated in European balladry; Catalina de Erauso, known as the lieutenant nun and a real-life adventuress in the New World; and several literary incarnations of the *serrana* [wild mountain girl]. All these women can be viewed as linchpins in a historical and thematic continuum that traverses fantasy, popular legend, song, and folklore: the genre-blurring mixture of fact and fable, history and fiction, lyric and drama, Spain and the Americas.

The Warrior Maiden in Iberian Balladry

The popular songs of the *doncella guerrera,* or warrior maiden, received consistent critical attention in William J. Entwistle's foundational study *European Balladry* (1939). Classical scholars such as Marcelino Menéndez y Pelayo (1900), Ramón Menéndez Pidal (1968), Américo Castro (1924), and Francisco López Estrada (1985) have also written about the *doncella guerrera*, and Stith Thompson (1989) provides a plethora of connections from the folk tradition.[1] This scholarly interest is prima facie evidence of the great popularity of the ballad of the *doncella guerrera*—one manifestation of the *mujer vestida de hombre* [cross-dressed woman] so ubiquitous in Golden Age literature—in European and other folklore from at least the sixteenth-century forward. Many hundreds of versions have been found not only throughout all regions of Spain (including Castile, the Canary Islands, León, Aragón, Galicia, and Catalonia), Spanish America, Portugal, the Azores, and Brazil but also in practically all Sephardic communities, including those in Morocco, Bosnia and the Balkans, Hungary, Greece, Asia Minor, and Palestine.[2] The breadth of the geographic area encompassed makes it difficult to establish origins and even more difficult to date the ballad (Delpech 1986, 58). It is for these reasons, in part, that the songs and tales of the *doncella guerrera* appear as a crossroads of subjectivities, themes, topics, and traditions—sometimes as high literature and sometimes folkloric, typically of rural provenance—that were concentrated around the Mediterranean basin at least as early as the end of the Middle Ages (Delpech 1986, 61). Although the ballad was known as early as the sixteenth century, it was not printed until the nineteenth century.[3] Why, then, is it of interest to us today?

One reason is that the *doncella guerrera* family of ballads, in spite of its widespread provenance, exhibits an underlying pattern or structure that functions formulaically and thus establishes fairly permanent cultural bridges. The ballad is a type whose hundreds of variants function as permutations of a recognizable tradition (see Dugaw 1989). In its most typical form the romance and Sephardic versions of the *doncella guerrera* ballad sing the tale of an elderly nobleman who is dishonored when war is declared between France and Aragon, because he has no son to send into battle. The youngest of his seven daughters (sometimes they are three, the other magic number) volunteers to go, disguised as a man in her father's clothes and using his name. She serves as a soldier for two years, during which time a young captain prince is captivated by her feminine eyes. Suspecting her true gender, he confides his hunch to his mother, who suggests a number of tests (of predictable semiotics) to determine the maiden's sexual identity. As it turns out, the girl is able to outwit them until the final test: bathing with the prince. At this point, in order to avoid being discovered in this manner, she admits her true gender, claims that her father has fallen ill, and gallops off toward home. The prince pursues her, and in many versions the poem ends enigmatically when the maiden takes up her distaff and the prince knocks on her door; in other versions the poem ends in marriage or betrothal. This progression is the palimpsest for the construction of subsequent plot variants, and it is in the concepts behind those changes that the lasting effects of the ballad reside. The following is a transcription, with translation, of the version of "La doncella guerrera" included in Menéndez Pidal's *Flor nueva de romances viejos*:

—Pregonadas son las guerras
de Francia con Aragón,
¡cómo las haré yo, triste,
viejo y cano, pecador!
¡No reventaras, condesa,

por medio del corazón,
que me diste siete hijas,
y entre ellas ningún varón!
Allí habló la más chiquita,
en razones la mayor:
—No maldigáis a mi madre,
que a la guerra me iré yo;
me daréis las vuestras armas,
vuestro caballo trotón.
—Conoceránte en los pechos,
que asoman bajo el jubón.
—Yo las apretaré, padre,
al par de mi corazón.
—Tienes las manos muy blancas,
hija, no son de varón.
—Yo les quitaré los guantes
para que las queme el sol.
—Conoceránte en los ojos,
que otros más lindos no son.
—Yo los revolveré, padre,
como si fuera un traidor.
Al despedirse de todos,
se le olvida lo mejor:
—¿Cómo me he de llamar, padre?
—Don Martín el de Aragón.
—Y para entrar en las cortes,
padre, ¿cómo diré yo?
—Bésoos la mano, buen rey,
las cortes las guarde Dios.

Dos años anduvo en guerra
y nadie la conoció,
si no fue el hijo del rey
que en sus ojos se prendió.
—Herido vengo, mi madre,
de amores me muero yo:
los ojos de don Martín
son de mujer, de hombre no.

—Convídalo tú, mi hijo,
a las tiendas a feriar;
si don Martín es mujer,
las galas ha de mirar.
Don Martín, como discreto,
a mirar las armas va:
—¡Qué rico puñal es éste,
para con moros pelear!
—Herido vengo, mi madre,
amores me han de matar;
los ojos de don Martín
roban el alma al mirar.
—Llevaráslo tú, hijo mío,
a la huerta a solazar;
si don Martín es mujer,
a los almendros irá.
Don Martín deja las flores;
una vara va a cortar;
—¡Oh, qué varita de fresno
para el caballo arrear!
—Hijo, arrójale al regazo
tus anillos al jugar:
si don Martín es varón,
las rodillas juntará;
pero si las separare,
por mujer se mostrará.
Don Martín, muy avisado,
hubiéralas de juntar.
—Herido vengo, mi madre,
amores me han de matar;
los ojos de don Martín
nunca los puedo olvidar.
—Convídalo tú, mi hijo,
en los baños a nadar.
Todos se están desnudando;
don Martín muy triste está:
—Cartas me fueron venidas,
cartas de grande pesar,

que se halla el conde mi padre
enfermo para finar.
Licencia le pido al rey
para irle a visitar.
—Don Martín, esa licencia
no te la quiero estorbar.
Ensilla el caballo blanco,
de un salto en él va a montar;
por unas vegas arriba
corre como un gavilán:
—¡Adiós, adiós, el buen rey,
y tu palacio real;
que dos años te sirvió
una doncella leal!
Oyela el hijo del rey,
tras ella va a cabalgar.
—¡Corre, corre, hijo del rey,
que no me habrás de alcanzar
hasta en casa de mi padre,
si quieres irme a buscar!
Campanitas de mi iglesia,
ya os oigo repicar;
puentecito, puentecito
del río de mi lugar,
una vez te pasé virgen,
virgen te vuelvo a pasar.
Abra las puertas mi padre,
ábralas de par en par.
Madre, sáqueme la rueca,
que traigo ganas de hilar,
que las armas y el caballo
bien los supe manejar.
Tras ella el hijo del rey
a la puerta fue a llamar.
(1976, 198–202)

[War has been declared between France and Aragon. "What shall I
do, wretched old white-haired sinner that I am! Why does your heart

not burst, Countess, since you gave me seven daughters and no son!"
Here spoke the youngest daughter, who in reason was the eldest:
"Don't curse my mother; I will go to war. You will give me your
arms, your trotting horse." "They will recognize you by your breasts
that show beneath your doublet." "I will flatten them, Father, next to
my heart." "Your hands are very white, Daughter; they are not like a
man's." "I will take off my gloves so that they become tanned by the
sun." "They will recognize you by your eyes; no prettier ones exist."
"I will change my expression, Father, as if I were a traitor." On saying
goodbye to all, she forgets the most important thing: "What shall
I call myself, Father?" "Don Martín of Aragón." "And when I enter
the court, Father, what should I say?" "I kiss your hand, good king,
may God guard the court."

She spent two years at war and nobody recognized her, except the
king's son, who was captivated by her eyes. "I am wounded, Mother;
I am dying of love. Don Martín's eyes are those of a woman, not a
man." "Invite him, Son, to go shopping in the market; if Don Martín
is a woman, she will look at fineries." Don Martín, who is discreet,
goes to look at arms. "What a lovely dagger this is to fight against the
Moors!" "I am wounded, Mother; I am dying of love. Don Martín's
eyes rob my soul with their glance." "Take him, Son, to the orchard
as a diversion. If Don Martín is a woman, she will approach the
(flowering) almond trees." Don Martín ignores the flowers and goes
to cut a rod. "Oh, what a fine little rod to whip my horse!" "Son,
throw your rings into his lap to play. If Don Martín is a man, he will
bring his knees together, but if she separates them, she will show that
she is a woman." Don Martín very prudently joins them together. "I
am wounded, Mother; I am dying of love. I can't forget Don Martín's
eyes." "Invite him, Son, to swim in the baths." Everyone is undress-
ing; Don Martín is very sad. "I have received letters, letters of great
sorrow, that my father, the count, is sick and dying. I request license
from the king to go and visit him." "Don Martín, I won't refuse you
license."

She saddles the white horse, leaps up and rides off. Up across the
meadows, she runs like a hawk. "Goodbye, goodbye, good king, and
your royal palace. For two years a loyal maiden served you!" "The
king's son hears her and rides out after her. "Run, run, prince; you
won't reach me until my father's house. If you want to, come and

look for me! Little bells from my church, I already hear you ringing. Little bridge, little bridge, over my river, once I crossed you a virgin; a virgin I cross you again. Open the doors wide open, Father. Mother, bring me the distaff; now I feel like spinning. I have handled arms and horse well." Behind her the king's son knocks on the door.]

Several traditions underlie this general theme: stories of daughters who aid their parents; themes of the warrior maiden, or Amazon; and a group of myths, stories, and legends in which transvestism plays an important role, often developing the symbolism of prenuptial separation and occultation and dilatory tests to which future marriage partners submit each other (Delpech 1986, 61–62).[4] However, the originality of the Spanish *doncella guerrera* ballad is that the protagonist joins together all three types, which usually appear independently and proceed from different cultural levels (Delpech 1986, 62). At the same time, as noted earlier, the *doncella guerrera* ballads form a distinct thematic family.

Of specific interest to the concerns of this book as an exploration of the erotics of sexual transgression are the two sequences in the ballad that describe the measures taken to disguise and thus foreground the erotic elements of female identity. The other sequence involves the ritualized, symbolic tests devised to determine the protagonist's sex. These tests differ greatly from the physical examination to which the real-life transvestite discussed in the following section of this chapter, Catalina de Erauso, was subjected in order to determine her true sex and virginity. In Erauso's case a rapid physical exam performed by a midwife verified the presence of an intact hymen. As the young woman in the ballad conceals her identity and the prince tries to reveal it, the readers or listeners are, of course, in on the secret, and they experience a sort of voyeuristic complicity with the narrator. This double process of concealment and revelation in the performance of gender (somewhere between a pose and a simulation in present theoretical terms) illuminates commonly held attitudes toward gender differences during the early modern period in Iberia and is the heart and nerve center of the ballad. These two moments also forge two contrasting filial bondings: that of father and daughter and that of mother and son, and both underline the foundational dialogic structure of the ballad.

The first movement, the disguise sequence, begins with a dialogue between father and daughter; it lists the means by which the daughter can conceal her sex in order to represent the father's line in the king's army, thus complying with a basic feudal pact that was deemed to conserve family honor. In this movement the maiden flouts the tradition of daughters who aid their fathers, since she actually replaces him by becoming him, appropriating his arms (a male symbol), his horse (a male icon), and even his name. The substitution involves transforming her identity—her sex—and fulfilling roles and activities commonly considered anathema to her female body and nature. At the same time, the girl vindicates and rehabilitates her mother, who the father blames for having failed to produce a male heir capable of defending the family name. Not only does the daughter vindicate women as capable of upholding family honor but she also ultimately proves that a *varón* [man] as heir is unnecessary.

It is worth noting within this scheme that the *doncella*'s mother is a mere shadow figure whose voice is never heard. In the first Spanish stage performances of the ballad, which were directed by Rafael Dieste in the 1940s, the wife—mirroring her impotence in the ballad—was mute and a purely decorative presence onstage: "La condesa aparecía en escena sentada, con la cabeza escondida entre los brazos, sin que se la viera la cara, y era un personaje mudo, puramente decorativo y testimonial. No tenía parlamento porque en el romance no lo tiene y . no se añadía nada nuevo" (Gibert Cardona 1986, 496). [The countess appeared seated onstage, with her head and face hidden in her arms; she was mute, a purely decorative and testimonial character. She had no speaking role, because she did not have one in the ballad and it would have added nothing new.] In this sense the ballad echoes most Golden Age texts in which young female characters tend to be motherless, as Anne Cruz (1996) has shown. Naturally, that fact might allow for an endless examination of psychological recesses with current interpretive tools; I prefer to perceive that critical venue as just one of the many that early modern Spanish literature offers. Little is risked by supposing that the loss of the mother—or father, for that matter—was bound to have an effect on a young girl, but rather than project current perceptions, I choose to examine the artistic and performative negotiations to which that absence led in the early modern period.

Without denying those psychoanalytical possibilities, what I find interesting in all versions of the ballad is the sensuality contained—and indeed exploited rather than concealed—in the text, as it is brought closer to the audience by the sexually suggestive and erotically titillating description of the young woman as male soldier.[5] Although her valor is not emphasized, her feminine attributes—through her attempts to suppress them—are. For example, the father's claim that the daughter will be recognized by her breasts, which show beneath her doublet, purposefully calls attention to them, providing one of the potently erotic moments noted previously. As Louise Vasvári has observed in her study of the "Mora morilla" ballads, the *jubón* [doublet], especially a tight one, was potentially titillating when worn by a woman (1999, 64). Because the warrior maiden's doublet was purposefully tight in order to flatten her breasts, these disciplined body parts are highlighted in the texts. Connections between clothing and sexual stimulation, as elucidated by John Carl Flügel in *Psychology of Clothes,* are surely pertinent: "Instead of reducing man's sexual desires, clothing actually increased them. Mankind, striving to rise above the call of the flesh, became one of the most erotic of all living creatures because of his clothing" (1966, 39). In fact, the erotic nature of the play between revelation and occultation provided by female cross-dressing was one reason behind the numerous attempts to remove actresses from the Golden Age Spanish stage.[6]

The maiden's other emblematic feminine features erotically accentuated in the text are her long hair, her delicate hands, her small feet, her fair skin, and (above all) her captivating eyes, which eventually enamor the captain and give her away. In this way the woman is textually dissected into a series of fetishized fragments whose recomposition helps to explain early modern notions of the eroticized female body. Perhaps the most iconographic of the feminine attributes, at least in this poem, are the woman's eyes. As the captain insists to his mother in one of the Portuguese versions, "Conheci-o pelo olhos, / Que por outra couza não" (Castro Pires de Lima 1958, 22). [I recognize her by her eyes alone.] In other words, only her eyes reveal her to be a woman. What is emphasized in many versions, as much as the physical appearance of her eyes, is their softness or expressiveness. Thus, when her father warns the girl that her eyes will give her away, she argues that she will change her expression to a harsh look or the look of a traitor; she will glance downward to avoid recognition or trust that her armor will hide her gaze. This final tactic appears in several Portuguese versions, which have been translated into French as follows: "Vous avez des yeux très vifs, / Ma fille, on vous reconnaitre." / "Quand je serai armée de toutes pièces, / Mes yeux ne luiront plus à travers" (Margouliès 1928, 304). ["Your eyes are too lively, Daughter; you will be recognized." "When I have on all my armor, my eyes will not shine through."] Candace Slater interprets this betrayal of the warrior maiden by her expressive eyes as "simply confirming the impossibility of disguising one's true nature" (1979, 175).

Be that as it may, the maiden's most feminine attribute, her eyes, will be concealed by the most masculine of attire, her armor. Armor is of great symbolic significance, representing not only the perfection and completion of the (male) body but also its protection. Armor also serves as a full body mask to conceal imperfections and perfect form. Here it is a particularly inspired anatomical fiction, since instead of hiding imperfections (its purpose), it conceals perfections—the maiden's beautiful and feminine eyes. At this juncture the warrior maiden becomes a sister of Joan of Arc, whose transvestism included the use of male field armor. In a similar vein, in several Portuguese versions collected by Fernando de Castro Pires de Lima, from Ilha Terceira, Trás-os-Montes, Portugal, the girl declares that she will use iron gauntlets, rather than the gloves that we find in most versions, to hide her soft feminine hands: "Venham já guantes ou mapolas de ferro / E compridas ficarão" (1958, 52). The textual move from glove to gauntlet would seem to be a case of hyper-masculinization rather than increased protection.

There is one final attribute that is central to the gender concerns expressed in the disguise sequence: the girl's dainty feet. In an Asturian version of the ballad ("Don Martinos") collected by Menéndez y Pelayo, the father warns his daughter that people will recognize her by her petite feet. The girl responds that she will wear her father's boots stuffed with cotton: "—Conoceránte en los pies,—que muy menudinos son. / —Pondréme las vuestras botas—bien rellenas de algodón" (1900, 120). Small feet were considered a particularly feminine feature in the early modern period, as they presumably were during Gustave Flaubert's time (the boot scene in *Madame Bovary*) and still are today. Women's feet were also considered to be a sexually provocative subject of fetish, of which shoes were a natural extension.[7] For this reason, in his anthology of erotic literature, Gregorio Morales comments that few people realize the degree of sexual fetishism attached to female feet in the Spanish Golden Age; feet, even when shod, were never shown. When they sat down, women would insert their feet into an inside hem on their skirts, and they would lock themselves away to put on their shoes (1998, 28). Shoes, as a result, often symbolize the vagina (Sieber 1978, 52–53), and the presence of an empty shoe in early modern painting sometimes indicated a brothel scene. Here the fact that the *doncella* will literally "fill her father's boots" suggests that she will easily find the supplement that will facilitate her transformation into a man.

The second, or test, sequence continues the dialogic production of gender in the text. The mother suggests a series of ingenious tests to which her lovesick son may submit the soldier in order to determine his true sex.[8] The first two in the Menéndez Pidal version test a woman's presumed preference for seeking out ribbons and personal adornments rather than arms in the marketplace and her natural inclination to gather flowers in a garden. Both tests fail, of course, since in the marketplace Don Martín chooses a dagger over ribbons and in the garden he cuts a rod as a whip for his horse instead of plucking flowers. This is a clear juxtaposition of the conventional female and male spheres: the softness of ribbons and flowers contrasts with the phallic dagger, rod, and horse. The *doncella* is effectively rebuffing the traditionally submissive female gender role and performing the active male social and sexual role, ostensibly in order to maintain her disguise.

In other versions, flowers are used to determine whether the young soldier menstruates. Because the actual biological function of menstruation was not yet known, it was viewed medically as a process of purging the blood, a way for the woman's body to release poisons. Thus, menstrual blood was considered unclean and corrupt, and while a woman was menstruating, she was seen as impure. One likely source of some of these beliefs in the Judeo-Christian tradition is the biblical proscription against sexual relations during menstruation. Leviticus 15:24, for example, warns that "if a man dares to lie with her [a menstruating woman], he contracts her impurity and shall be unclean for seven days; every bed on which he then lies also becomes unclean" (quoted in Niccoli 1990, 9). In addition to the religious proscriptions, menstruation carried a great many medical and popular taboos, since menstrual blood was generally considered to be somehow different from other bodily fluids and was considered dangerous to the point of being venomous.[9] According to popular belief, the touch, glance, or mere presence of a menstruating woman could rust iron, sour wine, spoil meat, dull knives, cloud mirrors, and fascinate others with the evil eye. Women who were menstruating were thought to spread illness via the corrupted vapors from their boiling menstrual blood, which were believed to ascend to the head and become excreted through the pores of the eye (Salmón and Cabré 1998, 63).

Such beliefs were especially pronounced in the rural societies where *romances* are traditionally preserved. At least two different versions of our ballad reflect such common superstitions. In one from the mountains of Cantabria in Northern Spain, the son timidly insinuates the topic of menstruation to his mother by noting the maiden's loss of color each month: "Todos los meses del año / se le muda la color" (Cossío 1942, 418). In a Sephardic ballad from Smyrna, one of the tests reflects the superstition that flowers wilt in the presence of a menstruating woman.[10] The mother tells the son to invite the soldier to his home and bed and to place fresh (that is freshly cut) roses in her room (presumably to see whether the flowers withered): "Hágale un convit' a casa, a la cama con siñor. / Métale í rosas frescas, ahí se ve si es varón" (quoted in Benmayor 1979, 147). Unfortunately, this fragmentary version ends with this verse, and the outcome of the test is not revealed. It is important to remember, however, that plucking flowers (particularly the rose) often symbolizes a prelude to sex or intercourse itself (literally the act of deflowering). In traditional lyric poetry, flowers mirror the idealized young woman with their beauty, fragrance, and appeal to the senses (Victorio 1995, 512). As the queen of flowers, moreover, the rose is the most intensely evocative of love and eroticism. Thus, in a Portuguese version of the ballad, the maiden claims that men prefer roses to carnations but for the purpose of plucking their petals: "Lindos cravos são p'ra damas, / Quem las for a convidar; / Los homens não querem cravos / Mas rosas . . . p'ra desfolhar" (Castro Pires de Lima 1958, 110).[11] Since in the previously cited Smyrna version the mother suggests that her son invite his soldier to bed, the interpretation of the rose as indicative of sexual play makes for a much more erotically, or more specifically homoerotically, charged trial; after all, the soldier's sex is still in doubt.

The ring test, in which the prince playfully tosses rings into Don Martín's lap, is also a common folk motif and gender determinant. A man will bring his knees together to catch something tossed into his lap, whereas a woman will open her legs to allow an object to fall into her skirts. This test is, in fact, performed on Huckleberry Finn early in Mark Twain's novel. The mother in the ballad suggests that her son throw rings, because the ring is a conventional symbol of the hymen. She (obviously much more knowledgeable than her son about female practices and symbology) is suggesting once again that he test the existence and availability of the *doncella*'s maidenhead. Are her legs open or closed to sexual play?

The final trial in Menéndez Pidal's version is the bathing test. In other accounts the maiden's sex will presumably be revealed by her natural fear of water if she is a woman. Of course, she confounds her testers by diving into the water and swimming off. However, the bathing test more often reveals a woman's fear of disrobing in front of a man. Here is where her body will finally be displayed and her gender will be exposed. This, of course, is the test that the maiden cannot pass, and the sequence comes to an end. The bathing test also allows for another interpretation, however. Public baths were also the place were the circumcised penis was revealed. Could this ballad be a transcoded Marrano text that metaphorically alludes to another type of concealment? Can the *doncella guerrera* and the tests to which she is subjected, and successfully manages to thwart, reflect another process of occultation in which post-1492 Spanish *conversos* engaged? Since the ballad has a very rich existence in the Sephardic tradition, this is a tantalizing possibility.

The *doncella guerrera* ballad is inscribed within the mythological and literary traditions relative to virile women and warrior maidens; however, the *doncella guerrera* is not the type of *mujer varonil* or *esquiva* who conventionally rejects men (that is, until she finds the "right one"). Although competent in masculine disguise and action, she wants to remain a woman. Thus, when she returns to her home and former identity, she reclaims her distaff and wishes to spin (*hilar*), a term that is charged with erotic references to heterosexual intercourse.[12] In this regard both Manuel da Costa Fontes (2000) and Ann Rosalind Jones and Peter Stallybrass (2000) have explored the erotic connotations of spinning and its tool, the distaff. Jones and Stallybrass point out that "the tools of spinning were also associated with flirtation and courtship" and that "through allegory or visual suggestion, spinning tools implied ungovernable female sexuality" (2000, 126).[13]

In these poems the *doncella*'s fragmented, eroticized body is foregrounded, whereas her warrior exploits go unmentioned. Instead, the poem centers on the physical constraints and the intelligence (some would say cunning) that she shows in keeping her true sex a secret.

Ultimately, the anatomic mobility that she embodies defeats the father's (and the epoch's) anatomic determinism. The captain prince and his mother see what has to be seen: the *doncella* has to be a woman; otherwise, the captain could not (or should not) have been erotically attracted to her. If he is a man, she has to be a woman. This, in turn, solidifies and ensures his masculinity, which has, of course, been called into question by his epistemological doubt regarding her sex.

The ballad of the *doncella guerrera* can also be read as an erotically charged seduction and courtship text in which the prince and the maiden pass through the various stages of courtship, each stage progressively more intimate. First is the suggestive description of her physical features; next come the "date" in the orchard, the imminent bathing scene, and the chase; and finally there is the seduction. The ballad ends with the girl calling to her father to throw open the doors of her house as the suitor prince arrives at the threshold. The denouement of the poem is an evident allusion to marriage rites, the crossing of the threshold, the symbolic passage from maidenhood to a married state, as Vasvári has shown. The man's knocking on the desired woman's door corresponds to his seeking entry into the house that is the female body (Vasvári 1999, 75). In this ballad the open door functions metaphorically as the maidenhead, the entrance to the vagina that this particular captain is invited to penetrate. Thus, the conclusion to the poem provides explicit sexual symbolism in which the outcome is nuptial expectation and bliss. In contrast to other traditional romance ballads, in which the suitor calls out for the woman to open the door, here the young girl is metaphorically arranging her own marriage. She orders the father to open wide the doors and enthusiastically welcomes her subsequent sexual penetration by the captain by calling out, "Abra las puertas mi padre, / ábralas de par en par."

In many aspects this ballad, whose female protagonist is competent in every way, displays a complete evacuation of the male role. The impotent father has not produced a son; instead, he has produced a strong-willed and competent daughter who has effectively replaced him as soldier in the king's army and displaced him as paterfamilias by arranging her own marriage. In this regard, Slater's study of several versions of "A Donzela que vai à guerra" from Bahia, Brazil, affirms that "on a deeper, sociological level, the ballad is about the chaos resulting from a refusal or inability to live out traditional sex roles equating masculinity with honor (willingness to defend both one's own good name and the reputation of one's family) and femininity with shame (chastity, reticence, deference to males)" (1979, 168). I would argue, however, that the *doncella guerrera* family of ballads embraces a figure deeply rooted in folk legend and mythology in order to celebrate the possibilities of escaping what are ultimately slippery and arbitrary gender roles while simultaneously exploiting their underlying erotic nature. The ballads reflect the gender play involved in cross-dressing as erotic game and pursuit.[14]

As the *doncella* states, she knew how to handle the masculine (the phallic arms and horse and the prince, whom she has effectively lured to her door), and now she is ready to control the feminine, her own body and choice of marriage partner. The warrior maiden has also skillfully usurped the masculine role and prerogative in another way: Her eyes not only "recall the medieval troubadour whose lady's fiery gaze wounds or slays him" (Slater 1979, 175); they also perform a phallic function by the very act of wounding and enamoring the prince. As he himself laments to his mother, he has been wounded and his soul stolen by Don Martín's eyes. In this sense the male figure is feminized, and his lack of sexual vigor is placed in counterpoint to the *doncella*'s forcefulness. The poem's repetitive, gender-marked imagery points insistently to the maiden's appropriation of the masculine. Besides wearing male clothing and armor, she jumps into the saddle and rides off on a white horse (a conventional phallic symbol), fast as a hawk—the nobleman's bird of prey and often a symbol of sexual predation.[15] At the same time, the prince is subordinate to and dependent on the other strong woman in the text, his mother. It is she who possesses the necessary sexual and cultural knowledge regarding femininity and she who plans the tests. In this sense she fulfills a function parallel to that of the *doncella,* and both transgress. Thus, the disguise and test sequences can be read as a series of feints by two skilled and knowledgeable female duelists.

The warrior maiden ultimately relinquishes her male disguise but not its prerogatives. She maintains control of her body, her sexuality, and her marriage as the seducer rather than the seduced, thus reversing conventional gender roles. In effect, she inhabits and mediates between both worlds—feminine and masculine—as daughter and soldier, upholding the familial honor that is attached to both. In this sense, the *doncella guerrera* is similar to other women of the *romancero* tradition who take matters into their own hands to resolve the predicament of having willingly lost their virginity and honor, by offering to their fathers the solution of marriage. This occurs, for example, with the princess in the ballad of Gerineldo "Parida está la infanta" and with Claraniña, Charlemagne's daughter and the lover of Conde Claros in "Medianoche era por filo."[16] At the same time, the *doncella guerrera* ballad can be read as a coming-of-age story in which the young girl leaves behind her world of childish dependence on and identification with the father to assume the familiar and societal role of a woman (Petrov 1993, 23).

The value of the *doncella guerrera* ballad cycle lies beyond its substantial aesthetic merits. In the final analysis, these are songs both of women's intercession in the salvaging of family honor and of their erotic empowerment. In all versions, the *romance* sings the tale of a patriotic and quick-witted soldier whose successful imposture reveals the precariousness and mutability of superficial gender determinants. Its successful gender masquerade and failed sex texts can be viewed not only as an invitation to gaze on the performance of masculinity but also as a claim of sexual elusiveness and corporeal mobility in an age of anatomic determinism. Such mind sets, which did not cede readily to change, caused women such as *la monja alférez* to seek escape by shedding their culturally and biologically imposed gender.

Crossing the Atlantic in a New Dress: La monja alférez

Another notorious cross-dressed warrior maiden in Hispanic literature takes readers from Spain to the New World, from lyric poetry to picaresque prose, from song to legend, and (perhaps most important) from fictional heroine to flesh-and-blood soldier. Long a mythical figure in Spanish America, Catalina de Erauso, the seventeenth-century ensign nun, or lieutenant nun, has received a flurry of critical attention in recent decades. Her exploits mutated over the years from "autobiography" into Golden Age theater (Juan Pérez de Montalbán's *La monja alférez*), early Spanish American prose (Ricardo Palma's *Tradiciones peruanas*), the nineteenth-century Spanish American novel (Lastarria's *El alférez Alfonso Díaz de Guzmán*), and (in the twentieth century) cinema and comics.[17] Erauso continues to serve as muse for fiction writers today, as in Juanita Gallardo's 2005 historical novel, *Confesiones de la monja alférez*. Lately, her life story has been perceived as fictional and has thus been viewed as a forerunner of the Spanish American short story.

Perhaps the most dramatic and colorful interpretation of Erauso's story, however, is still the one that the late María Félix brought to the screen as the lead in the 1944 Mexican film *La monja alférez,* directed by Emilio Gómez Muriel. The voluptuous Mexican diva was, in one sense, an unusual choice to play a woman who was said to have been quite manly; however, Félix was also known for wearing pants at a time when doing so was not the norm for women. When she was questioned about her penchant for trousers, she is reported to have said, "Yo me pongo los pantalones porque quiero. Que ellos se pongan faldas si quieren" (quoted in Taibo 1985, 60). [I wear pants because I want to. Let men wear skirts if they want.] When pressured by one of her biographers about whether her preference for pants was a subconscious sign, she responded, "Mis pantalones son femeninos siempre. Los pantalones que yo uso no los podría poner un hombre sin parecer marica" (quoted in Taibo 1985, 60). [My pants are always feminine. A man could not wear the pants I wear without looking like a fairy.] Félix's initial comment about wearing trousers is an emblem and a conceptual parallel of the character she brought to life on the screen in 1944, one that is usually applicable to cross-dressed women in the theater or other early modern genres in which masculine disguise generally heightens their erotic allure. The pages that follow explore the hermeneutic complexities that surround a precursory figure for the type of gender transgression and independence that Félix and Erauso embody still.

Strictly from the umbrella concept of the literary, Erauso—like Hernán Cortés, Bernal Díaz del Castillo, and many other authors before her who still compose the colonial literary canon—is a Spaniard whose only work (whether or not she wrote it herself) is now being studied as part of the first foundational literature of Spanish America. In no small measure, this is due to an ongoing interest in gender studies (an element that informs my own work to an extensive but not exclusive degree). Her "Spanishness" is not an irrelevant issue, since the national alliances and location of culture that were clear during her time are diffused when authors are viewed as part of the zeitgeist of the new continent. As purported narrator and protagonist of her own story,

Erauso clearly sees herself as a Spaniard, and—to an even larger and quite chauvinistic extent—as a Basque. In fact, throughout her story, she accentuates the national and regional allegiances that provided the cohesiveness and privileges that got her out of more than one tight spot. Once her text leaves her hands, however, the locus of her narrative is Spanish America, and her readers confront that social and cultural space as their main referent.

Moreover, and despite the several contemporary *relaciones* [accounts] that disseminated her story, it is difficult to discern how her contemporaries perceived her life. In this sense, hers is no different from the fictional lives examined in other chapters of this book. A fuller picture emerges, however, if we contextualize her overall behavior within the epistemological constraints of her time. Erauso is, above all, a prima facie baroque transgressor and storyteller on several levels: laws of literary history and production, gender and sexuality, genre, institutional law, narrative voice, and social expectations. Erauso crosses continents, dress, people, social mores, and dates; as a consequence, her work straddles literary histories and handbooks of both of the continents that she inhabited. The following discussion weaves these crossings with the elements that subsume them to focus on the issues of sexual otherness and eroticism that her text raises.

In 1829, Joaquín María de Ferrer published the first modern edition of Erauso's text, entitled *Historia de la monja alférez, Doña Catalina de Erauso, escrita por ella misma, é ilustrada con notas y documentos.* He proposes that Erauso wrote her partial memoir in Madrid, a short time before her definitive return to America. Her motivation might have been to support her request to the Spanish king for a pension (which we know to have been granted in 1626), by providing a written chronicle of her military service in the New World. To date no edition from that period has been found, although traces of a manuscript exist. Rima-Gretchen R. de Vallbona (1981, 1992) provides the editorial details, idiosyncrasies, and history of the text, basing her 1992 edition on the manuscript *Vida i sucesos de la monja alférez* held in the Biblioteca de la Real Academia de la Historia de Madrid. This manuscript was reproduced, with some variants, by Ferrer in his 1829 edition. Erauso's story is also included in Ángel Esteban's edition (see Erauso 2002), which is based on Ferrer's edition, Vallbona's edition, and all available manuscripts and *relaciones* that have come to light since.

With respect to Erauso's inclusion in specifically Spanish American literary history, it is worth noting that toward the end of her story—after she has more or less outed herself by confessing that she has spent most of her life dressed as a man—the narrator-protagonist asserts that her newly found fame has spread throughout the Indies: "Y los que antes me vieron, y los que antes y después supieron mis cosas, se maravillaron en todas las Indias" (Erauso 2002, 162). [And those in the Indies who saw me before, and those who knew of my exploits before and after, were astounded.].[18] Her fame would subsequently reach far beyond the Indies. By 1830 her story had already been translated into French and German, and Thomas de Quincey published his own fittingly romanticized version, "The Nautico-Military Nun of Spain," in the June and July 1847 issues of *Tate's Edinburgh Magazine*. Erauso's statement regarding her fame in the Indies and the many years of her adult life that she spent in the New World would seem to justify the inclusion of her work in histories of Spanish American literature. As Clement Moisan's recasting of what constitutes literary history generally reminds us, other complications can inform Erauso's place in those histories. One important, albeit hackneyed, consideration is whether her story belongs to the realm of history or fiction. Another is that her work was first published in book form at the beginning of the nineteenth century. In recent years, and almost single-handedly, Walter Mignolo (1981, 1982) has attempted to resolve such issues by referring to "historiographic metatexts," a phrase that conflates the blurring of fictional, colonial, (auto)biographical, and historical codes by resemanticizing what, up to that point, had been understood as chronicles, histories, letters, or *relaciones* of the period. It is surely appropriate to view *Historia de la monja alférez* as a hybrid text that melds forms of history and fiction in a very effective way. Its very hybridity increases its value as a sociological document.

But let us, for a contemporary moment, take history away from the text and see what happens. It is the seventeenth century, and we face the narrative of a woman who tells about her life spent as a man. Nobody seemed to be aware of or even to suspect her true sex until the body in question, as it were, confessed to leading a double life. In our historical and critical period we would speak about difference, otherness, gender-bending, transgression, transvestism, and transgenderism. There is no doubt that in the almost four hundred years of its existence, and the almost two hundred years of its reception (the *Historia*, or *Vida*, was recovered in 1829), this text and its author have been given various disguises. The lieutenant nun's life defies belief at every step, yet to this day it is a life that draws us powerfully into her stratagems (see Merrim 1994).

According to Erauso's own narration in her purported "autobiography," she was born in 1592 into a well-to-do family from San Sebastián in the Basque region of northern Spain. Placed in the San Sebastián el Antiguo convent as a little girl, she flees at age fifteen (before taking her final vows), cuts her hair short, and adopts male dress. Except for during a brief period when the authorities return her to the convent, she will employ this "disguise" until the end of her days. According to the plot of the *Historia,* for three years she leads a picaresque life in Spain, serving as a page to various masters. Her narrative makes it clear that from an early age she chooses to follow adventure, wandering as a vagabond without a fixed course or reason. Her brief stories contain no psychological explanation for or analysis of her life choices. The narrator states simply that she took to the road "sin saberme yo qué hacer ni adónde ir, sino dejarme llevar del viento como una pluma" (Erauso 2002, 97) [without knowing either what to do or where to go, but instead letting the wind carry me like a feather]. This does not necessarily mean, however, that she was a free spirit. Considered within the framework of the period, her attitude differs little from that of many of her compatriots who simply opted to try their luck "elsewhere," which at the time generally meant the New World.

Consequently, at the age of sixteen, she takes a job as a cabin boy and embarks for America. During the next twenty-one years, she works throughout the Americas as a shopkeeper, businessman, minor circuit judge, and (most important) a soldier in the final wars of conquest in Peru and Chile. (Her narrative never explains how she is able to establish her many connections at such an early age.) Erauso's story is similar to that of Inés Suárez, who also participated as a soldier in the conquest of Chile and who was, for a time, the mistress of Pedro de Valdivia, the first royal governor of the terrritory. After distinguishing herself in battle as courageous, daring, and bristling with sangfroid, especially in the battle of Paicabí, Chile, Erauso is promoted to the rank of ensign, or lieutenant—hence her sobriquet, the lieutenant nun. In a letter of recommendation supporting her petition to the king requesting a military pension, Juan Recio de León, quartermaster and captain general of one of the Peruvian provinces, evaluates her services as follows: "Le conocí al dicho Alférez en las guerras de Chile, haciendo su deber como el más valerosso y onrrado soldado, resistiendo a las yncomodidades de la milicia como el más fuerte varón" (quoted in Vallbona 1992, 146). [I met said Lieutenant in the Chilean wars, performing her duty as well as the bravest and most honorable soldier, enduring the discomforts of military life like the strongest man.] Statements such as León's provide the gist of what was and was not acknowledged in Erauso. She/he seems to have been judged for what *he* represented on the surface, with barely an indication (" como el más fuerte varón") of any difference.

Her military exploits, which constitute much of her story, reveal a fundamental concern with the depiction of military values. Therefore, they are narrated in an aggressive tone, which is in perfect accord with Erauso's bellicose nature and with the varied roles that women assumed during and after the conquest (which included, according to Delamarre and Sallard 1992, translator, companion, lover, governess, conqueror, pioneer, and *adelantada* [scout]). Erauso's combativeness is evidenced by her many gambling hall arguments and fistfights. These and other occurrences on the road become opportunities for Erauso to defend her honor with her sword. Even when she wounds or kills her opponents (among whom is her own [inadvertently] mortally wounded brother), however, no clarification of her reason for or effect from the killing is offered. She simply states that she is defending herself, as is any man's right.

Although she is repeatedly arrested for her acts of violence and is even condemned to death for murder, she generally manages to escape justice—often by seeking asylum in churches, where invariably she is protected, her wounds are nursed, her immediate future is secured, and she even receives aid in fleeing her captors. Around 1622 the bishop of Guamanga saves her from arrest for killing a man in a gambling brawl. In view of the injuries she sustained during the fight and the saintly (as she puts it) nature of the bishop—and undoubtedly to avoid the punishment she faced—Erauso confesses to the bishop her true sex, her previous status as a nun, and her virginity.

For a few years, Erauso is confined to convents in America. Then she returns to Spain, where she requests and obtains from Philip IV a pension for services rendered in America. She leaves for Rome, where (after becoming involved in altercations with Italians in defense of Spanish honor) she receives a dispensation from Pope Urban VIII to continue her life dressed as a man. As Mary Elizabeth Perry reports, "In 1630 she was licensed to dress as a man, and she was formally invested with this privilege in a ceremony in the Cathedral of Seville" (1980, 216).[19] Thus, after experiencing few problems living her life as a man at a time when the church condemned cross-dressing and after receiving a military pension from the Spanish king, Erauso finally seeks to legitimize her status.

In my view, Erauso experienced few problems living as a man only in the sense that there exist no textual references to the material difficulties inherent in passing as male. In contrast to the *doncella guerrera,* whose many versions center specifically on the obstacles to passing, all such experiences (which would be of primary interest to readers today) are elided from the *Historia.* Only in a 1626 letter from the Italian Pedro de la Valle is mention made of a procedure that Erauso allegedly used to flatten her breasts (quoted in Erauso 2002, 202). In this regard Erauso's story conforms to the genre that Estelle Jelinek has accurately called "disguise autobiographies." Jelinek describes the texts of this genre as written by women who chose to masquerade as men in secret out of desperation and in defiance of society's mores. The works that she refers to (most of them by English or American women from the nineteenth and twentieth centuries) seem to have been "written expressly to describe the women's disguise adventures . . . [and] actually reveal very little about the disguise experiences" (1987, 54). Again, in Erauso's *Historia,* the inevitable disguise experiences are left unmentioned.

Erauso ends her story abruptly, in 1626 Naples. The empirical data available in historical archives (traced in Vallbona 1981, 1992) indicate that she returned to America in masculine dress in 1630 and established herself as a mule driver in Veracruz, where she died in 1648 or 1650. Erauso's story is, perhaps, typical of the unknown transgressions and transgressors that managed to cross continents and set up a sort of beachhead for unknown desires and perceptions that literary histories and even general readers ignore. What did Erauso look like, and why should she matter to us? According to Fray Nicolás de Rentería, who met her in Veracruz, "Era sugeto allí tenido por de mucho corazón i destreza: i que andava en hábito de hombre, i que traía espada i daga con guarniciones de plata: i le parece que sería entonces como de cinquenta años, i que era de buen cuerpo, no pocas carnes, color trigueño, con algunos pocos pelillos por bigote" (quoted in Vallbona 1992, 126). [She was considered a person of great courage and ability who went around dressed as a man, carrying a sword and dagger trimmed in silver. I thought she was about fifty years old then and had a sturdy build, not thin, and was neither dark nor fair skinned, with a few hairs serving as a mustache.] Rentería's description is brought to life on canvas in Francisco Pacheco's 1630 portrait of Erauso (painted in Seville before her definitive return to America),[20] which has become the palimpsest for our visualization of her. Nevertheless, the portrait has not prevented pictorial idealizations such as the one reproduced in Pumar Martínez 1988 (6) or even the screen images of María Félix.[21]

Pacheco's portrait seems to capture the essence of this enigmatic figure, who Valle, her contemporary, described as follows:

Ella es de estatura grande i abultada para muger, bien que por ella no parezca no ser hombre. No tiene pechos: que desde mui muchacha me dixo haver hecho no sé qué remedio para secarlos i quedar llanos, como le quedaron: el qual fue un emplasto que le dio un Ytaliano, que quando se lo puso le causó gran dolor; pero después, sin hacerle otro mal, ni mal tratamiento, surtió el efecto.

De rostro no es fea, pero no hermosa, i se le reconoce estar algún tanto maltratada, pero no de mucha edad. Los cabellos son negros i cortos como de hombre, con un poco de melena como hoi se usa. En efecto, parece más capón, que muger. Viste de hombre a la Española: trahe la espada bien ceñida, i así la vida: la cabeza algo baja, un poco agoviada, más de Soldado valiente, que de cortesano i de vida amorosa. Sólo en las manos se le puede conocer que es muger, porque las tiene abultadas i carnosas, i robustas i fuertes, bien que las mueve algo como muger. (Quoted in Vallbona 1992, 128)

[She is tall and bulky for a woman, and in any case she does not appear not to be a man. She does not have breasts; she told me that as a very young girl she used some remedy to dry them up and flatten them as they are now. This remedy was a poultice that an Italian gave her, and it was very painful when she used it, but afterward it worked without causing her any further harm. She is neither ugly nor pretty, and she looks a little worn but not very old. Her hair is black and short like a man's, slightly long as is fashionable today. She actually looks more like a eunuch than a woman. She dresses like a man, in the Spanish style; she keeps a tight grip on her sword and her life; she carries her head low and is a little stooped over, more like a brave soldier than a courtier or a lover. You can tell she is a woman only by her hands, because they are full and fleshy and strong and robust, and she moves them in a somewhat womanly way.]

It is interesting to note here how Erauso deviates from the conventional and idealizing norm of cross-dressed women in literary description.[22] The *doncella guerrera,* whose problems center on concealing her feminine beauty, and the extensive cast of female cross-dressers in Golden Age theater are women whose stereotypical beauty shines through, and in spite of, the male attire. In most theatrical and literary cases, crossdressing served precisely to enhance women's beauty and figure, since it revealed parts of the female body that were usually covered. Consequently, Golden Age moralists consistently denounced women who appeared onstage dressed as men. The real *mujer varonil*—Erauso—in contrast, is the type of woman who rarely appears in Golden Age or colonial literature: the plain woman. Erauso was far from the swashbuckling and voluptuous beauty depicted by Maria Félix.

As expected, given the exceptional nature of the already legendary figure of the ensign nun and the events narrated in her *Historia,* some critics have questioned the authenticity of the book.[23] Even in a critical period when the "death of the author" alters literary genesis, others maintain that the text is a true autobiography. Their assertion is based on research allegedly conducted by Malcolm K. Burke and recorded in documents that purportedly verify the existence of virtually all of the characters and events described in the text. These elusive (and probably spurious) documents have never surfaced.[24] After an exhaustive investigation of the official archival documentation and a comparison of historical data with the text of the manuscript *Vida,* Vallbona concludes that there is no doubt that Erauso existed and enacted the majority of the deeds that the narrator-protagonist of *Vida i sucesos* relates in autobiographical form (1992, 3).

In a contemporaneous study that addresses the text's baroque frame, Stephanie Merrim outlines the three plausible theories of authorship that scholars commonly propose: (1) Erauso herself wrote the work, (2) Erauso told her tale to a more cultivated author, who then penned the story, and (3) a later author elaborated on Erauso's original, interpolating episodes (1994, 196). Merrim posits that whatever the theory, Erauso had a direct hand in constructing the *Historia*. More important, however, Merrim states that "the text reflects—*be it metonymically or metaphorically*—Erauso's larger strategy vis-à-vis her own anomaly" (196, original emphasis). What becomes more pertinent, then, is that Erauso existed beyond her conflictive narrative and that the majority of the events that her "autobiography" retells are undeniable facts or snippets of fact. I say "autobiography" (in quotation marks) not merely because of the inherent problem of that genre regarding mimetic contracts with the reader but also because of the seemingly superficial and brief nature of the text (as autobiography), which has not merited study by specialists in the field. In light of the differences between Spanish and English attitudes in Erauso's time, it is not inconceivable to propose that the success of autobiographies such as Erauso's depends on her ability to reconcile generic ambivalences by imposing on the material a narrative structure that entails a coherent vision of herself as a unique, integrated human being (M. B. Rose 1986, 248).

Also at stake here is the generic consideration of attributing to a narrative that, at best, is a long picaresque-type short story the capability of containing enough content to construct a life. In comparison with other narratives of that or earlier periods (such as Teresa of Avila's *Libro de la Vida*), Erauso's short novel lacks both the characteristics of the best seller that she wants her life story to be and the aesthetic value that is generally attributed to a canonical narrative. Although Pérez de Montalbán's *La monja alférez,* a play based on Erauso's life, was performed in Madrid during her lifetime (possibly while she was there), it was clearly her life, not her "literature," that achieved notoriety. Erauso's sexual, baroque alterity can certainly be aligned with the dilemma of the Renaissance storytellers who preceded her and who struggled to find ways to authorize fiction.

Erauso's *Historia* provides a module that allows us to examine and revise transgressions of the gender canon. The "autobiography" and the lieutenant nun's petition to Philip IV reveal the careful construction of a positive masculine identity in accordance with the patriarchalism of the period on both sides of the Atlantic. The psychological underpinnings that led Erauso to assume a fairly stereotypical masculine life for the period aside, the petition to the king requesting a military pension

explains that she left for America "en ávito de Barón, por particular yn-
clinacion que tuvo de exercitar las armas en defenssa de la fee católica,
y emplearsse en servicio de vuestra merced sin que en el dicho Reyno
de Chile todo el tiempo que asistió fuesse conocida sino por hombre"
(quoted in Vallbona 1992, 132) [in male dress following a particular
inclination that she had to take up arms in defense of the Catholic faith
and enter into your service and that during the whole time that she
served in the Kingdom of Chile nobody knew her as anything other
than a man].

The explanation is too pat, in large part in that it follows the code
and reasoning acknowledged by most of the exclusively male partici-
pants in the Conquest: We are acting for God, country, and Crown.
However, Erauso is balancing carefully on the tightrope of generic and
gender expectations of the "historiographical metatexts" of the period
(two authors of which—Bernal Díaz del Castillo and El Inca Garcilaso
de la Vega—come immediately to mind). It would appear that all her
merits are, of necessity, masculine, since feminine merits have no place
in the life that she forged. Living as a man liberated Erauso from many
of the limitations of sexual ideology. In this way, she could (1) live free
from the constraints of femininity and (2) produce her "autobiography."
In other words, because her story (whether or not she wrote it herself)
is a male-focused autobiography that reflects what was considered to
be a male sensibility, it was worthy of being written and disseminated.
After all, Erauso openly displays decidedly unfeminine traits for the period: anger and hostility. Her petition states, "Fue con particular valor,
resistiendo a las yncomodidades de la milicia, como el más fuerte varón,
sin que en acción ninguna fuesse conocida sino por tal" (quoted in Vallbona 1992, 132). [She was particularly brave, enduring the discomforts
of military life like the strongest man, and at no time was she known as
anything but a man.] It is not surprising that the overemphasis on her
masculinity was one of the main bases for her request, but was it mere
cynicism or opportunism? Seemingly it was not, because Erauso further
supports her request by reminding the king of the military service of
her father and brothers. That is, she sees herself, or at least depicts herself, as part of a military tradition that, in principle, had no place for
women.[25]

Erauso ends her petition to King Philip with her request for rec-
ompense for her long service to the Crown, for her acts of bravery, for

the exceptional quality of her discourse *sensu strictu* ("la singularidad y prodigio que biene a tener su discursso" [quoted in Vallbona 1992, 133]), for her status as noblewoman, and "más, por la singularidad y rara limpieça conque ha vivido y bibe" (133) [more for the singular and rare purity with which she has lived and lives]. Even if we could account for the selectivity that defines autobiographical discourse or the moral sense with which it might be accepted, Erauso's positioning in that subjectivity of being is never questioned. Thus, what appears in her petition as a brief passing reference is of undeniable importance: her virginity. Erauso astutely leaves a record of the sine qua non for women of her historical period: chastity. All early modern Spanish moralists invoke the importance of female sexual purity as the requisite basis on which all other womanly traits are constructed. In his *Formación de la mujer cristiana* (1523), for example, Juan Luis Vives notes that female virginity represents integrity of mind, spirit, and body: "Llamo virginidad a la integridad de la mente que se extiende hasta el cuerpo; entereza total, exenta de toda corrupción y contagio. . . . Por lo demás, la parte más principal de esta purísima entereza radica casi totalmente en el alma, manantial de todas las virtudes" (Vives 1947, 1006). [I call virginity that integrity of mind that extends to the body, totally free from any corruption and contagion. Regarding the rest, the principal part of this pure integrity pertains almost totally to the soul, the source of all virtues.]

Once a woman is married, the maximum wifely virtue is sexual fidelity to her husband, since a wife is to her husband as the church is to Christ: "En una y otra virtud refleja la imagen de la Iglesia, que es castísima y guarda tenacísimamente a Cristo, su Esposo, una fidelidad sincera" (Vives 1947, 1076). [In her chastity and love of her husband the wife reflects the image of the Church, which is absolutely chaste and sincerely faithful to Christ, its Husband.] For a woman to offend her husband through sexual infidelity is not only to dissolve the most sacred of human bonds but also to "dirim[ir] una sociedad civil; viol[ar] las leyes y ofend[er] a la patria" (1077) [dissolve civil society, break the law, and offend the fatherland]. Thus, female chastity is inextricably bound up in notions of personal virtue and in notions of family, church, and state. Seen as a barricade that safeguarded women from assault by other vices, chastity granted Erauso a type of protective and protected subjectivity. In her case, her status as virgin and nun effectively exempted her from the punishments commonly invoked for the types of transgressions she committed.

As important as Erauso's self-concept and representation as a man, or at least as a masculinized woman, is that the same individuals who had a stake in her identity always assumed her to be and treated her as a man. Even after her "true" identity became known in Spain and the Americas, various documents of the period gave an official and public patina to her alleged masculinity by treating and gendering her as a male (Castresana 1968, 82). For example, although she was named as a daughter in her father's will (1611), her mother's will (1612) includes her as a son, under the name that she used during the rest of her life, Antonio de Erauso (Berruezo 1959, 21). In addition, many letters of recommendation support her petition to the king by invoking her manly courage and her exemplary behavior as a man.

Erauso's construction of a male identity, even when it can be attributed to political expediency, leaves the reader wondering about her sexual orientation. A reasonable assumption, given certain explicitly homoerotic moments in her *Historia* and the *relaciones,* is that she was what today we would call a lesbian (recall the reservations expressed in Chapter Three about the use of anachronistic terminology for sexual identities). In a study of the extant psychological and physiological data that surround the ensign nun, Dr. Nicolás León, extrapolating from the text, observes, "Catalina jamás tuvo la inclinación a los hombres, amistad estrecha o marcada simpatía por ellos. Por el contrario, le agradaban las mujeres, pero las de 'buenas caras'" (1973, 126). [Catalina was never attracted to men; she did not have close friendships with them or like them very much. To the contrary, she liked women, but pretty ones.]

In her 1981 dissertation, Vallbona interprets Erauso's habit of flirting with other women and then retreating immediately before consummating the sexual act: "Subyace en toda esta pose una serie de signos que connotan una complacencia lesbiana reprimida por la protagonista hasta en el discurso narrativo (palabras referidas a sí misma) debido al peligro que corría si en aquellas circunstancias se llegaba a descubrir su sexo" (1981, 299 n. 2). [Underlying this pose is a series of signs that connote a lesbian complacency that was repressed by the protagonist even in the narration (words referring to herself) because of the danger she risked in those circumstances if her sex was discovered.]

The repression that Vallbona adduces may have been caused by Erauso's fear that her disguise and her biological sex might be discovered. After all, given the inquisitorial climate of the period, attempts at sexual intimacy with the wrong woman would certainly have been risky. The punishments for such behavior were surely deterrents to open sexual transgressions. In Serge Gruzinski's statistical study of the "many faces of sin" during the period that Erauso lived in the New World, among the most common sexual and sociocultural transgressors cited as exhibiting the most egregious behaviors are effeminates, cross-dressers, and transvestites (1986, 271–72). The model of bad conduct represented by male cross-dressing is doubly deviant for the role inversion that it implies and for the feminine referents chosen, since some of the transvestites' nicknames ("La Conchita," "La Zangarriana," "La Estampa") refer explicitly to an already marginal space in novo-Hispanic society: the world of female prostitution (273).[26]

As noted in previous chapters, during this period male homosexuality was considered a much more serious transgression than female homosexuality. After all, in the collective mentality of the age, a desire to be female signified a desire to be inferior. Erauso's reaction to a pair of prostitutes in the last section of her final chapter might come from an awareness of this state of affairs with respect to deviance or, since her own life was not necessarily exemplary, from a contradictory stance toward difference: In Naples, Erauso interprets the laughter of two prostitutes as an affront. Addressing her as "Doña Catalina," they ask her where she is going. She answers, "Señoras p . . . a darles a ustedes cien pescozadas y cien cuchilladas a quien las quiera defender—. Callaron y se fueron de allí" (Erauso 2002, 175). ["Madame whores . . . to give a hundred blows to the neck to you and a hundred stabs to whoever defends you." They shut up, and they left.] These are Erauso's final words, and if they are not sisterly, it is because she seems to share no solidarity with women who are neither of her original social standing nor, in this case, Spaniards. Her utterance has no moralistic overtone; she has simply assumed her male identity in full.

With respect to the consideration of Erauso's sexuality, her autobiographical tale relates a number of episodes of clearly homoerotic transcendence. The most evident of these occurs in Lima, when the young unmarried sister-in-law of Erauso's master, the merchant Diego de Solarte, falls in love with him/her. Solarte walks in on them and finds Erauso reclining in the maiden's lap "andándole en las piernas" [stroking her legs] (Erauso 2002, 109). Dismissed by Solarte, Erauso resolves the sentimental dilemma in a typically and romantically masculine manner: She enlists as a soldier and goes to war, since "era [su] inclinación andar y ver mundo" (110) [her inclination was to see the world]. Of course, what can be placed in checkmate immediately is the fact that Erauso controls the point of view.[27] What has been even more difficult for her critics to contextualize, however, is why Erauso would, as a way of daring to narrate what at the time were deviations against nature, create the tension of providing details and then sweeping them away. Had these details of her story been published during her lifetime, the revelation of her transgressions would surely have come at a high price.

José Toribio Medina, perhaps the best critic of Erauso's life and times in the New World, traces the risk of being under even the slightest suspicion for crimes punishable by the Inquisition. Among the punishments were public exposure and disgrace, flogging (women were whipped in the streets, naked from the waist up and mounted on pack animals while the town crier shouted out their crimes), and prohibition from mounting a horse or wearing silk (Medina 1952, 132). As discussed in Chapter Two, when it came to accusations of sodomy, the Inquisition had no time for subtleties; had she been accused of this crime, Erauso would have risked, at the very least, being returned to Spain.[28] In the end, however, it mattered who the woman in question was and what she did, because as an institution the Inquisition in the New World was as arbitrary, and gendered, as anywhere else. Women were generally considered to be weak, ignorant, and capricious, and their testimonies were viewed as less reliable than the testimonies of men. This disdain was by no means limited to the Inquisition; it was universally held. As a result, accused women received at least a little leniency because their presumed inferiority also diminished their guilt: A child is not punished with the same severity as an adult (Alberro 1987, 91).

One case illustrates the punitive norm for such transgressions: A man who in 1530 fought in the conquest of New Spain dressed as a woman, since he had been raised that way and lived by prostitution, was ordered by the general to be burned alive, despite the fact that he had distinguished himself as the bravest in battle (Orozco y Berra 1853–56, 354; see also Vallbona 1992, 52). It is important to remember here, as we have discussed, that at that time neither homosexuality nor lesbianism existed as a sexual category, much less as a social identity. What did exist was the category of sodomite, which, as we have seen, encompassed both men and women. Given the distance that made enforcement of the law unfeasible, whatever Erauso's transgressions may have been, they must be viewed in the context of the perception of women at a time when fighting bodies were greatly needed in the Americas. It is a mental outlook that has crossed not only continents but also interpretive views. Thus, with reference to women warriors in Peru, Nancy O'Sullivan-Beare comments that it is possible that none of these bold women was a model of honesty, since not one said that her companion was her husband (ca. 1956, 254). It is interesting that there remain no records to indicate any denunciations of sexual transgression against Erauso during her lifetime; at least none is recorded in the documentation that has so far been gathered around her history. As a result, Erauso's sexuality has been obliterated, and she has been interpreted not as a lesbian but rather reticently or euphemistically as a woman who attempts to become hypermasculinized.[29]

We might ask, as a parallel source of inquiry, why Erauso was never punished for adopting male attire and habits. At the time, cross-dressing was, after all, prohibited by both canon and civil law. The Old Testament is quite explicit in this regard: "A woman must not wear men's clothing, nor a man wear women's clothing, for the Lord your God detests anyone who does this" (Deut. 22:5). Despite these proscriptions and even considering the church as the ideological state apparatus that it was and is in the Hispanic world, Erauso's exemplary performance in the military may have been given greater weight than her cross-dressing transgressions. This possibility is reinforced by such considerations as the various recommendations from her superiors and her status as a member of an *hidalgo* family that had already sacrificed male children to the service of the Crown. In fact, Erauso was a celebrity, a heroine who, as previously noted, saw the playwright Pérez de Montalbán, a disciple of Lope de Vega, transform her into a legend on the contemporary Madrid stage.[30]

In his study of Spanish American history as a source for Spanish theater, Medina traces the reception of Erauso's deeds and puts them into perspective. Conceding that she is a Spaniard of second order (vis-à-vis the conquistadors), Medina places the conclusion of the feat period of the Conquest at the end of the sixteenth century. During the subsequent colonial era, he notes, there were no more deeds from the vast continent to be celebrated. Thus, peninsular theater topics drawn from Spain's experience in the Americas seemed to dry up, except for the occasional event or exceptional character that cropped up during the first half of the seventeenth century. Erauso was one of these (Medina 1970, 152–53). In other words, she was exceptional in a very diminished milieu, when the great adventures had already been mined. Her disguise was not as shocking as she may have thought it would or wanted it to be, but she was also a woman who was celebrated and entertained by the upper echelons of the ecclesiastical hierarchy in Rome and who presumably enjoyed the admiration of the people and the king as a warrior returning from the American campaigns. It is reasonable to believe, then, that the laws that governed common people could hardly be applied to her. That acceptance was not seventeenth-century clairvoyance; rather, it was a way of co-opting the capacity of any human being at the service of the state.

Merrim argues that Erauso was unlocking a zone of permissiveness and flexibility that was reserved for the prodigious and the unusual in the baroque period. In explaining her transgressive infiltration of baroque society, Merrin comes to the conclusion that "in writing herself as a man and in mining her own masculine/feminine difference, Erauso has achieved fame, a space which in the Baroque Age, thanks to its penchant for the bizarre, lay beyond the pale of normative social codes" (1994, 197).

In this regard it becomes possible to go against the hermeneutical current and posit that seventeenth-century transvestites can be considered, in a certain sense, among the first feminists. According to Lillian Faderman, although they were silent and without any umbrella ideology to help them express their convictions, female cross-dressers saw women's roles as boring and limited. At the time, the only way to expand these roles was to become a man. Only by donning convincing male attire could they claim for themselves the privileges generally accorded to the men of their class. For many adventurous young women who understood that as women they could hope for little latitude or liberty in their lives, transvestism must have been a temptation or at least a favorite fantasy (Faderman 1981, 61). Of course, in addition (or perhaps first), it is fitting to ask why a woman would want to become a man, even in the seventeenth century. Unfortunately, however, the historical conditioning of women tempers any projection about the matter made from this contemporary reading moment.

In her study of transvestism, *Vested Interests: Cross-Dressing and Cultural Anxiety* (1992), Marjorie Garber affirms that critics look *through* the transvestite rather than *at* him. Garber deals mainly with the man who dresses as a woman, devoting very little attention to the female cross-dresser. The critic's gaze becomes a way to determine the transvestite's "true" sex in order to place him in one of the two traditional categories: male or female, man or woman. Garber's book tries to see the transvestite as *he* is, as the signifier of a space of possibilities that blurs categories, sexual as well as cultural. In other words, for Garber the transvestite questions, destabilizes, and represents a crisis in a binary system. As a consequence, sexual indeterminacy questions the social order, and the transvestite becomes an indicator of a crisis. Garber avoids the issue of whether such queries are possible without the knowledge that one is dealing with a transvestite. Also neglected is the importance of sociohistorical context: Will the meaning of transvestism be unchanged across uneven cultural developments and cultures? When we insert theories such as Garber's into the material world, when we confront them with a historical reality such as Erauso's, doubts arise. Therefore, a transvestite who provides no inkling of his or her cross-behavior cannot provide us with a crisis in the way that perhaps a patently fictional character such as the *doncella guerrera* or the numerous cross-dressed women in Spanish Golden Age theater can. In fact, the cross-dressed woman's conduct, as character and actress, contains a significant (heterosexual) erotic charge, which Garber's study, in its ahistorical insistence on the alleged destabilization of binary systems, neglects to analyze.

In the everyday sphere, we rarely *see* a transvestite or *observe* an androgynous person; rather, we perceive a person of one sex imitating the other sex. Erauso's disguise was the essence of her being, and only she could deconstruct what she had created. What makes her, and perhaps all cross-dressers, interesting across historical periods is precisely the enigma that she presents or how convincing she is as the person she has self-fashioned, to say nothing of the erotic possibilities involved in the imposture. This would never have been a questionable fact of her life had she not revealed the device (in the formalist sense applied to narrative) of being a woman dressed as a man. It is clear that, when we deal with previous historical periods, when gender and sexual codes were very different from what they are today, the motivation and possible benefits—both social and literary—of assuming a different sexual identity become equally important determinants.

From Christopher Columbus to Alexander von Humboldt—a historical and literary period that encompasses the attitudes that governed the world that surrounded Erauso—Europeans found themselves translating into practices of their own a variety of experiences from an alien, totally new world. According to Anthony Pagden, this crossing was carried out by analogue or metaphor, a process that avoids the linguistic connection. Erauso's comportment does not fit neatly into this interpretative construct; rather, it fits into the device that Pagden offers in opposition for an understanding of the subsequent progression of the crossing of cultures in the New World. What Pagden calls the principle of attachment he defines as follows: "What is familiar, abstention and self-denial, is employed to 'attach' one unfamiliar action to another familiar one. The stark incommensurability of the two is, or seems to be, dissolved in the supposed common recognition of the danger of sex and of the cosmic worth of gold" (1993, 21).

For Erauso her lieutenant status had the cosmic worth of gold; thus, she recognized the danger of sex in terms of practical rather than moral consequences. In other words, she could easily violate most norms of comportment and social expectations. This is a feasible act in a social sphere created by the attitudes that inform the everyday behavior of her historical period. It is not feasible in the context of early modern balladry or theater, where there is a cultural, aesthetic, and perhaps generic (i.e., literary) imperative for a woman to act like a woman at the end. As a matter of fact, Erauso's case was not isolated; there were many women in Europe who lived for years, if not for their whole lives, dressed as men. This occurred with some frequency in Erauso's time, and the women's true sex was often discovered only after their death. The confirmed cases of women who lived as men are only the tip of the iceberg, since they constitute only those cases in which the women's identity was discovered (which often occurred when they attempted to court or marry other women). If Erauso's case provides any sort of measure or precursory advantage, it is also possible that the better-known cases may well have been the less typical ones.

In this regard it is revealing that the majority of cases that Rudolf Dekker and Lotte van de Pol investigated in *The Tradition of Female*

Transvestism in Early Modern Europe involved soldiers or sailors.[31] The authors state categorically that until the nineteenth century, women were found among the dead on battlefields throughout Europe (1989, 22), thus revealing their "true" sex. At the same time, a great number of young women abandoned their homes and countries to live at the margins of society, infiltrating groups of male adolescents as they boarded ships or joined armies. All this crossing of peripheries occurred in the midst of the strict differentiation between the sexes regarding codes of dress and behavior in the early modern age.

It would be wise to emphasize in our unisex age that during early modern times dress clearly distinguished not only the social classes but also the sexes. A person who dressed as a man, therefore, would have been assumed to be a man. Moreover, Mariló Vigil observes that Fray Hernando de Talavera's *De vestir y de calzar, tratado provechoso cómo en el vestir e calzar comunmente se cometen muchos pecados y aún también en el comer y beber,* written at the end of the fifteenth century, remained quite influential in the sixteenth and seventeenth centuries:

> Las mujeres "fueron hechas" para estar encerradas y ocupadas en sus casas por eso "a donde quier que hay seso" se usa que lleven ropa luenga, que refrena la ligereza que naturalmente tienen las mujeres. Estas han de llevar ropa que las pueda "empachar." . . . Los hombres, según Fray Hernando de Talavera, deben llevar ropa corta y la cabeza descubierta, puesto que están llamados a una vida más activa. (Vigil 1987, 194)

> [Women were made to be enclosed and occupied in their homes. This is why, wherever reason reigns, they wear long dresses that inhibit their natural movement. Women should wear clothing that impedes them. . . . Men should wear short clothes and leave the head uncovered, because they are called to a more active life.]

Sandra Gilbert (1982) notes, in a similar vein, that until the middle or late nineteenth century, clothing was a clear indicator of class, age, and occupation. She comments that Virginia Woolf's view of clothing in *Orlando* implies that costume is inseparable from identity, that it creates identity. In *Renaissance Clothing and the Materials of Memory,* Jones and Stallybrass, who have done formidable research in this regard, explain the extent to which clothes "permeate the wearer, fashioning him or her within" and the way they "inscribe themselves upon a person who comes into being through that inscription" (2000, 2). This is certainly the case in any number of literary texts from Golden Age Spain in which clothing made the man or woman. So powerful was gendered attire that, as Will Fisher affirms in *Materializing Gender in Early Modern English Literature and Culture,* it was thought to effect sex change (2006, 12–15).

The transvestite warrior maiden is neither a historical rarity nor a mere literary or theatrical cliché. Indeed, she goes beyond the type of mythical and fictional heroine celebrated in the *romancero* to form part of a long tradition that Erauso herself helped further concretize. Female tranvestism offered a viable and real option for escaping from poverty and other difficult circumstances. Erauso's case proves that it also provided an untold opportunity to become liberated from the rigorous bounds that confined women, especially if their sexual preferences were not the hetero norm. Erauso is, therefore, more than a critical curiosity for baroque studies. Her importance lies, perhaps, in truly bringing to life the figure of the warrior maiden and manly woman as a cross-cultural element of literary history. In various ways Erauso proved that a woman could be a soldier, a conqueror, a merchant, and perhaps a lover of other women, and she could lead an independent life. Erauso seems to have internalized the external behavioral codes of patriarchy, but the system was so obsessed with these codes that it was unable to grasp or even recognize the ease with which Erauso subverted the very exteriority that defined her. She further confounded the European centrality of her being by coming to a New World overcharged with representations of alterity. Hers is a hidden *mestizaje* that brings to the fore the complexities of cultural identity by adding a sexual element.

If Erauso freed herself from the cultural and societal centrality of masculine control, however, she could not discard the weight of her sexuality. Her virginity, duly examined by a midwife and certified by church and king, was what ultimately protected her from civil and ecclesiastical censure. Her heterosexual chastity together with her paradoxical virility were her guarantees as an exemplary royal subject. During the time that she passed as a man, she did not interrupt the social order or gender hierarchies. Ironically, she received the highest possible license to circumvent that order from the traditional keepers of patriarchy: the pope and the king. In fact, as I have argued, Erauso never comes full circle in her search for a cross-identity. In contrast to the *doncella guerrera,* who, having proven herself as a man, gladly returns to life as a woman, Erauso is inscribed as an honorary member of the masculine gender. This is ultimately her most personal and unacknowledged quandary, and it is also one of the many paradoxes of transgression.

The Murderous Serrana, *from Juan Ruiz to Luis Vélez de Guevara*

In his novels, Donatien de Sade, known as the marquis de Sade, defines murder as the culmination of erotic excitement. In *The Tears of Eros,* Georges Bataille's study of the relationship among violence, eroticism, and art, the French philosopher asserts, in turn, that medieval art relegated eroticism to hell (1989, 82). During the Renaissance, he continues, "the violence of passion played a part in this erotic art born from the night of the religious world, which piously cursed all works of the flesh" (83). Since the moment that a distant and often brutal eroticism entered this world, Bataille concludes, we have had to face a terrible alliance between eroticism and sadism. The Hispanic literary tradition, as we know, has not been reticent about the representation of violence or eroticism, and there is little risk in postulating that this tradition has much to offer with respect to the association between the two, especially during the medieval and Golden Age periods.

For example, in the fourteenth-century erotic masterpiece *Libro de buen amor,* we read, "Yo só la Chata recia que a los omnes ata" (J. Ruiz 1988, 306, strophe 952).[32] ["I'm the rugged country girl who ties men up"] (J. Ruiz 1972, 254). By proclaiming to the world her rough and fearless nature, the Chata emblematizes the violent mountain girl known as the *serrana.* Although we tend to associate erotic violence with aggression inflicted by men on women, these belligerent women turn the tables by assaulting men both sexually and physically. Thus, they provide a fascinating variation on the theme of fighting women and their particular connection to eroticism.

To trace a genealogy of this devourer of men and link three of her different types, we begin with the origins of the earliest figure in those horrific *serranas* portrayed by Ruiz. From there we move briefly to the legendary *serrana* from the ballad tradition and conclude with Vélez de Guevara's Gila, the manly woman and assassin of a thousand men who is the protagonist of *La serrana de la Vera*. To begin with, an explanation of sources and precursors is necessary to clarify what is understood by the concept of *serrana*. Most critics who have studied medieval *serranillas*—those brief songs and lyric compositions (*villancicos*) in which we find the *serrana* figure—believe that, for the most part, the poems are derived from the Provenzal *pastourelle*. This class of courtly lyric describes the encounter between a gentleman (*chevalier*) and a peasant girl or shepherdess whom he seduces, deceives, or rapes in order to satisfy his base and immediate needs. As Nancy Marino points out in her study of the Spanish *serranilla*, in Spain the shepherdess becomes a *serrana*, the mountain woman native to the Iberian Peninsula who not only can be less refined, shy, and delicate than the Provenzal *bergère* but can even be grotesque. Because of her lack of refinement, the *serrana* has been identified with the monstrous women of the medieval tradition, such as the *selvaticae*—the tenth-century demon women who personified the forces of nature—or with the legendary folk figure the *serrana de la Vera*, who attacked and killed men who traveled through the mountains (Marino 1987, 5–6). The *serrana de la Vera* figure is depicted in Vélez de Guevara's play. The rough mountain women, along with the fearsome *serranas* depicted by Ruiz, lack the conventional beauty possessed by the shepherdesses of whom the Provenzal troubadours sing; they are, instead, the antithesis of the ideal woman.

Of course, not all *serranas* are of the violent and ferocious variety examined here. According to Marino, for fifteenth-century poets such as Íñigo López de Mendoza, the marqués de Santillana, the *serranas*—despite their rural provenance—tend to be pretty and somewhat refined. Although at first the *serrana* protagonists of pastoral poetry were portrayed as grotesque caricatures of the *bergère*, or reproductions of the horrific women from medieval myths, the shepherdesses of lyric poetry from the end of the Middle Ages in Spain share more, in terms of their looks and behavior, with their precursors from the other side of the Pyrenees (Marino 1987, 7). Marino also asserts that at first the female protagonists of *serranillas* were portrayed as frightening women who terrorized men; this type of *serrana* reached its maximum expression in Ruiz's fourth *cantiga de serrana* (8). Despite this character shift from rough mountain dweller who enjoyed terrorizing men to more delicate shepherdess, authors did not forever abandon the violent features. Thus, a timeline between the *serranas* studied by Marino and Gila as portrayed by Vélez de Guevara shows that Gila embodies characteristics present in earlier depictions—most notably the *serranas* from Ruiz's *Libro de buen amor.*

Erotic Adventures in the Sierra: *Ruiz's* Libro de buen amor

In Ruiz's *Libro de buen amor,* the narrator—speaking in the first person and in *cuaderna vía,* followed by a *cántica* or lyric composition—relates his amorous adventures with four brutal *serranas* after he gets lost in the high mountain country in early spring. Denise Filios's study on Iberian lyric poetry and sex, *Performing Women in the Middle Ages,* which very perceptively examines these adventures in the sierra, illustrates how the mountainous landscapes form a fully erotic topography. Filios affirms that "the landscape in which the *serrana* is located resounds with erotic significance. The pass she defends is that between her legs as much as the literal road on which the traveler walks; mounds signify breasts and the forested *mons pubis* or 'mound of Venus'" (2005, 133). Thus, the mountain passes that the protagonist of Juan Ruiz's book crosses when he decides to "try out the mountains" are not simply Somosierra and other similar locales but also the secret passages of the *serranas* who attack the narrator and carry him off to their huts to feed him and later "wrestle" with him. The attacks are both violent and sexual; La Chata de Malangosto tells the traveler, for example:

> "Yo guardo el portadgo e el peaje cojo;
> al que de grado me paga, non le pago enojo;
> el que non quiere pagar, priado lo despojo.
> Paga me, si non verás commo trillan rrastrojo."
> (J. Ruiz 1988, 306, strophe 953)

> ["I'm in charge of the toll, and I collect the toll fees; if a person pays me willingly, I don't bother him; if he refuses to pay, I strip him

.clean instantly. Pay me; if not, you'll see how a stubble patch gets threshed."] (J. Ruiz 1972, 254)

As Filios argues, the performances of aggression and monstrosity by *serranas* make possible the performances of submission and passivity of the narrator-protagonist: "He gets to perform as a weak, impotent fool, and also have sex, because they are monstrous" (2005, 148). According to Filios, this is because the narrator presents the *serranas* as monsters, subhuman in their bestiality and stupidity and superhuman in their size and strength. Filios reaches this conclusion by beginning with the premise that poetry about *serranas* is always about sex, gender, class, and social sphere and almost always about violence. If her view seems categorical, it is because she intuits that poets from this period project their desires, fears, and frustrations onto the eroticized mountainous terrain and onto the *serrana* herself (131). Her psychological reading is convincing and supported by the text, if not—at least for the extra-textual context—with respect to the empirical author (which would be impossible to ascertain).

The monstrosity that can be attributed to the *serrana* is, at the same time, a myth and metaphor for the "world upside down" concept created by sociocultural processes that include rural superstition and ruling-class fears of mass rebellion. In this regard, Filios argues that the *serranas* engage in a ritualistic behavior that reflects the cult of Saint Agatha, on whose feast day—February 5—women attack men (2005, 149). Thus, it is not surprising that the episodes begin with a suggestive epigraph: "De como el Arçipreste fue a provar la sierra, e de lo que le contesció con la serrana" (J. Ruiz 1988, 305) ["How the Archpriest went to make a trial of the mountains, and on what happened to him with the mountain girl"] (J. Ruiz 1972, 252).

When the author says that he "went to make a trial of the mountains," however, what is he alluding to, and what is he anticipating? Several possibilities come to mind within the sociocultural and sexual context of the *Libro*—for example, the commonplace of woman-as-nature, the cultural meaning of mountains with a shape akin to breasts, and a type of sexual alpinism that rewards the man who reaches the highest peak, the mons veneris. During Ruiz's time, mountains were feared and marginal places, not only because they were difficult to access and their terrain was arduous to traverse but also because they were inhabited by wild beasts, bandits, and unofficial toll collectors such as La Chata and Gadea de Río Frío (Filios 2005, 135). The inhabitants of the Old World were terrified of wild forests, isolated areas, the unexplored highlands, and the wilderness. In European folklore, such topographies are populated by evil spirits, demons, and witches (Short 1991, 6–8). Perhaps for this reason, Ruiz refers to his *serranas* as "devilish." In this context, a "monster" like the *serrana* is born out of the pleasures and perils of difference, the dangerous classes that are a source of transgression, and the dark zones of exploitation.

In addition to being dangerous and forbidding, however, the mountains in pre-eighteenth-century Europe have also been interpreted as being a deformed and sinful place, a landscape that is neither appealing nor sublime, a malformed wasteland that threatens heaven with its height. With respect to this topography, Michael Ferber notes, "Because of their impassable homeland, mountain people have preserved their independence more effectively than people of the valleys or plains, or so it has seemed" (1999, 131). From these conflicting perceptions arise not only an obvious opposition between civilization and barbarism but also (since the medieval period) the tendency to depict sierras in Spanish lyric as inhospitable wastelands inhabited by monstrous and violent women who beat and rape male travelers (Filios 2005, 138).

It is also worth mentioning that current criticism pretty much takes for granted the notion that mountain ranges follow the contours of a woman lying supine in the prescribed position for sexual intercourse. Accordingly, the mountain in popular lyric poetry *is* the female erotic body par excellence. *Copla* number 980, for example, is one of many similar *coplas* collected by Margit Frenk in her *Corpus de la antigua lírica popular hispánica (siglos XV a XVII)*:

Montaña hermosa,
alegre y muy leda,
la tu arboleda
cómo es deleytosa.
(Quoted in Frenk 1987, 469)

[Beautiful mountain, happy and content, how delightful is your grove of trees.]

Returning to Ruiz's *Libro de buen amor,* and taking the first of its *serranas* as a model, la Chata de Malangosto finds the archpriest lost in the sierra and exposed to the elements, snow and hail. Vasvári has shown the parallel between suffering from cold and hunger and feeling sexually frustrated; she asserts that the lodging that the traveler requests of the *serrana* alludes to the sexual refuge of the female erotic triangle (1977, 1566). The mountain girl responds as follows:

> Echó me a su pescueço por las buenas rrespuestas,
> e a mí non me pesó por que me llevó a cuestas;
> escusó me de passar los arroyos e las cuestas.
> Fiz de lo que ý passó las coplas de yuso puestas.
> (1988, 308, strophe 958)

[She threw me over her shoulder for giving a nice answer, and it didn't hurt my feelings that she was carrying me on her back: it spared me from going on foot over the brooks and the slopes. Out of what happened there, I composed the verses written below.] (1972, 254)

The *cántica* that follows expands on the archpriest's story. He asks La Chata to warm him up: "Querría estar al fuego" ["I'd rather be by the fire"], he says, in strophe 964, in an obvious reference to her inner fire. The *serrana's* reply telescopes the entire encounter, so to speak: Not only will she be the active partner but she will also feed him after "burning him." In her words:

> "Yo te levaré a casa,
> e mostrar te he el camino;
> fazer te he fuego e brasa;
> dar te he del pan e del vino."
> (1988, 309, strophe 965)

["I'll take you to my house, I'll show you the path; I'll build you a fire with hot coals; I'll give you some bread and wine."] (1972, 258)

The path or way to which she refers is that of her own body, more specifically her vagina, whose fire and coals will warm the traveler.[33] For her, preambles are unnecessary, and while the narrator remains passive, she gets right down to business:

Tomó me rrezio por la mano,
en su pescueço me puso,
commo a çurrón liviano,
e levom la cuesta ayuso.
(1988, 310, strophe 967)

[She took me firmly by the hand, threw me around her neck like a light shepherd's bag, and carried me downhill.] (1972, 258)

The *serrana* carries him this way "downhill" to her hut, where she feeds him a meal that is both rustic and erotic: "mucho gazapo de soto, / buenas perdizes asadas, / fogaças mal amassadas, / e buena carne de choto" (1988, 310, strophe 968) ["plenty of rabbit meat from the forest, good roast partridges, poorly kneaded bread, and good kid meat"] (1972, 258). As other critics have pointed out, foods such as bread, rabbit, and partridge can have secondary meanings, referring to the female sexual organ. In fact, Ruiz makes the connection between food and sex throughout the *Libro*.[34] After this alimentary foreplay, La Chata invites the traveler to engage in other activities: "Hadeduro, / comamos deste pan duro; / después faremos la lucha" (1988, 311, strophe 969). ["Hard-luck man, let's eat some of this hard bread, and afterwards we'll do some wrestling"] (1972, 260). Once the *serrana* is aroused, she says:

"Luchemos un rrato:
lieva te dende apriesa,
desbuelve te de aqués hato."
Por la muñeca me priso,
ove de fazer quanto quiso;
creo que fiz buen barato.
(1988, 311, strophe 971)

["Let's wrestle a bit: get up from there fast, and get out of those clothes." She grabbed me by the wrist; I had to do what she wanted. Believe me, I made a good bargain.] (1972, 260)

What we see here, once again, is a sensual game illustrating the "world upside down" theme, in which the woman takes the place of the man as sexual aggressor, while the man enjoys playing the submissive role. He congratulates himself, in the end, for making a good bargain, since the sexual encounter has cost him very little.

For Ruiz, then, the *serrana* is aggressive, both sexually and physically, but not to the point of killing her sex partner. The archpriest's *serrana* is the opposite of a passive object; instead, she is the actant in an assumed sexual quid pro quo—a rather inconsequential game based on the exchange of conventional sex roles. As such, Ruiz's *serranas* are perfectly adapted to the self-burlesque tone, the wild atmosphere, and the amorous-sensual themes of that hybrid and multifaceted *ars amatoria* called the *Libro de buen amor.*

The Serrana *as Maneater in the* Romancero

The second milestone in the *serrana*'s metamorphosis in pre- and early modern Spain is the *serrana de la Vera* from the ballad or *romancero* tradition. The legendary character from Extremadura emerges from the region of La Vera de Plasencia, an area that Julio Caro Baroja describes as "sierra, pure sierra" (1974, 3). This manly woman from the village of Garganta la Olla is the protagonist in a series of well-known ballads with a plot structure that contains many common motifs.[35] In contrast to the rough, feral mountain women depicted by Ruiz, the *serrana de la Vera* is a rare beauty, almost always with fair skin, blonde hair, and dark eyes—in spite of the fact that in several versions she is born of the strange coupling of a shepherd and a mare. Caro Baroja has noted that this freakish parentage may be intended to reveal the consequences of a tremendous offense against nature frequently attributed to lonely shepherds—the crime of bestiality (1974, 294). The *serrana*'s characteristic weapons and apparel vary throughout the different versions, although a certain preference for the slingshot, arrows, and traditional shepherd's garb is apparent. Partridges and rabbits, the same animals that are intimately associated with eroticism and that provide sustenance for the medieval *serrana,* hang from her waist.[36]

This individualized *serrana* from the ballad tradition attacks the unsuspecting traveler and takes him off to her hut or cave to satisfy her sensual desires. According to a version from the oral tradition, "Cuando tiene ganas de agua / se baja pa la ribera; / cuando tiene ganas de hombres / se sube a las altas peñas" (see Hernández Hernández and Martínez Terrón 1993, 171–72). [When she wants some water, she goes down to the riverbank; when she wants a man, she goes up to the rocky cliffs.] Once in her hut or cave, she and the man dine on rabbits or capons (once again, eroticized animals). Sometimes she offers the man a drink of water out of a skull, or she asks him to light a fire out of skulls and bones. After eating, she falls asleep, and he escapes with his shoes or underpants [bragas] in his hand. Sometimes the serrana slumbers from the sedative effects of sexual intercourse; other times the sexual element is linked metaphorically to the music of stringed instruments. The traveler often plays a rebec [rabel] while she plays a vihuela, an ancient guitar. In a study of the serrana myth, Jean-Pierre Vidal notes that the rebec is a masculine instrument played with a bow, whereas the vihuela is open and feminine. He concludes that in these ballads "il devient clair que c'est sexuellement qu'il s'agit de vaincre l'adversaire. Il faut venir à bout de ses résistances et partant s'en rendre maître" (1975, 82) [it becomes clear that one must sexually conquer an adversary. By confronting her resistance, one becomes the master]. This musical contest is a preamble to the amorous battle that will subsequently take place.

Lyrics collected by María Goyri de Menéndez Pidal say:

Le trajo un arrebolillo,
para que se entretuviera,
y al son del arrebolillo
jizo que durmiera ella.
(Quoted in Caro Baroja 1974, 279)

[He brought her a little rebec, so she could entertain herself, and with the music of the rebec, he put her to sleep.]

The rabel and the vihuela may also refer to the two passages into the female body—vaginal and anal. These are the symbolic caminos through which the mountain girl will guide the protagonist. As noted in Chapter Two, in erotic-burlesque poetry (especially in the works of Luis de Góngora), the word rabel becomes fused with rabo [tail, anus] in a common pun. The ballads from this tradition usually end with the serrana thundering through the mountains after the traveler, leaping from boulder to boulder, and trying in vain to trick him into returning.

In these poems the level of sexual violence increases as the Extremaduran *serrana*, after satisfying her sexual appetite by means of the intruder, tries to kill him to protect her secret. As a result, the mountains are strewn with stone crosses or her lair is filled with skulls and skeletons that evidence her ferocity. She taunts the man with these, telling him that death awaits him too; however, he astutely manages to escape the trap unharmed. In this version of the *serrana,* the meal as erotic preamble and the ensuing episode in bed lead to the sacrifice of the traveler. This particular type of mountain woman, with her insatiable appetite for both sex and blood, is the one who most merits the epithet of "man-eater." Similarly, François Delpech notes that in these ballads the more or less regimented game of the *pastourelle* has evolved into conflict and violence: We have moved from a ludic cultural code to the evocation of a savage nature whose driving forces are primitive instincts, desire, or fear (1979, 25). At this point in her development within peninsular literature, the *serrana* has metamorphosed into a desirable but dangerous sexual predator from whom men must flee—but not without first sharing her bed. The only element of the medieval *serrana*'s monstrous nature preserved in the ballads is her sexual hunger, and her charms prove fatal. In a certain way hers becomes a *vagina dentata,* and she becomes a human version of the black widow spider, which kills the male spider after mating. It is of no little importance that the plays written by Lope de Vega and Luis Vélez de Guevara incorporate verses from the ballads.[37] With them the bloodthirsty legendary figure will be reborn in a different context, one in which the *serrana* similarly lures and then kills the man, but this time for different reasons.

Violence and Eroticism: La serrana de la Vera

The end point of my exploration of the transformations in the *serrana* figure during the Spanish Golden Age is Vélez de Guevara's 1613 play *La serrana de la Vera*. Vélez de Guevara's *comedia* requires a change of focus in which literariness cedes to theatricality and performance. As early as 1949, René Wellek and Austin Warren warned that "the whole tendency of dramaturgic doctrine today is against any judgment of a play divorced from, not inclusive of, its stagecraftness or theatreness" (Wellek and Warren 1977, 307 n. 15). In more recent years, José Luis García Barrientos has asserted that unlike logocentric approaches to theater, the "scenocentric" view considers performance, spectacle, or staging as the first, principal, and autonomous quality of the work. This means that performance is neither dependent on nor subordinate or subsequent to the literary work. Scenocentrism [*escenocentrismo*] recognizes that it is not the written text that produces or contains performance; rather, the theatrical spectacle determines and to a certain extent produces the text (García Barrientos 2004, 53). I concur with the view that literary critics must not disregard the performative aspects of the production of meaning in what is, after all, a *dramatic* art. It is crucial, therefore, to take into account the staging of Velez de Guevara's play—not only to reveal the techniques and significance of the weaving of eroticism and violence in the drama but also to round out the multiple meanings generated by the *serrana* figure.

Velez de Guevara's play is a tragedy that presents a conventional conflict that involves deception and honor. Don Lucas, a nobleman, seduces Gila—a beautiful, manly, and indomitable woman of superhuman strength—through a false promise of marriage. Gila then takes refuge in the mountains in order to single-handedly avenge the offense committed against her. The dishonored and abandoned *serrana* explains:

> Que por estos brazos mesmos
> mi agravio quiero vengar,
> que sólo a todos les ruego
> que vengan a ser testigos
> de la suerte que me vengo.
> Y guárdense de mí todos
> cuantos hombres tiene el suelo
> si a mi enemigo no alcanzo,
> que hasta matarlo no pienso
> dejar hombre con la vida.
> (147, vv. 2129–38)[38]

[With my very own arms I want to avenge the offense committed against me. I ask all to come and witness how I get my revenge. And may all men on this earth beware of me if I don't catch my enemy, because until I kill him, I will let no man escape alive.]

Faithful to her word, Gila stations herself in the wilds of the Extremaduran sierra, where she tempts all the unwary men who wander in the mountains and cross her path. She lures them to her hut, only to toss them over a cliff to their death. Among the one thousand men she kills is her enemy, Don Lucas. Gila is finally arrested by the Holy Brotherhood and executed publicly by being garroted and pierced with arrows—but not onstage. Before we return to this highly suggestive ending, it is important to note that Gila, like the *serranas* before her, embodies an irresistible fusion of eroticism and violence. René Girard has presented the notion that cultural traditions stem from the disorder, the actual or potential violence that is experienced when mimetic desire (or desire based on rivalry, appropriation, and violence) is exaggerated and human beings discover that converging on a victim provides them with unanimity and therefore alleviates the violence (2000, 69). That is to say, the *serrana* is a sort of necessary evil who functions as the scapegoat and, once expelled, provides order and relief from conflict and violence to the community that she threatens. The theatricality with which Gila is portrayed demonstrates this philosophy.

Before we return to the notion of scapegoating, the performative aspects of the play must be examined. In this regard it is imperative to remember that Vélez de Guevara wrote *La serrana de la Vera* expressly for the actress Jusepa Vaca. Vélez de Guevara dedicates the play to Vaca on the title page of his manuscript, and his construction of the plot is geared specifically toward her acting skills (Vélez de Guevara 2002, 17–18). For example, one of the stage directions in the first act takes into account Vaca's particular style of acting: "*Éntrase el CAPITÁN, retirando, y GILA, poniéndole la escopeta a la vista, que lo hará muy bien la Señora Jusepa*" (92). [Enter the CAPTAIN, moving backwards, and GILA, raising her shotgun to his eyes, which Señora Jusepa will do very well.] The editors of the 2002 edition—William Manson and George Peale—point out that the role of Gila, a multifaceted character, required an extraordinary range of acting skills. In addition to portraying the typical *serrana,* the actress was also required to play the role of a manly woman, a beautiful huntress, a flirty peasant girl, a bandit, and a murderess. In this female lead character, masculinity and femininity, aggression and passivity, strength and beauty, contradiction and consistency are summed up and fused together (2000, 18). What merits emphasis is that literary critics tend to relegate or disregard entirely the material aspects of the performance of a dramatic text that can elicit readings centered on the real-life performer who is displayed onstage. Vélez de Guevara evidently believed that Vaca possessed all the necessary qualities to project these characteristics, and his detailed stage directions testify to the importance of costumes and visual effects.

This said, it is also important to keep in mind Vaca's enormous popularity as an actress—not only because of her great talent (especially in roles that required her to cross-dress) but, perhaps more important, because of both her notoriety as a courtesan and the bad reputation of her husband, the theatrical producer Juan de Medrano Morales. In a study of Vaca, Mercedes de los Reyes Peña writes that she had a reputation for having loose morals because of the number of noblemen she entertained and that this behavior provoked her husband's jealousy. The situation turned into fodder for gossipmongers, and she became the target of pasquinades and satirical compositions by such writers as Luis de Góngora, Francisco de Quevedo, and (above all) Juan de Tassis, conde de Villamediana (see the text of these *sonetadas* in Reyes Peña 1998). In these ad hominem satires, the poets revel in the case, mocking Medrano Morales as a husband who consents to and profits financially from his wife's affairs. This type of notoriety, as we well know in our age of tabloid press, can launch an actress to stardom. It should be emphasized that, at the time, actresses were viewed as little more than prostitutes. With Vaca in the role of Gila, an even greater dose of sensuality was added both to the figure of the *serrana* and to the play itself. In fact, Vaca did not create the role of Gila; on the contrary, the role of Gila was written specifically to exploit Vaca's theatrical and erotic talents. The notorious actress was the living model for this *serrana de la Vera*: one more example of how art imitates life.

Given this context, Gila/Jusepa's first entrance onto the stage in act 1 is eminently spectacular. The stage directions specify:

Suenen relinchos de labradores, y vayan entrando por el patio cantando toda la compañía, menos los dos que están en el tablado, con coronas de flores, y uno con un palo largo y en él metido un pellejo de un lobo con su cabeza, y otro con otro de oso de la misma suerte, y otro con otro de

jabalí. Y luego, detrás, a caballo, Gila, la Serrana de la Vera, vestida a
lo serrano, de mujer, con sayuelo y muchas patenas, el cabello tendido,
y una montera con plumas, un cuchillo de monte al lado, botín argen-
tado, y puesta una escopeta debajo del caparazón del caballo, y lo que
cantan es esto hasta llegar al tablado, donde se apea. (Vélez de Guevara
2002, 86–87)

[*The joyful shouts of peasants are heard, and the entire troupe enters the*
courtyard, except for the two onstage with wreaths of flowers. One holds
a wolf pelt and head inserted on a long pole; another carries a bearskin
in the same way, and another a boar skin. And then, behind them, Gila,
the Serrana de la Vera, appears on horseback, dressed as a woman in
highlander's attire, wearing a peasant tunic and many medallions, her
hair loose, and a cap adorned with feathers, a hunting knife at her side,
shiny boots, a shotgun placed under the covering of the horse's saddle. They
sing the following until they reach the stage, where she dismounts.]

The conjunction of several visual elements is quite evident here. First,
the skins and heads of wild beasts nailed to poles are a violent emblem
of the hunt; then there is Gila's ostentatious entrance, like a Roman
centaur astride the horse, another symbol of her masculinity. We know
from José María Ruano de la Haza's study of staging practices, *La puesta*
en escena en los teatros comerciales del Siglo de Oro, that horses entered
the courtyard of the *corrales* [playhouses] and that there was nothing to
prevent a small horse from passing through the main door of either of
Madrid's main playhouses—the Corral del Príncipe or the Corral de la
Cruz—into the central courtyard, where functions were held. According to Ruano de la Haza, the horse could cross through the rooms on
the lower level of the *corrales* (which were about 3.5 meters high). Once
in the courtyard, the groundlings would open the way for the actors and
the horse to approach the stage (2000, 271–74).

As Vaca gradually approaches the stage, always astride and thus elevated, the remaining actors sing a song that exalts the beauty of the
serrana de la Vera and directs the audience's gaze toward the physical
charms of this actress turned Amazon: "*ojos hermosos rasgados . . . lisa*
frente, . . . rojos labios, . . . pelo de ámbar, blancas manos, . . . cuerpo

genzor y adamado" (Vélez de Guevara 2002, 87, vv. 213–19) [beautiful almond-shaped eyes . . . smooth forehead, . . . red lips, . . . amber hair, white hands, . . . handsome and adored body]. It is not difficult to imagine the excitement and arousal that the spectators experience as they view this triumphal procession, which culminates with the actress reaching the edge of the stage and dismounting. All in all, the scene is, as the song by the Cuban singer La Lupe says, theater, pure theater. Upon seeing the *serrana* for the first time, the captain, Don Lucas—highlighting this dazzling spectacle—exclaims, "¡De puro admirado callo! / ¡No he visto en un hombre jamás / tan varonil bizarría!" (2002, 88, vv. 247–50). [I'm speechless out of sheer astonishment! I've never seen such virile gallantry in a man!]

Throughout the rest of the play, a series of spectacular appearances by Gila/Jusepa fuse and never separate eroticism and violence. At various moments we see her defeat men in sword fights, tame a bull with her bare hands, beat up oxen, push her victims off a cliff (Arellano 1995, 315), and—in the finale—bite off her own father's ear. Even before she appears onstage, she is presented as a beautiful woman whose strength and abilities far exceed those of any man: "De bueyes, detiene un carro, / de un molino, la violencia" (Vélez de Guevara 2002, 85, vv. 147–48). [She holds back a cart pulled by oxen and the asps of a windmill.] We also read or hear the following:

Corre un caballo mejor
que si en él cosida fuera,
y en medio de la carrera
y de la furia mayor,
que parece que al través
a dar con un monte viene,
suelta el freno y le detiene
con las piernas y los pies.
(2002, 85, vv. 149–56)

[She gallops a horse better than if she were sewn to it, and in the middle of the race, at top speed and when it seems she's going to crash into a mountain, she lets go of the reins and stops the horse with her legs and feet.]

Notice the insistence on legs and feet, which—being, as previously noted, two great sexual fetishes during the period—were normally hidden from view. These are the legs that the audience will see when this virile woman enters the stage, whether as a huntress, a swordsman, a bullfighter, or a murderess. Throughout this play, it bears repeating, it is crucial—even in narrative episodes—to imagine the gestures and the performance. It is precisely in the gestures and movements of the actress, rather than in the conventionally chaste dialogue, that the eroticism of the play becomes evident. For example, Vaca's movements when Gila relates the boar hunt were surely worthy of note:

> Vuelvo las ancas, aflojo
> el freno, doyle al ijar
> la espuela, y vuélveme a dar
> asalto, en su sangre, rojo.
> (2002, 90, vv. 309–12)

[I turn the horse's haunches and loosen the reins; I spur him in the flanks, and the boar attacks me again, red with blood.]

But the final image of Gila, the one that the members of the audience will take away with them, is unforgettable and occurs in an *apariencia* [discovery]. Ruano de la Haza asserts that the purpose of *apariencias* was to surprise and amaze the audience by means of the sudden unveiling of a memorable image (2000, 228). Vélez de Guevara gives explicit stage directions for the scene in which the dead *serrana* appears on high in an *apariencia*: "*Entre don Fernando, y doña Isabel, y el Maestre, y los que pudieren de acompañamiento, corren el tafetán, y parezca Gila en el palo arriba, llena de saetas y el cabello sobre el rostro*" (2002, 185). [*Enter King Ferdinand and Queen Isabel, and the Maestre, and all the extras who can. They draw the curtain, and Gila appears high up on a post, full of arrows and with her hair hanging over her face.*] This gruesome *tableau vivant* exploits the allure of this particular actress in order to create a suggestive spectacle that is both violent and morbidly erotic. Matthew Stroud has made the very obvious connection between Gila's pierced body and the martyrdom of Saint Sebastian. In the art of the period, this saint was usually portrayed as a nude or seminude male figure in the most erotic pose possible. Stroud notes that "piercing her body through with arrows is a way to eliminate Gila and feminize her at the same time: the one who is penetrated is dominated" (2000, 65).[39]

There is no doubt that the unveiling of Gila executed in this manner is carefully staged to make the strongest possible impact on the audience in the *corral*. In his study *El actor en el teatro español del Siglo de Oro,* Josef Oehrlein explains that the highest level of erotic stimulation for audiences during this period came from the onstage appearance of women who imitated masculine gestures and wore male attire (1993, 225). We can only imagine the effect, then, when a veritable star of the stage appeared half-naked, showing her legs, with her hair loose, her breasts pierced through and bleeding, in a pose that probably imitated that of Christ on the cross. Whether the protagonist was interpreted as a cruelly and unjustly martyred victim or as a deservedly punished assassin, the mix of violence and eroticism must have been a tremendous draw that, just as it does today, guaranteed success at the box office. Evident in this play is that the *serrana,* as a type and as a character, had moved far beyond her initial representation in the archpriest's *Libro de buen amor.* Although both texts equally combine violence and sex, the presentation of this fusion on the public stage carries a highly provocative charge.

What Vélez de Guevara does, then, is to modify and adapt the legend according to the technical and physical qualities of Vaca, a flesh-and-blood woman. This, rather than a "realistic" transposition of what passed as a *serrana* at the time, is what would draw people to the theater. This is why the character acts as she does, functioning as a sensual magnet onstage to then be sacrificed in a spectacularly cathartic manner. In Vélez de Guevara's play, the crude lasciviousness of the earlier *serranas* becomes a carefully choreographed sensuality that inevitably leads to Gila's final galvanizing appearance, lifeless and pierced with arrows, above the audience.[40]

This highly dramatic denouement reinforces male dominance over women in an ambiguous confrontation that probably would be read differently by the men and women in the audience. The mythical image of the wild woman has changed, cosmetically, to be sure. However, we cannot say that from a female perspective it has improved. Vélez de Guevara, in sum, humanizes the *serrana* by fleshing out her history, but he also disciplines her character flaws (aggression, dominance, arrogance) via an exemplary sacrifice, whose message serves as a warning to the woman who dares to deviate from social and gender norms. Her execution, we know from Girard's studies on the double transference of the scapegoat (2000), serves to transfer to the victim the disorders and the offenses produced by collective violence. However, to end on a positive note and to paraphrase Girard, we can also say that the aggressors transfer to the victim the peace that they have just found in abusing her, attributing to her the power that this peace produces.

CHAPTER FIVE

Eros and the Art
of Cuckoldry

Sabed que tanto los hombres como las mujeres sienten
el deseo como el placer.
   Speculum al joder

[Know that that both men and women feel desire and pleasure.]

In an influential 1963 talk, subsequently translated and published in
1968 as *Critical Reconstruction vs. Historical Reality of Spanish Poetry in
the Golden Age,* the respected philologist and bibliographer Antonio Rodríguez Moñino alerted Hispanists to the urgent task of searching out,
cataloging, editing, and studying the thousands of poetic manuscripts
that languish, overlooked, in libraries throughout the world. Only by
doing so, he said, can we construct a true history of Golden Age poetry.
Unspecified, however, was the need to revive a tremendously fertile and
historically neglected province traditionally stored in manuscript form:
explicitly erotic poetry. Along with the texts that we have examined thus
far, erotic poetry and prose—which enrich and renew the field of early
modern cultural studies by expanding our knowledge of the spirit of the
times—must be unearthed, edited, and studied in greater depth. Most
important, this genre of texts includes works that not only flout the accepted norms of the Golden Age Spanish canon (after all, no literature
is more transgressive than the erotic) but also more accurately reflect
contemporary poetic tastes and reading practices and allow for revision
or expansion of that canon. More than four decades after Rodríguez

Moñino's proposition, despite the fact that official censorship has long since ceased to exist, the study of early modern erotic literature in Spain remains in the incipient stages.

By questioning previous knee-jerk interpretations of an obscurantist early modern "Inquisitorial Spain" (in both the political and sexual sense), however, several studies and compilations published (mainly in Spain) since 1990 are gradually expanding and changing our critical horizons. Ameliorating the paucity of attention that this literature has received are such works as *El erotismo y la literatura clásica española* (Jauralde Pou 1990), *Hispanic Marginal Literatures: The Erotic, The Comics, Novela Rosa* (Pérez and Pérez 1991), *Discurso erótico y discurso transgresor en la cultura peninsular: Siglos XI al XX* (Díaz-Diocaretz and Zavala 1992), *Erotismo en las letras hispánicas: Aspectos, modos y fronteras* (López-Baralt and Márquez Villanueva 1995b), *Literatura erótica en España: Repertorio de obras, 1519–1936* (Cerezo 2001), and *La poesía erótica del Siglo de Oro: Crítica y antología* (Martín 2006), a special issue of the journal *Calíope* on Golden Age erotic poetry for which I served as guest editor (see also works listed in the Preface herein).[1] Signaling a further opening of the aforementioned anti-canon are erotic anthologies on particular poets, such as J. Ignacio Díez Fernández's edition of *Poesía erótica* (Hurtado de Mendoza 1995), Adrienne Martín's and Díez Fernández's *La poesía erótica de Fray Melchor de la Serna* (2003), and Emilio Palacios Fernández's edition of *El jardín de Venus* (Samaniego 2004). Thus, shopworn and outdated Black Legend notions of Spanish literature as a sort of post-Tridentine erotic wasteland can no longer be seriously sustained.

In fact, from the Middle Ages on, eroticism is a particularly rich vein in Spanish literature. Canonical medieval works such as Juan Ruiz's *Libro de buen amor,* Fernando de Rojas's *La Celestina,* and Francisco Delicado's *La Lozana andaluza,* alongside lesser-known and lesser-read works such as the *Speculum al foderi,* reflect an appreciation of sensuality that Spain inherited in part from the Arabic erotic tradition and in part from Western classics such as Ovid's *Ars amandi.*[2] This literature flouts moral and social conventions in favor of a witty spontaneity that Western criticism persists in viewing through the lens of didacticism (for example, it insists on interpreting Juan Ruiz strictly as a moralist) and a simplistic perception of Otherness. Much of pre- and early modern Spanish literature is not, in fact, didactic, at least not in the moralistic, admonitory sense in which didacticism has traditionally been interpreted. Rather than being exempla of sin and repentance, these earlier works and much Golden Age verse reflect the existence of a complex set of surprisingly tolerant attitudes toward the literary representation of sexuality and eroticism in early modern Spain. In fact, the Inquisition, otherwise engaged in ferreting out and punishing religious heterodoxy, rarely attempted to censor the type of literary eroticism that stressed weaknesses of the flesh (López Baralt and Márquez Villanueva 1995a, 13). These attitudes changed with the onset of modernity, which Michel Foucault has famously called the age of repression. Early modern Spanish erotic texts, in contrast, are not only abundant but also still understudied.[3]

Scholarship must, therefore, advance in those areas of sexuality and eroticism in literature that have been largely ignored, misrepresented, or deprecated by certain sectors of criticism and literary historiography. In that spirit, I explore here the mechanisms of sexual humor in a variety of early modern literary genres: the world of cuckolds, female tricksters, and erotic tricks commonly found in Golden Age poetry, short novels, and dramatic interludes.

Humor and Eros in the Verse Novella

At this point the reader may question the interlacing of humor and eros. My answer is a simple, pragmatic one that speaks to the conceptual framework for the discussion at hand: Several Golden Age literary critics (including me) have pointed out the marked preference for the burlesque mode in Spanish erotic literature, especially poetry. For example, in an article published in *Edad de Oro 9*—in many respects a foundational volume for the renewed study of eroticism in classical Spanish literature—Christopher Maurer notes that a primary characteristic of erotic poetry is its close proximity to burlesque (Jauralde Pou 1990, 157). In the introduction to his critical edition of Diego Hurtado de Mendoza's erotic verse (1995, 12), Díez Fernández concurs, and in a study of *El jardín de Venus,* María Cristina Quintero notes that the characteristic discourse utilized in these poems is typical of burlesque genres, whose purpose is to provoke laughter (1996, 241).

In a particular sense, much erotic verse can be analyzed as a subgenre of the burlesque, since it partakes of the same expressive license that we find in humorous literature in general. Of course, not all erotic literature is burlesque, but "serious" erotic poetry—whose boundaries are not well delimited—is much more difficult to analyze. For example, how do we distinguish, with any specificity, between love poetry and erotic poetry? Eroticism is a vague, unstable concept grounded in contemporary notions of sexuality and the personal, moral, and literary standards of its readers. The lack of substantive lexicographical, stylistic, and sociolinguistic studies through which we can examine erotica and contextualize it appropriately within the current Golden Age canon also hampers analysis of works in the field.[4] Critiques and studies such as those discussed throughout this book, however, are gradually chipping away at the barriers that hinder our understanding of erotic literature. We are now becoming better equipped to analyze not only the types of humorous erotic texts examined herein but also the erotic output of our most canonical Golden Age poets: Lope de Vega, Francisco de Quevedo, and Luis de Góngora (to name just three).

By tracing the close relationship between humor and eros signaled by a number of scholars, we can appreciate the value of the literature as amusement, its quality and capacity to stretch the limits of the "literary," and its function as a means of suspending socially accepted values and transgressing established literary norms and codes. As I have previously contended (see Martín 2005, 87–88), among the roles of erotic poetry are to reflect human nature more authentically and to illuminate the long-standing debate on the alleged sobriety, chasteness, and "morality" of Spanish literature. Accordingly, Melchor de la Serna's narrative poems serve as an entry point for the appraisal of the implications of hybrid erotic texts for literary history.

In Golden Age literary historiography, the verse novella has, at worst, been marginalized and silenced in response to prudish and misplaced accusations of obscenity or pornography. At best, it has been dismissed as a mere literary curiosity whose art is unsophisticated and imitative and whose value lies principally in its status as a precursor of the great Golden Age Spanish dramatists who perfected the wedding of verse form with content inherited from Italian *novellieri* (see McGrady 1968, 14–15, 23). This is the assessment of Donald McGrady (the only critic to have written extensively on the genre), who has examined the novellas written by Cristóbal de Tamariz, perhaps the best-known author of verse novellas to date. McGrady's critique is typical of the negative evaluation reserved for erotic literature, as contrasted with the greater critical deference with which the reams of mediocre and derivative Petrarchan poetry produced during the same period are treated. Erotic literature, I maintain, deserves scholarly attention not simply for its status as precursor but also as a unique form of narrative verse that accommodates skillful displays of erotic linguistic play, telling considerations of context and reception, and refreshingly direct expressions of human emotion and sensuality.

Since metrics are always integral to the meaning behind poetry, it is revealing to note that most erotic verse novellas—including those by Tamariz and Hurtado de Mendoza—are written in *octavas reales,* a classical adaptation of the Italian Renaissance ottava rima, which dominated Italian narrative verse. In Spain this strophe was generally employed for epic and lyric verse that was elevated in content and solemn in tone; therefore, the use of *octavas* in burlesque and erotic narrative verse serves to parody and undermine established paradigms of form and content. Other novellas, especially Serna's, are composed in tercets, following Italian terza rima, another refined meter that learned poets often used parodically in their burlesque verse.

The themes of these brief, witty, and ingenious tales are illicit love, erotic adventures, trickery, deceit, and cuckoldry. Always narrated in a comic tone, they are written to amuse rather than edify. Or, perhaps as in the exemplary novels of Miguel de Cervantes, their lessons are less obvious and are revealed only by reading between the lines. Their discourse ranges from the use of somewhat guarded euphemisms to the most explicit depictions of sex. Infrequently adorned with mythological allusions and references, this verse (although not without its own sophisticated, codified system of metaphors and symbols) most often contains few poetic tropes or erudite allusions and reads like versified prose. A curious combination of oral and written, popular and cultured literature, these tales closely approximate the prose novella in content, if not language, since the sheltered nature of poetry enables the inclusion of much more explicit eroticism than is available to its prose counterparts. This is the transgressive, burlesque world of sexual tricks, unfaithful wives, and cuckolded husbands: *burlas, burlados,* and *burladoras.*

The authors of these novellas are obviously learned (often men of the cloth) and skilled in creating the most exquisite parodies of serious love poetry. Accordingly, their verse required the type of cultured, humanistic audience found in university towns such as Salamanca. A short who's-who list of known sixteenth-century Spanish erotic verse novelists includes Serna ("El sueño de la viuda de Aragón," "Novela de las madejas," "Novela de la mujer de Gil," and "Novela del cordero"), Hurtado de Mendoza ("Fabula del cangrejo"),[5] and Tamariz ("Novela de la tinta," "Novela de Mathea y su marido," "Novela de un estudiante y una dama," "Cuento de una burla que hizo una dama," and "Novela del enamorado de la mujer del cirujano").[6] Other *novelas en verso* of uncertain authorship populate manuscript *cancioneros* housed in numerous European libraries. Since comic and erotic works could be ephemeral—destined as they often were for oral transmission in private and thus rarely transcribed or preserved and almost never published during their time—the corpus of works of which we are aware is probably only the tip of the iceberg.

One of the principal if not the best of the early modern proponents of the genre is Serna (whose "Sueño de la viuda de Aragón" is discussed in Chapter Three). Serna was a cultured Benedictine friar, a humanist, and an orator, who resided in Valladolid; later (from approximately 1571 to 1595) he became a professor of Latin (and probably a friend of Fray Luis de León) at the University of Salamanca. Serna's birth date is unknown; José Luis Gotor (1980) places his death sometime after 1606. From the biographical details that Gotor and others have gathered and from the friar's surviving works, we conclude that Serna was a skilled commentator and translator (having translated Ovid into Spanish) and an acclaimed humorous erotic poet and author of the notorious collection of erotic poems known as *El jardín de Venus*.[7] An assessment made by one of his contemporaries, Juan de la Cueva, is indicative of Serna's fame as author of *El jardín:* "El que hizo el *Sueño de la viuda,* / y a Venus el *Jardín* tan deshonesto. / Que siempre fue su musa tosca y muda, / en no siendo lasciva y descompuesta, / y en siendo obscena, fácil fue y aguda" (quoted in Labrador Herraiz and DiFranco 1989, xxix). ["Creator of *Sueño de la viuda* and Venus's dishonest *Jardín,* when not lascivious and crude, his muse was always coarse or mute, and when it was obscene, it was quick and sharp.] Evidently, despite the fact that Cueva brands Serna's erotic verse as obscene (a generalized tendency in the historiography of literary eroticism), his opinion of it is, on the whole, positive. José Labrador Herraiz and Ralph DiFranco have collected and edited Serna's verse in several volumes published in recent decades.[8] Most recently, I have co-edited with Díez Fernández a collection of critical essays dedicated to Serna's literary works, accompanied by a selection of his poetry (Martín and Díez Fernández 2003).

The novellas that we can attribute to Serna with a degree of certainty are, as previously noted, "El sueño de la viuda de Aragón," "Novela de las madejas," "Novela de la mujer de Gil," and "Novela del cordero." In addition to appearing in the codices edited by the Labrador and DiFranco team, they have appeared in limited editions, articles, and critical notes.[9] They are also reprinted, with modernized spelling, in Martín and Díez Fernandez 2003; all textual quotations from Serna's novellas are taken from that volume. Current tastes tend to expect and appreciate totalizing novels such as *Don Quixote,* and the scarcity of verse novellas or short stories in the twentieth and twenty-first centuries could lead to the assumption that the genre has little worth rescuing.[10] However, with the realization that its hybrid form owes to the poets of the ancient world the emphasis on the quotidian above the heroic, it is easy to see that these works are novelistic in scope, if not in method. It is also clear that in daily life humor and sex have been and will continue to be powerful forces that channel human actions. Nevertheless, because this genre has been largely hidden from the literary history of the period, to write of the Golden Age verse novella is to transgress that history.

As noted, these texts—and others explored in the pages that follow—which narrate brief tales of illicit sexual encounters, are (at least on the surface) Italian in inspiration and style, following in the tradition of Renaissance *novellieri* such as Giovanni Boccaccio, Matteo Bandello, Masuccio Salernitano, and Ser Giovanni. According to McGrady, in his introduction to Tamariz's verse novellas, the genre was imported from Italy, where an enormous stock of verse *novelle* composed in ottava rima (although eclipsed, in modern times, by novellas written in prose) enjoyed great popularity during the fourteenth and fifteenth centuries.[11] Other probable influences on and sources of the polygenesis of the genre include the works of Ovid; Juan de Timoneda's *Patrañuelo;* Pedro Alfonso's *Disciplina clericalis;* Far Eastern sources such as the *Sendebar;* oral folk traditions; and the jokes, fables, anecdotes, and fabliaux that enriched medieval and Renaissance narrative material. Here that largely inherited raw material is refashioned in verse; in other words, it becomes original in the Renaissance sense of the notion—especially since poetry is particularly receptive to and appropriate for erotica. Sources and influences aside, however, Serna excels in this genre because of the highly suggestive, humorous, and natural eroticism that characterizes his verse. Unfortunately, despite the popular reception of Serna's poems during their time, many have been censored, some to the point of mutilation, by excessively scrupulous modern editors, and even appropriated by readers who are anxious to transfer his works to their private collections.

The first novella, "Novela del cordero," or "Cuento del pintor," narrates in greater detail the Pitas Payas story from Ruiz's *Libro de buen amor* (probably the oldest written Spanish version of the tale). Both José Fradejas Lebrero (in his 1985 edition of the sixteenth-century short novel) and Donald McGrady (in his 1978 monographic study of the novella) have examined this short text. The core tale, of course, exists in all great European literatures: The painter paints a lamb on his wife's belly before he leaves home, to prevent her from being unfaithful, and he returns to find painted in its place a full-grown ram with tremendous horns, symbolizing his cuckolding. According to McGrady, because multiple folk versions of the tale are found in Italy, Germany, France, and England from the fourteenth through the eighteenth centuries (1978, 3–5), it is difficult to identify the original source.

In Serna's version the poetic voice begins the tale by rejecting the conventional Renaissance sources of poetic inspiration (the fountains of the muses called Hippocrene, Castalia, and Aganippe) in order to invoke Venus, a parodic procedure that the poet will follow in his other novellas and that introduces the sensual theme of this poem. The tale contains a few perfunctory and requisite misogynistic touches, such as the conventional notion of women's fickle and sexually insatiable nature. For example, the narrator says, "Primero se verá el abril sin flores / que esté firme la hembra en un intento / y no apetezca más nuevos amores" (quoted in Martín and Díez Fernández 2003, 68, vv. 13–15). [We will see an April without flowers before we find a constant female who does not desire new lovers.] The poet emphasizes, however, that the husband in this tale deserves to be punished for his jealousy, which is—at least at first—unfounded. The drawing of the ram grazing in the wife's pubic hair ("los cuernos inclinados al florido / valle por cuya causa los tenía" [71, vv. 140–41]) is obviously a pure *bufonada* perpetrated by the lovers; the only thing the husband can do, therefore, is try to conceal his disgrace by refusing to acknowledge that he has been tricked (which would be to acknowledge his dishonor). Instead of perpetrating the type of grotesque bloodbath that occurs in Golden Age drama in the wake of wifely infidelity (even when it is merely suspected), the adultery in this purely comic genre is followed by the gullible and mistrusting husband being mocked and the lovers' wit exalted. Thus, we can add this story to the numerous Golden Age texts that ridicule the universal figure of the excessively jealous husband as fabricator of his own dishonor, which culminate in Cervantes's matching protagonists: Carrizales from *El celoso extremeño* and Cañizares from *El viejo celoso* (discussed in the final section of this chapter).

Serna's skillful creation of witty and sensual verse in "El sueño de la viuda de Aragón" (analyzed in Chapter Three) prompted Rodríguez Moñino to comment, "No hay duda alguna de que a través de *El Sueño* se incorpora a las letras españolas un nuevo modo de narrar en verso, hábil, artificioso y elegante dentro de su manifiesta crudeza, que doscientos años después dará como fruto *el Siglo de Oro*" (quoted in Labrador Herraiz 1989, 51). [There is no doubt that *El Sueño* incorporates into Spanish letters a new modality of verse narration, one that is skillful, ingenious, and elegant within its manifest crudeness and that two hundred years later will give rise to the Golden Age.] The Benedictine friar's erotic qualifications, however, extend far beyond the widow of Aragón's tale.

The Art of Cuckoldry: "Novela de las madejas" and "Novela de la mujer de Gil"

Serna's "Novela de las madejas" is a tour de force of erotic deception. The novella elaborates on the conventional scenario of the simpleton husband who is deceived by a wife who is always more astute and clever than he. In a 1978 article the French critic Yvan Lissorgues examined the numerous possible precursors and epigones of similar theme, including Francesco Bello's 1509 "Cuento de los tres maridos burlados," the fourth story of the seventh day of Giovanni Boccaccio's *Decameron,* and Tirso de Molina's "Los tres maridos burlados" from *Cigarrales de*

Toledo. However, because the connections are tenuous between these works and Serna's novella and because the basic plot is found in a great number of tales and could therefore have emerged from the popular tradition, Lissorgues is forced to conclude that there is no direct source for the "Novela de las madejas." He affirms, "Sobre esta trama nuestro poeta puso 'carne' verdaderamente original . . . tanto en el desembarazo de la expresión como en la ingeniosa desenvoltura de las burlas" (1978, 3). [Our poet fleshed out the plot in a truly original way . . . as much in the ease of expression as in the ingenious naturalness of the tricks.] And the tricks are, without a doubt, the sine qua non of this type of composition.

The poem narrates the tale of three married women (*dueñas*) who squabble over some skeins of yarn that they have come across by chance. A deputy decides that whoever plays the best trick on her husband will win the skeins. Written in tercets, this composition—parodying the epic beginnings of ancient poetry—opens with an invocation to the muses imploring them to inspire the poet. Gotor has determined that the structure of Serna's novels consists of an invocation as *captatio benevolentiae,* the narration of the case (of the novella as something singular and new), and the moral of the story. However, I find no standard, gratuitous, or repressive moral in the tales, which I view as exalting the joys of sex with unbridled enthusiasm. Immediately following the invocation, the narrator addresses the ladies who will listen to his verses, suggesting that those who are scrupulous take their leave, since it is possible that he, converted into a siren, may frighten or bewitch them: "A las damas requiero de delante / se quiten las que son scrupulosas, / guárdense de mi voz, no las espante" (quoted in Martín and Díez Fernandez 2003, 116–17, vv. 7–9).[12] At the same time, he invites discreet ladies (that is, those who are knowledgeable and prudent in the arts of love) not only to lend loving ears to his song but also to eliminate their need for go-betweens when they pursue illicit sexual relations, by imitating the ingenious protagonists of his tale. This is the type of erotic "moral," which is didactic in a manner very different from that of conventional wisdom, that Serna provides.

This invitation to a female audience or reader is not a mere narrative cliché; rather, it suggests another social horizon (or, in the words of Roger Chartier and other theorists, another "community of readers") in which erotic poetry was not necessarily (as has often been assumed) restricted to male consumption. Tamariz adopts the same technique in his stories, often directing his words to the "señoras" or "damas" who constitute his public. For example, he begins his "Novela del torneo" with the following gallant *piropos:*

Damas, que soys al mundo en hermosura
no menos que en abril las nuebas flores,
dad fabor a mi pluma, que procura
contino engrandeser vuestros loores.
Dalde parte de aquella gran dulzura
que tienen vuestras gracias y primores,
porque desta manera enriquecida
aquello que escribiere tenga vida.
    (1974, 303)

[Ladies, you whose beauty is no less to the world than are new flowers to April, grant favor to my pen, which ever strives to sing your praises. Grant it part of that great sweetness possessed by your grace and exquisiteness, because thus enriched my writing will come alive.]

Given the implicit and explicit female audience for these stories, it is important to keep in mind the relationship between the written word and female experience in early modern Spain, since understanding women's activity as readers is just as important as unearthing texts written by women authors. As María del Mar Graña Cid comments in her essay on writing and female experience in the sixteenth century, "Las líneas femeninas de recepción y transmisión de la escritura de mujeres no son un dato baladí. Sobre todo porque esta escritura de mujeres pudo actuar como palanca para el escribir de otras, bien al nivel de aprendizaje, bien de creación" (1999, 233). [The female lines of reception and transmission of women's writing are not negligible facts, because writings by women could act as a springboard for other women to write, either as apprentices or creators.]

It is pertinent that in his study and edition of Tamariz's novellas, McGrady observes that they were not written for publication but to be read aloud at literary gatherings (see Tamariz 1974, 28). Not unlike the *saraos* in the frame story to María de Zayas y Sotomayor's novella collections, in which young men and women gather to tell tales of love, the gatherings to which McGrady refers very likely included women. The popularity of erotic literature with women should not surprise current-day critics. Palacios Fernández (2006) indicates that women's eighteenth-century literary *tertulias* were circles in which erotic verse was composed and recited. Also, it is well-known that even the illiterate in early modern Europe had access to texts through the common cultural practice of reading aloud. Thus, Maritornes and Juan Palomeque from *Don Quijote,* both profoundly illiterate, are well versed in the popular (and erotic) chivalric romance. The practice of reading aloud is related with great realism when the priest reads the interpolated novel *El curioso impertinente* [The Man Who Was Recklessly Curious] to the mixed group of men and women gathered at the inn (*Don Quixote,* pt. 1:33–35). It is easy to imagine Serna's verse being read aloud in the same manner.

The underlying issue here is the still unresolved question of female literacy rates in Golden Age Spain, about which texts such as those discussed here can be illuminating. Pedro Cátedra and Anastasio Rojo's 2004 study on women's libraries and reading practices in the sixteenth century points out the difficulty of obtaining reliable data because of historiographical distortions. For example, book inventories rarely included women's libraries (a gap that their volume tries to fill). Books were also relatively expensive and were often borrowed from people or even from bookshops. Owning no books, manuscripts, or other reading materials did not necessarily indicate illiteracy. Sara Nalle comments that in the sixteenth century someone could learn to read using inexpensive primers (*cartillas de leer*) without ever owning a book (1989, 70). Inquisition interviews, in which the subject was required to state whether or not he or she could read and write (even assuming that the answers were truthful), are statistically negligible: What percentage of the population, after all, was interrogated by the Inquisition? Moreover, the spectacular growth of the Spanish university system during the sixteenth century could not have occurred in an educational or cultural vacuum (Nalle 1989, 65). A concurrent growth in secondary and primary education, to which women had access, was requisite. Literary documents (and paintings) that showcase women reading and writing can, therefore, relativize "official" records showing low female literacy rates. Thus, the oral, almost jongleuresque qualities of these narrative poems, such as the narrator's tendency to address his listening public (which is generally and implicitly female) directly, can provide valuable insights into the nature of female literacy and reading tastes.[13]

McGrady notes that the publication of Tamariz's novellas permits the twentieth-century public to attend, in spirit, an intimate sixteenth-century reading (1968, 29). The same is true for twenty-first-century readers of Serna's novellas: We enter a virtual literary salon accompanied by gentlemen and ladies of the time. We can thus conjecture with little risk of presentism that verse tales in which ingenious and sexually daring wives stage elaborate tricks to cuckold their husbands would probably have enjoyed popularity among sixteenth-century salon-going women, especially since the tales represent women as not only clever tricksters but also active agents in questions of love. In addition, however, it is likely that the stories would entertain men as well, since they confirm the presumed or real masculine fantasy of the sexually insatiable woman.

The three tricks that shape the "Novela de las madejas" follow a minimal pattern in which the wife makes a pact with her lover and they subsequently deceive the husband, who unknowingly witnesses or even actively participates in the trick that will cuckold him. It is perhaps a primitive mechanism whose humor resides in the manner of its telling. As Jean Sareil has commented in his book *L'écriture comique,* in every comic masterpiece what is original is not the idea but its expression, the mise-en-scène, the perspective, the imagination, the laugh (see Huerta Calvo 1990, 117). What should be added to Sareil's observation is the notion that linking the comic to the erotic affirms a certain type of subjectivity: that of women. Of course, here female subjectivity is filtered, if not invented, by a male author.

As expected, all Serna's novellas are characterized by multiple and irreverent sexual allusions. For example, "Madejas" begins under the sign of Capricorn (a horned sign), an obvious allusion to the imminent cuckolding of the husbands. The three women are described from the beginning as deceitful *dueñas,* always suspect figures in Golden Age literature, since they are often assumed to be the conduit through which illicit suitors gain access to young virgins. At the same time, these three women are *panaderas* [bakers]:

Casadas todas tres y muy matreras,
pienso yo que el oficio que tenían
debía ser, sin falta, panaderas.
    Las cuales juntas iban y venían
a una cierta ciudad desde su aldea
y allí, juntas también, su pan vendían.
(Martín and Díez Fernandez 2003, 117, vv. 19–24)

[All three were married and very cunning, and I think that without a
doubt they must have been bakers by profession. They would travel
back and forth together from their village to a certain city, and there,
also together, they would sell their bread.]

As noted in Chapter Two, in burlesque literature the woman baker is
notorious for being a procuress and/or prostitute (for selling her own
pan [bread, vagina]). Thus, Serna's narrator is clearly indicating that the
three *dueñas* are prostitutes.

Moreover, of all possible items they might come upon while traveling to the city where they ply their trade, fortune places balls of yarn in
their path: "[Fortuna] les ofreció, caídas en el suelo, / unas madejas de
hilo bien curadas; / las cuales, de sus asnos, al señuelo / se abalanzaron
luego codiciosas / de añadir a su tela un pedazuelo" (117, vv. 29–33).
[Fortune offered them some well-cured balls of yarn that had fallen on
the ground, and they jumped from their asses and fell upon the lure,
greedy to add a little piece to their fabric.] The disputed objects, *madejas
de hilo,* resonate with particular significance in early modern Spanish
erotic literature. The most potent and well-known example is the *hilado*
sold door-to-door by Celestina as a pretext for entering the homes of
the young virgins she wants to procure. Alan Deyermond (1977) has
shown the relationship between *hilado* and images of hunting and trap-
ping and, in the case of Melibea's girdle, the relationship between *hilado*
and sorcery. The findings of Manuel da Costa Fontes (2000), Rosario
Ferré (1983), and Otis Handy (1983), who have analyzed *hilado* as a
metaphor for lust, are relevant to Serna's use of *madejas de hilo.* According to Costa Fontes, Ferré "shows that *hilado* also constitutes a metaphor for *cupiditas,* both as a 'tejido de lujuria' [fabric of lust] and as a
'tejido de codicia' [fabric of greed], being textually and metaphorically
woven into the fabric of *La Celestina* as a whole" (2000, 56).

The same might be said of "Novela de las madejas," in which the skeins of yarn become a metaphor for the lust and greed that construct the story's frame. The term *madejas* is also suggestive, given its sexual connotation (testicles)—here we literally have balls of yarn. Costa Fontes has found this erotic metaphor in several folkloric sources—among them, Portuguese folktales that continue to circulate today and in this conundrum:

—Que diferença há entre o bébé e a capa que veste?
—A diferença que há é que a capa é feita com um novelo e duas agulhas. O bébé debe ser o contrário: dois novelos e uma agulha.
(Quoted in Costa Fontes 2000, 62)

[What's the difference between a baby and the clothes he wears? The clothes are made with a ball of yarn and two needles. With the baby, it must be the other way around: two balls of yarn and a needle.]

We should keep in mind that Serna wrote for a cultivated audience in the know—in other words, for an audience familiar with and entertained by the sexual innuendo and particular metaphoric system that is expected of erotic literature. Costa Fontes points out in his essay on erotic sewing metaphors that folktales, riddles, jokes, and legends played a central role in Golden Age texts and were familiar to all—both the untutored masses and the learned authors who incorporated them into their writings (2000, 55). Given the highly eroticized atmosphere and language of Serna's novellas, therefore, it is easy to see his double entendres for the sexual jokes that they are.

All the lovemaking in "Novela de las madejas" is narrated using a plethora of expressions signifying fornication that are common in erotic poetry: *cabalgar, atacar, brincar, abrir el camino, sanar, rempujar* [ride, attack, bounce, open the way, push]. For example, in the first trick, the husband—thinking he is helping his widowed neighbor to tame his aloof new bride—grasps his own disguised wife (who is betraying him with the neighbor) as follows:

Y convidando al bueno del viudo
de los pies y las manos la tenía,
dándole el cuerpo franco y sin escudo.

El viudo, que aquello sí quería,
cabalgóse en la yegua que le daba
el que de los estribos la tenía.
(Martín and Díez Fernandez 2003, 120, vv. 136–41)

[And inviting the good widower, he held her by her hands and feet,
giving him her body freely and without a shield. The widower, who
desired precisely that, rode the mare that the gentleman offered him,
while the other held the stirrups.]

Setting aside for the moment the patent linguistic reification of the
woman (who, let us keep in mind, coordinates the trick) and given
the self-assured content and tone of this novella, it is clear that the
fundamental notion here is the *burla* [trick], which is, by definition,
aggressive and cruel. In fact, in her study of the *burla* in Golden Age
literature, Monique Joly (1982) observes that sexual tricks or practical
jokes were classified at that time as *burlas pesadas* [dirty tricks]. Instead
of being portrayed as the type of venal sexual predator that we find, for
example, in Quevedo's satirical works, the women are presented here as
true Doña Juanas, since they are motivated by the desire to trick their
spouses in order to possess the skeins and, metaphorically, the lover's
body. In fact, the sexual pleasure they receive from their lovers appears
to be subordinate to the enjoyment they get from duping their dim-
witted husbands. At the same time, the tricks have an added element of
cruelty; the second *dueña's* trick is especially imaginative, for example.

In this *burla,* the wife, in league with her lover, a Benedictine friar,
pretends to suffer from severe menstrual cramps that seemingly have her
at death's door. Here the metaphorical menstrual pain is thinly disguised
sexual longing, for which the "cure" is legendary: sexual intercourse.
Thus, in act 7 of the *Tragicomedia de Calisto y Melibea,* Celestina advises
Areúsa that intercourse with Pármeno would be the most expedient
cure for her cramps. In Serna's poem the suffering wife dispatches her
husband to fetch the friar to hear her confession. The friar pretends to
be lame, and the husband is forced to carry him on his back, effectively
being transformed into a beast of burden—a mule. Once the friar has
"cured" the wife, the husband carries him back to the convent. Thus,
the friar has symbolically and literally ridden both the husband and his
wife. When the husband returns home, he discovers the *pañetes* (a type

of underpants generally worn by fishermen, tanners, and other men whose work requires that they disrobe) that the friar has left behind in his bed. The wife, deceiving with the truth, tells the husband that the underpants are the holy flannels that the priest uses to perform his cures and obliges the husband to go back to the convent to return them. The double trick, narrated in a language redolent with sublime irony and double entendres, generates the connections that readers can readily make with the context of the Salamancan convent (within which and for whose residents the story was written):

> Y los paños benditos son aquéstos
> con que han sido mis males remediados.
> Sabed, si no sabéis, marido, que éstos
> son los que San Benito se vestía,
> y así sanan del mal donde son puestos.
> (Martín and Díez Fernandez 2003, 122, vv. 218–22)

[These are the holy flannels that have remedied my ills. You should know, if you do not know, husband, that these are the same ones that Saint Benedict wore, and they cure the ills of the spot whereupon they are placed.]

Serna's transformation of the friarly flannels (the same term for which—*pañete*—is used for the loincloth that hides Christ's genitalia from view on the cross) into a sort of miraculous, sexual relic characterizes the type of burlesque transgression of religious orthodoxy found in this novella. Thus, this episode would have resonated with particular significance at that time and in the context of the University of Salamanca, where Serna was a professor and—like the lover in the story—a Benedictine friar. He and his colleagues and students were acutely aware of the eroticized atmosphere that characterized Salamanca, with its proximity to the picaresque sectors of society and to prostitution. It was precisely the lively and peculiar commingling of university, convent, and brothel in Salamanca that facilitated and encouraged this parody of religious convention.

Golden Age erotic verse novellas are rarely original in their themes, since adultery, deceit, sexual tricks, and cuckoldry are common in satirical-burlesque literature—from folktales and the medieval fabliaux through the works of the Italian *novellieri,* the writings of François Rabelais, and the Spanish Golden Age theatrical interludes.[14] In fact, these brief verse novellas share many characteristics with the *entremés*—the most obvious being their dramatic, representational technique and privileging of the theme of marital betrayal. In this regard, María Grazia Profeti has correctly pointed out that the most frequently used technique in erotic poetry of the sixteenth and seventeenth centuries is precisely representation, with the use of verbal and symbolic media that hark back to the theater (1980, 104). This representivity can be appreciated in each trick that appears in the "Madejas" novella—especially the last one.

In this *burla,* at the wife's insistence, a husband challenges his young field hand to a test of strength: The lad must immobilize the married couple beneath him. The prize, a kid and a lamb, suggest that the unwitting spouse will soon wear horns. The husband lies down, the wife lies face-up on top of him, and the young man positions himself over the wife, with the woman effectively sandwiched between the two men in a position that could be described only as a sexual crucifixion. The narrator details the action as follows:

> Boca arriba se echó y luego sobre ella,
> que ya tenía las faldas regazadas
> el garañón que había de ponella.
>   Y como ella sintió las espoladas:
> "¡Tened, tened, marido—voceaba—,
> que tiene éste unas fuerzas endiabladas!"
>   Y así, el mozo de arriba rempujaba,
> y el marido, de abajo, resistía
> y ella, en medio de entre ambos, se brincaba.
> (Martín and Díez Fernandez 2003, 123, vv. 274–82)

[She lay down face-up, with her skirts tucked up, and the stud lay on top of her. And feeling his spurs, she shouted, "Hold on, hold on, husband, this one is as strong as the devil!" But the lad pushed down from above, and the husband resisted from below, while she bounced up and down between the two.]

The episode ends with a play on words in which the lover loses the bet, overcome not because he lacks strength but because he is sexually spent:

> Mas llegando la lucha al dulce instante,
> alzóse el mozo y dijo: "Estoy molido;
> ni puedo más, por Dios, ni soy bastante".
>   "Pues ¡sus!—dijo la dueña—, ¡alzaos, marido,
> que la apuesta los dos hemos ganado,
> pues se rinde y se da ya por vencido!"
> (124, vv. 289–94)

[But when the battle arrived to the sweet final moment, the lad picked himself up and said: "I'm exhausted; I can't go on; I have nothing more in me." "Well, cheer up," said the lady. "Get up husband; we've won the bet, since the lad says that he gives up because he's been beaten."]

This scene is a highly visual, representational *burla erótica,* but the joke is not only on the husband; it is also on the church in a moment of comic teasing. Clearly, the immediate audience for these jokes and parodies—both Salamanca's young students, who learned their Latin by reading the classical erotic-didactic writers, and Benedictine and Augustinian clerics—would understand and appreciate quite well this type of comedy.

The "Novela de las madejas" concludes with the judge deciding in favor of the third woman and awarding her the skeins. Serna closes his poem, at least in this version, with a conventional comment on women's diabolical nature: "Ve con Dios, que según eres / miedo tengo de sólo escucharte: / que más sabéis que el diablo las mujeres" (124, vv. 302–4). [Go with God, because given the way you are, I am afraid even to listen to you, since you women know more than the devil.] Thus, the authority figure caps the tale with the type of moral rebuff that often appears in erotic literature as a sort of obligatory (if unconvincing) writerly disclaimer in the introduction or addendum—not unlike Ruiz's exquisitely ambiguous defense of "good love."

In "Novela de la mujer de Gil," Serna tells the story of an excessively modest husband, who limits himself to chaste kisses with his young and beautiful spouse, Elvira. We should keep in mind that Gil is a name typically associated with witless rustics, who, because they are foolish, are easily cuckolded. The sexually frustrated, desperate wife transfers her erotic desires to their farmhand, Pedro. This dark, virile, and robust young man, who contrasts sharply with the conventionally pallid and submissive courtly lover, is a perfect sex object.[15] With a wealth of erotic metaphors gleaned from nature and agriculture that fill the poem with Ovidian echoes, Serna fragments and eroticizes the body that Elvira exhibits in order to seduce Pedro.[16] Then, in a scene filled with sensual wit, the poet describes the lovers' initial sexual encounter on a staircase:

> Sucedió que, bajando una escalera,
> Fortuna le dio medio conveniente
> para poner a Pedro en la carrera.
> Al cual—como por caso contingente
> subiese por la misma—Elvira, alzando
> la pierna con un pie, le dio en la frente.
> Ya él, de la ocasión no le pesando,
> como ella alzó la pierna, extendió el brazo,
> y en los carnosos muslos no parando
> arribó a Montenegro, y de un pedazo
> asiendo de la grama blandamente
> al cuello le acudió con un abrazo
> (Martín and Díez Fernandez 2003, 74, vv. 92–103)

[It so happened that while she was descending a staircase, Fortune offered her a way to coax Pedro into the game. Since he was coming up the staircase at the same time, Elvira lifted her leg and struck him in the forehead with her foot. And he, glad of the opportunity, extended his arm and, not stopping at her fleshy thighs, went all the way up to Montenegro, softly grasping the grassy tuft and embracing her neck.]

This encounter—with its arm and leg swings, its lascivious blows and embraces—evokes the celebration of the mass, with the priest's bows, gestures, and genuflections before the altar and the altar boys' movement to and fro. It imitates the conventional saintly poses found in religious images as well, but with erotic gestures. The passage also recalls Ovid's extraordinary instructions in Book 3 of *The Art of Love* about the various sexual positions that are suitable for women of diverse builds and statures. He recommends that women with shapely legs elevate them in a way similar to Elvira's: "Milanion bore Atalanta's legs on / His shoulders: nice legs should always be used this way" (1982, 237). Our poet's humor lies precisely in mixing the profane with the sacred and in combining the evident theatricality of the liturgy with the liveliest expression of sexual drives.

Serna's novellas and his erotic poetry in other meters are characterized by candid eroticism delivered in frank and accessible language interspersed with abundant rapid dialog, which adds humor, immediacy, and dramatic potential to his tales. His discourse is bold and irreverent, as befits the convent cloister or university café. The friar's principal theme is sensual, sexual pleasure and anecdotes that relate the play of passions to which the clergy would have been privy via the confessional: their library and their private archive. However, although the poems generally feature scant ornate language, devices, and tropes and few elaborately descriptive passages, they resonate with the type of wit found in baroque dramatic interludes. Such humor, it is worth mentioning, comes from the displacement of the narrative and poetic genres of the time. This said, I should note that "Novela de la mujer de Gil" mentions a good many mythological characters, all of whom are connected in some way to sexual love: Venus, Cupid, Mars, Lucretia, Penelope, and Isis, among others. Such allusions are, of course, to be expected from this Ovidian poet. In the majority of Serna's works, however, the rapid and fluid verses are appropriate for a narrative poem without serious scholarly pretensions beyond a rhetorical exercise. Written to be recited in public, doubtless accompanied by appropriate gestures, they lack a greater purpose beyond amusement. Texts such as these flourish safeguarded, in large measure thanks to the freedom and privacy provided by oral and manuscript transmission, the common medium by which erotic poetry circulated. As with all erotic humorous poetry of the time, because its purpose is to entertain, it would be difficult to detect a sexually moralizing purpose. Thus, like much of the literature and writers studied in this book, these texts and their authors offer a burlesque counterpoint not only to classical, courtly, and Petrarchan love poetry and its creators but also to the professional moralists of the epoch.

Nevertheless, the hybrid nature of these verse novellas makes them a promising avenue for actualizing studies of Golden Age literature. This updating, viewed as a trigger of the modern era, can be appreciated in the gullible husbands who are punished by their sexually frustrated and energetic wives in an explosion of irrepressible sensuality that, even in Tridentine times, is difficult to smother. As Luce López Baralt and Francisco Márquez Villanueva comment about Golden Age eroticism, "Tales y tan brillantes desenfados de nuestros clásicos revestían para ellos el carácter de una espontánea lealtad a la verdad de la vida y del lenguaje, que para nada tenía por qué interferir con sólidas convicciones morales y religiosas, que eran en todo caso harina de otro costal" (1995a, 13). [The many brilliant diversions written by our classical authors represented for them a spontaneous loyalty to the truth of life and language, and this in no way interfered with solid moral and religious convictions, which were, in any case, another matter.]

In contrast to Golden Age plays (the most public of performative genres) in which wives merely suspected of infidelity are put to death or locked away in a convent, in these texts wives are inevitably sexually rewarded for their quick thinking and ingenuity in betraying their foolish spouses. The fact that absent from this genre is the figure of the unfaithful playboy husband, however, tells us a great deal about what was considered funny at the time. The cuckold is the risible figure in this comic world whose underlying motivation is sexual fulfillment, mainly for women. Thus, today's readers should not be shocked or even puzzled by the burlesque-erotic poetry that we find in the Golden Age verse novella. After all, in many cases—as we have seen briefly with Serna—the connection of this poetry to the monastery and the university is what sustains it and gives it meaning. It was in precisely those intellectual spheres that the texts of the classical and Renaissance authors (Virgil, Catullus, Ovid, Petrarch, Boccaccio) who provided the literary model for the expression of erotic love in Spanish circulated.

Seduction and Adultery in the Burla Erótica

As we have seen, in the art of cuckoldry in verse tales and many other Golden Age popular and cultured literary genres, from novel to theater, the *burla erótica* is a popular, essential, and defining element. As Stith Thompson has pointed out, to the unlettered storyteller and story listener and to the writer of literary tales, deceptions connected with sex have always held greater interest than any other conduct (1946, 202). Such *burlas* can be somewhat elaborate (though spontaneous) sexual tricks played on credulous spouses by their headstrong wives, either in order to castigate their husbands for such faults as excessive jealousy or age or lack of sexual vigor or prowess or to submit the notion of conjugal honor to a process of subversion and degradation by simply cuckolding and making fools of them. The origins of the *burla* (an element found throughout various literatures), although most likely literary rather than oral, are hidden in the recesses of folklore and the popular tradition. *Burlas,* which can be variations on previous texts from the various aforementioned sources, are found in *facecias, cuentecillos,* jokes, short stories, novels, plays, and interludes with themes of adultery and erotic adventures.

As noted, these works belie prevailing social-sexual norms that attempted to channel sex into chastity or marriage and corroborate the acceptance of sexually explicit erotic literature in Golden Age Spain. Consequently the sexual jokes therein, whose principal theme is female infidelity, are light years away from didactic and moralistic literature (much of which revolves around the honor theme) that for many critics is still a parameter of the time. Sexual tricks that involve the beguiling of cuckolded husbands, of course, have existed since antiquity and have been especially popular with the writers of fabliaux, novellas, and jest books (S. Thompson 1946, 202). Although generally orchestrated to take revenge for masculine failings, the jokes are also sometimes motivated simply by the pleasure gained from tricking and from exacting punishment for the sort of male presumption and machismo that Golden Age literature foregrounds. At times the tricks are devised to get the woman out of a tight spot—for example, when she is with her lover and her husband returns home unexpectedly. Caught *in fraganti,* she nonetheless inevitably manages to delude and consequently shame her husband or lover or both.

This scenario, which has been exploited to the saturation point in both literature and cinema, is the topic of the following pages. Two types of *burlas* exemplify some of the most successful female erotic tricks: those that are structured around keys and those that are structured around beds. Rather than trace their sources, the discussion focuses on some of the most developed versions that appear in popular

Golden Age texts. Because (once again, it bears repeating) the formula clearly demarcates the parameters of humor during their time, the *burlas* exploit the theme of men who are tricked by women.

Key Tricks and Bed Tricks

The key trick, which exists in multiple incarnations, appears in at least two well-known texts of the period. Designed to punish men, it provides a moral and suggests better ways to treat women. The first text is a narrative poem by Tamariz (whose erotic verse novellas are somewhat more chaste than and rarely as witty or explicit as those of such poets as Serna and Hurtado de Mendoza). The key trick occurs in his "Cuento de una burla que hizo una dama a un caballero que andaba de tierra en tierra con un libro, escribiendo faltas de mujeres, por vengarse de una de quien fue despreciado." In this tale an insistent suitor falls in love with a young woman who rejects his advances. Eventually, his love turns to hatred, and—in an attempt to avenge his tarnished honor and pride—he travels from place to place, collecting stories of women's sexual transgressions and registering them in an enormous ledger. The central *burla* is enacted by a wealthy and clever noblewoman in an effort to chastise the protagonist for his presumption and malice in writing negatively about women. She invites him into the house during her husband's absence, and when her spouse arrives unexpectedly, she hides her would-be lover in a chest (a scenario reminiscent of a tale from Boccaccio's *Decameron* in which the friend and wife of a man who is locked inside a chest make love on top of the chest and him).[17]

In Tamariz's story the lady invites her unsuspecting spouse to sit on top of the chest with her. She proceeds to coax her husband into betting who can go the longest without mentioning an object made out of metal. Then she deceives him with the truth, telling him that she has fallen in love with a young traveler who arrived to the house and that she hid him in the chest when her husband arrived. When the angry spouse demands the key, he loses the bet and his wife convinces him that it has all been a practical joke:

> "Y no penséis que el galán se os aya ydo,
> que aun está todavía en esta sala,

aquí dentro en esta arca está metido".
"¡Pese a tal, ello sea enhoramala,
dadme la llaue!", dice el buen marido.
Riendo le responde la zagala:
"A, mi señor, pagadme lo apostado,
perdido avéis, en hierro avéis tocado".
No se pudo tener que no riese,
viendo el señor la burla bien compuesta,
y sin que otra ves se lo dijese,
él se dio por vencido en el apuesta.
(Tamariz 1974, 197)

["And don't think that the young man has left, for he is still in this room, here inside the chest." "To the devil with him; give me the key!" says the good husband, and the lady answers him laughing, "Pay me my money, sir. You lost the bet, since you mentioned iron." The husband could not contain his laughter, seeing the ingenious joke, and without waiting for her to repeat her demand, he gave up.]

Worth noting in Tamariz's poem is the lively wordplay on *arca* and *llave*, transparent erotic euphemisms for vagina and penis. Ultimately, however, the joke is on the man hidden trembling inside the chest, and the lesson he learns is this:

Si no se quiere ver de allí adelante
en otro tal peligro, se guardase
de ser ynjurioso y cruel amante.
Y en yerros de mugeres no tocase,
mas siempre en su loor escriua y cante
y en confusión de su dañoso yntento,
ponga en fin de su libro aqueste cuento.
(Tamariz 1974, 197)

[If he doesn't want to find himself in another dangerous spot, he should be careful not to be insulting and cruel. He should not touch on women's faults but always write and sing their praises. And to overcome the harmful intent of his book, he should include this tale at the end.]

Finally, as McGrady (editor of Tamariz's novellas) has pointed out, both lover and husband are defeated in the perennial but unequal battle of the sexes (see Tamariz 1974, 47). It is worth noting, however, that Boccaccio's tale ends very differently. The two betrayed husbands, Spinelloccio Tavena and Zeppa di Mino, decide to forgo vengeance and salvage their honor and friendship by agreeing to share, each husband keeping two wives and each wife keeping two husbands (a happy arrangement for all). Thus, rather than a battle of the sexes, we have in Boccaccio's tale a type of merry early modern wife swapping.

The popularity and persistence of this plot is demonstrated by the fact that María de Zayas recreates it, to similar effect, in her short story *El prevenido, engañado,* the fourth of her *Novelas amorosas y ejemplares.* In this novella the protagonist, Don Fadrique, is a young nobleman from Granada who falls in love with and is deceived by several women. These experiences convert him into a profound misogynist, and he determines to seek out and marry a simpleton in order to mold her to his ways and live in peace. The narrator stresses the flawed reasoning in Don Fadrique's insistence on speaking badly of all women, pointing out that for every bad woman there are a hundred good ones and that it is unfair to blame all for the actions of a few (2000, 300). Later in the story a duchess lures Don Fadrique into her bed and then hides him in a wardrobe when her husband arrives home unexpectedly. She proceeds to trick her husband by inventing a game in which they have to write down everything they can think of that is made of iron. When the duke does not come up with the word *keys,* the wife deceives him with the truth by telling him everything that happened before he arrived. Don Alonso, the tale's narrator, explains:

> Alborotóse el duque, empezando a pedir aprisa las llaves, a lo que respondió la duquesa con mucha risa:
> —Paso, señor, paso, que ésas son las que se os olvidan de decir que se hacen del hierro, que lo demás fuera ignorancia vuestra creer que había de haber hombre que tales sucesos le hubiesen pasado, ni mujer, si no fuera muy necia, que tal dijese a su marido, si fuera verdad; pues cuando lo hubiera hecho, lo callara.
> (Zayas y Sotomayor 2000, 332–33)

[The duke became agitated and started to demand the keys, to which the duchess responded, laughing: "Calm down, sir, the keys are what you forgot to name as something made out of iron. Besides, it would be foolish to believe that such things could happen to any man or that a women would tell her husband if it were the truth, because if she had really done such a thing, she would keep it quiet."]

Zayas castigates Don Fadrique for his pursuit of ignorant rather than discreet women, the purpose of her story apparently being to provide a moral and to suggest a different way for men to think about women.

Tamariz's novellas also contain introductory strophes that express a moral. At the beginning of the "Cuento de una burla que hizo una dama," for instance, the narrator advises, "No seas injurioso contra ella, / queriéndola infamar, que las mugeres / por su valor merecen ser amadas / y en gran veneración muy estimadas" (1974). [Don't insult her and seek to dishonor her; women are worthy and should be loved and venerated.] Subsequently, the poet employs immoral adventures to illustrate principles of conduct. However, the comic tone that characterizes his tales undermines any serious intent. The main purpose of Tamariz's and other erotic verse novellas is clearly to entertain, to amuse an audience with clever stories that ridicule male presumption or pride.

Both versions of this key trick (Tamariz's and Zayas y Sotomayor's) are clearly Boccaccian in following his leitmotif of hiding the lover in a piece of furniture in the presence of the spouse.[18] In the second story of the seventh day of the *Decameron*, Peronella puts her lover in a tub and then tells her husband that she has sold the tub to the man and he is inside the tub inspecting it. A typical procedure of this joke is for the trickster to flaunt the husband's own dishonor before him, without his realizing it or at least without his acknowledging it. We have already seen one of the most ingenious examples of this technique of deceiving with the truth in the episode of the Benedictine friar in Serna's "Novela de las madejas." In the three episodes (by Tamariz, Zayas, and Serna) the modus operandi for deceiving with the truth is irony, which serves to transform the women into resourceful leaders instead of passive followers in issues of love and trickery. Thus, complicity is established between author and reader or listener, whether man or woman, who is entertained at the expense of the victim of the trick.

At the risk of overstating the obvious, I believe it is necessary to insist on the fact that the mechanism that generates these tricks is precisely a conventional phallic symbol in erotic literature (see, for example, several uses of *llave* or *clave* as penis in *PESO*).[19] For this reason, the sexually emancipated women in these stories control the rules of the game by obliging their husbands to enter into a contest that revolves precisely around his remembering or not remembering, of naming or not naming a key. Seen in this light, the men's masculinity is clearly precarious or at least at risk. As in the priapic verse and eulogies of the phallus that Díez Fernández has analyzed so sensibly (2003, 289–324), here the metaphorical phallus is also the central element of the stories, but it is, of course, ridiculed quite cleverly. Thus, these fables can be read as a sort of anti-eulogy or dethroning of the phallus. Within this context, and expanding the semantic field, the concealment of the lover in a closed and asphyxiating space (a wardrobe, tub, chest, or trunk) can be viewed as a questioning of or response to contemporary apologists of female enclosure. The confined female whose intimacy is besieged and penetrated by a young gallant would be the reverse of the same coin; both motifs are characterized by the suspense and mounting tension produced by the threat of being discovered in a compromising situation.

The key also functions as a leitmotif in two Cervantine tales on the theme of female adultery precipitated by male jealousy. In both the theatrical interlude *El viejo celoso* and the exemplary novel *El celoso extremeño*, Cañizares's and Carrizales's respective obsessions compel them to lock up their young wives at home and never relinquish the key. Javier Huerta Calvo has noted that Golden Age interludes stage stories from the Boccaccian tradition or from the Spanish tradition of witty tales and anecdotes (1995, 69). This relationship can be appreciated in *El viejo celoso*, which begins with the following words spoken by Doña Lorenza to her neighbor: "Milagro ha sido este, señora Ortigosa, el no haber dado la vuelta a la llave mi duelo, mi yugo y mi desesperación" (1980, 203). [It is a miracle, Señora Ortigosa, that my grief, my yolk, and my desperation has not locked the door.] Young Lorenza fuses perfectly the notion of the key with her aged husband, foreshadowing the complaints that will lead to his victimization.

Inevitably, the *senex* character in *entremeses* is the victim of all possible tricks, beatings, and affronts for repressing his wife's irrepressible instincts (Huerta Calvo 1995, 71). Doña Lorenza continues to insist on the same object, noting, "Siete puertas hay antes que se llegue a mi aposento, fuera de la puerta de la calle, y todas se cierran con llave; y las llaves no me ha sido posible averiguar dónde las esconde de noche" (206). [Besides the front door, there are seven other doors before reaching my chamber, all locked with a key, and I haven't been able to discover where he hides the keys at night.] When Doña Lorenza's niece Cristina says to her ironically, "Tía, la llave de loba creo que se la pone entre las faldas de la camisa" [Aunt, I think he hides the master key between his shirttails], Doña Lorenza answers, "No lo creas, sobrina; que yo duermo con él, y jamás le he visto ni sentido que tenga llave alguna" (206). [Don't believe it, niece; I sleep with him, and I have never felt any key on him at all.]

It is obvious that we are dealing with language and dialogue loaded with double entendres, whose meanings are communicated and emphasized by the performers via the appropriate gestures and expressions. The wordplay on the notion of the key as an object that holds the power to open and close, to liberate or incarcerate is easily transported to the erotic sphere. In erotic symbology the key also denotes liberation, knowledge, all types of mystery, and even initiation. Just as in the spiritual realm Saint Peter's keys open the door to Paradise to the faithful, in the temporal world man's key opens (or should open) the earthly paradise that is woman's sex. Hurtado de Mendoza alludes to this in his burlesque sonnet "Preciábase una dama de parlera," in which a lively lady who enjoys nicknaming quips to a young gallant that he looks like Saint Peter. The man responds with an erotic joke that is easy to decode: "Mi reina, aunque San Pedro yo no sea, / a lo menos aquí traigo la llave / con que le podré abrir su paraíso" ["My Lady, although I may not be St. Peter, at least I have the key that will unlock your paradise"] (text and translation in Martín 1991, 196–97). The key is clearly a potent sexual symbol within universal erotic symbology.

The Cervantine *entremés* key that functions as a metaphor for the old man is, however, as bent [*doblada*] as the fruits of matrimony that Cañizares swears that his wife enjoys in double measure. The key that opens the house and that synechdochically should open the young wife's body is a nonviril member that cannot open the desired lock. We are dealing with a *burla* of the decrepit husband's sexual impotence (an inexhaustible source of literary jokes) and a total rejection of both unequal marriage (that of a young woman with an aged man) and forced marriage (we should remember that the marriages of Doña Lorenza and Doña Leonor [from *El celoso extremeño*] were arranged by their parents). Since here the women exercise full rights to sexual satisfaction, which is exalted over abstinence, the *burla* also questions the notion of women as sensually inferior to men. Cervantes is not defending female promiscuity or anything even approximating it; rather, he is defending women's right to pursue sensual satisfaction in human relationships. Ultimately, he is recognizing and touting the naturalness of desire over the imposed celibacy recommended by Golden Age moralists and by the church

The key, as such, permits access to another nucleus or locus of human desire: the bed. In this regard a motif exists that appears in innumerable versions but with the same basic structure: "You go to bed with someone you think you know, and when you wake up you discover that it was someone else—another man or another woman, or a man instead of a woman, or a woman instead of a man, or a god, or a snake, or a foreigner or alien, or a complete stranger, or your own wife or husband, or your mother or father" (Doniger 2000, 1). Wendy Doniger discusses the bed trick, a popular literary motif based on masquerade, the substitution of one bed partner for another. In this trick a sexual encounter occurs in which one of the partners is unaware of the true identity of the other. The tricked person expects a certain individual, but since the encounter takes place in the dark, the substitution goes undetected.[20]

As Doniger points out, the basic plot "should make it onto anyone's list of the Ten Greatest Hits of World Mythology" (2000, 1). It is woven through texts as varied as the *Arabian Nights,* the Bible, the legends of King Arthur, Shakespearian drama, a Japanese novel from the eleventh century, popular folklore, Boccaccio's *novelle,* and the *Canterbury Tales.* Naturally, the motif has served cinema endlessly, perhaps most prominently in Billy Wilder's *Some Like it Hot* and most spectacularly in Neil Jordan's *The Crying Game* (see Doniger 2000, 1–2). If many of the bed tricks are characterized by misogyny—by centering on male rivalries, by the reification of women, by the inevitable and perhaps predictable victory of the man, leading to acts of bloody vengeance—some provide a space for female sexual agency.

Rather than itemize the occurrences of this leitmotif in Golden Age Spanish literature, I examine a single and unique example, another tale from Zayas y Sotomayor's *El prevenido, engañado.* The fact that this improbable situation may require some suspension of the reader's belief does not detract from its psychological and narrative depth. In Zayas's story, the same Don Fadrique and his cousin Don Juan become enamored of two beautiful and discreet cousins, Doña Violante (who rejects marriage because she fears losing her freedom) and Doña Ana (who is engaged to a man in the Indies). When Doña Ana marries the *indiano,* an older and jealous man, she enters into an obligatory confinement that separates her from her lover. Soon, however, Doña Ana devises a plan to reunite with Don Juan and, at the same time, amuse herself at the cost of the misogynist Don Fadrique. She asks Don Fadrique to occupy her place in the marriage bed while, elsewhere in the house, she receives her lover, Don Juan. The narrator sets the scene as follows:

[Aquella noche Doña Ana] le abriría la puerta [a don Juan], mas que había de venir con él su primo don Fadrique, el cual se había de acostar con su esposo, en su lugar; y que para esto hacía mucho al caso el estar ella enojada con él, tanto que había muchos días que no se hablaban; y que demás de que el sueño se apoderaba bastantemente de él, era tanto el enojo que sabía muy cierto que no echaría de ver la burla, y que aunque su prima pudiera suplir esta falta, era imposible respecto de que estaba enferma, y que si no era de esta suerte, que no hallaba modo de satisfacer sus deseos. (Zayas y Sotomayor 2000, 324)

[(That night Doña Ana) would open the door for Don Juan, but his cousin Don Fadrique had to accompany him and take her place in bed with her husband. A crucial element was the fact that she was angry with her husband, so angry that they had not spoken for several days, and besides he was a heavy sleeper. Their anger was so great that she was sure that he would not notice the trick, and although her cousin might have taken her place, this was impossible because her cousin was ill. Without this plan, she and her lover would be unable to satisfy their desires.]

That night Doña Ana strips Don Fadrique and places him in bed with her husband in the darkened room. Don Fadrique "estaba tan temeroso y desvelado que diera cuanto valía su hacienda por o haberse puesto en tal estado" (Zayas y Sotomayor 2000, 325) [was so fearful and anxious that he would have given all he had not to have placed himself in such a situation]. Don Fadrique spends a tortured night with the sleeping husband throwing his arm around Don Fadrique's shoulder, trying to get closer to the person he believes is his wife: "El engañado marido, extendiendo los pies los fue a juntar con los del temeroso compañero, siendo para él cada acción de éstas la muerte. En fin, el uno procurando llegarse y el otro apartarse, se pasó la noche" (325). [The deceived husband stretched out his feet and touched those of his terrified companion, each of these acts causing a living death for Don Fadrique. Finally, they spent the night with the one attempting to get closer and the other trying to get farther away.] The hoax is revealed the following morning when Don Fadrique sees that his bed partner was Doña Violante; the lover is humiliated, and the women celebrate the success of their prank.

Zayas inverts or complicates the standard erotic trick in which a masquerade facilitates sex with a stranger. Here it is a matter of trying to avoid a sexually threatening situation, either the possibility of an unwanted homosexual encounter or the violence that could result if the husband discovered a strange man in his bed. The protagonist is doubly deceived, because he is forced to sleep with a person he believes to be a man but in reality he has spent the night in bed with his lover without making love to her. The proximity and touch of the female foot, which Don Fadrique does not recognize, that pursues him in darkness plays with what was a common Golden Age sexual fetish. The episode ridicules Don Fadrique's sense of masculinity and intelligence (after all, he cannot distinguish between a man and a woman or a female foot and a male foot in bed). Here his manhood is placed in doubt by a woman who is much more astute than he and who literally leaves him in the dark.

As noted, the main purpose of these tricks is to amuse, to make the reader or listener laugh rather than to moralize or to teach a conventional lesson. Nevertheless, as Robert Jammes has pointed out, laughter is an essentially subversive act. Tricks represent rebellion against order, and those who laugh—the public—are complicit with this rebellion (1980, 9). Thus, these stories of sexually and socially transgressive tricks differ significantly from stories of female adultery (such as those in Golden Age theater and ballads) that are characterized by extreme violence. These episodes of real or suspected female adultery generally culminate in murder, as in Pedro Calderón de la Barca's honor plays or in the popular ballads on Blancaniña. In the Blancaniña *romances* she is courted by Don Carlos, the emperor's son, and the adulterers spend the night together during her husband's absence. When he returns unexpectedly, the lover hides, but then he sneezes and the story ends in a bloodbath.[21] The husband kills the lover or both the wife and the lover, or in another version he returns Blancaniña to her father, who stabs her to death or cuts off her hands and feet before killing her (Armistead 1978, 2:48).

Another similar ballad on the theme of adultery narrates the story of a wife who admits her lover through a window when her husband exits through the door. When the husband returns home, she hides the lover in a box used to store pepper, and he starts to sneeze. When the husband asks who is sneezing, the wife replies that it is the neighbor's cat, who is hunting mice. Up to this point the trick seems similar to those that we have examined, but in this ballad, instead of allowing himself to be tricked, the husband breaks open the box, invites the neighbors to come and see "un gato con barba y mostachitos retorcidos" (quoted in Armistead 1978, 2:54) [a cat with a beard and twisted whiskers], and then kills the unfaithful wife. Clearly, although both involve marital deceits, the ballads represent an alternative current to the tricks that we have examined. In the ballad adulteries not only is the development and wit of the novelistic *burlas* lacking but the comic ludic spirit is also transformed into violence and extreme tragedy. In the final analysis this development represents an inversion in the structure of power and sexual control, which can evidently take different paths and have different results. Curiously, the more forgiving literature (for women) is also the more cultured, whereas the popular *romancero* seems to mercilessly disallow female infidelity.

The erotic tricks examined here constitute another model of female sexual comportment that is in opposition to what Enrique Martínez-López calls a mentality founded on the identification of sexuality with obscenity, a mentality in which the woman is, par excellence, the origin and receptacle of dishonest desires (1995, 369). These *burlas* are characterized by the exaltation of sex as a natural instinct and the ludic interpretation of life. Although some may view the message of these tricks as conservative—beware of women's wiles—the female astuteness, intelligence, and wit that dominate in them (even though, in others, men will triumph as tricksters) reveal a tendency to vindicate an expression of female power and subvert the dominant ideology (especially as it relates to the honor theme).

In the upside-down world that characterizes these sexual tricks, the woman is portrayed as a self-sufficient, resourceful, and daring trickster who easily outsmarts men, and she occupies a space—an erotic space— in which she teaches men lessons (whether moral or not). Perhaps above all else, these *burlas* can be seen as an expression of female independence in response to the social norms that bind female sexuality. Sexuality, as the cliché goes, brings power, and, as we have noted, such female tricks destabilize male hegemony.[22] It is crucial, however, to contextualize these female erotic tricks within the wider current of *burlas* in which women are the victims of male deceit. Although they may offer a brief comic respite to certain conventional attitudes, they must be framed within contemporary revisions of Golden Age literary history—above all with respect to the multiple erotic currents that clearly flow through it.

Notes

CHAPTER ONE

1. In *Love and the Law in Cervantes,* Roberto González Echevarría ponders
the intimate connections between desire, interdiction, and the law in works
by Spain's greatest Golden Age novelist. My approach is similar in that I
examine the type of sexual traffic that legal proscriptions tried to control
and literary criticism has often denied or attempted to camouflage under
the cloak of didacticism. As González Echevarría notes, "Literature becomes
an archive of the forbidden, counterbalancing the copious repository of the
pious, generally the context that has been used to read Cervantes because
of its availability. The forbidden, on the other hand, tends by nature to be
scarce in its public displays and leaves a scant record. There is a surfeit of
information about the law, about how to suppress and punish crime and sin,
but scant contextual documentation about the allure and manifestations of
desire" (2005, xv–xvi). Although I agree that literature is the great repository
of the forbidden, I disagree regarding the absence of manifestations of desire
in literature, especially early modern Spanish texts, which are particularly rich
in eroticism. As I argue herein, what we lack is an appropriate methodology
for analyzing and evaluating erotic literature. This issue is addressed further in
Chapter Five.

2. The following are important among the studies that shape the novella's
critical history: Raymond Foulché-Delbosc's classic essay (1899), José Toribio
Medina's extensive essay included in his edition of the novel (see Cervantes
1919), Jorge García López's discussion in his edition of Cervantes's *Novelas
ejemplares* (2001), and the studies by Julián Apráiz (1906), Francisco A. de Icaza
(1916), Manuel Criado de Val (1953), Luis Astrana Marín (1953, 391–408),

Alan Soons (1970), E.T. Aylward (whose 1982 postulates are reviewed in Geoffrey Stagg's 1984 study), Mary Gossy (1989 and 1993), Pedro Tena (1990), Francisco Márquez Villanueva (1990), Carmen Hsu (2002), and José Luis Madrigal (2003).

3. My understanding of the Foucauldian notion of discourse is informed by Michel Foucault's "The Discourse on Language" (1972), "What Is an Author?" (1977b), and "Truth and Power" (1980) and by Robert D'Amico's "What Is Discourse?" (1982) and Manfred Frank's "Sur le concept de discours chez Foucault" (1989). Works by Diane MacDonell (1989) and Timothy W. Crusius (1986) provide a greater context.

4. William Nelson, who discusses the progress of changing attitudes with respect to "invented history," has called this ambivalence the dilemma of the Renaissance storyteller (1973). Regarding Cervantes, see pages 32–33, 63–64, 70, and passim. The subtitle to *La tía fingida* clearly locates the reader in a given sociohistorical moment, a "chronotope," which could interfere in the narrative strategies that can be perceived in the text. This and subsequent chapters quote parenthetically from García López's 2001 edition of Cervantes's *Novelas ejemplares*. Unless otherwise indicated, all translations in this book are my own.

5. Cervantes did not totally disregard the *cortegiana onesta,* however, since Estefanía de Caicedo from *El casamiento engañoso* falls within the parameters of this literary and historical figure. See Hsu's 2002 study of courtesans in Spanish Golden Age literature.

6. See Gossy 1989 on the relationship between "text" and "hymen."

7. In his examination of the Salamancan society depicted in *La tía fingida,* Francisco Márquez Villanueva (1990) has concluded that the work corresponds to the genre of university literature and is intimately linked to the Celestinesque novel. For the greater context of student life in Salamanca, see Luis Cortés Vázquez's 1989 study; regarding the relationship between prostitutes and students in that city, see pages 121–32.

8. As the textualization of prostitution, *La tía fingida* reflects the common distinction made in Western culture between man as mind and woman as body. Esperanza's corporeality is constantly thrust before the reader in this text as her body is acted upon and treated as an object of exchange. In *Volatile Bodies* (1994), Elizabeth Grosz studies the philosophical bases of corporeality in an attempt to recover the female body for feminism.

9. This type of unattached, autonomous woman who plays sexual tricks on men is discussed in Chapter Five.

10. Regarding legal prostitution in Spain at this time, see Perry 1985, Perry 1990 (37–152), and Sánchez Ortega 1995. The situation was similar in other European countries. Legalized prostitution in France as a means of social control is discussed in Rossiaud 1988. Prostitution in England and Europe within the general context of social marginality is examined in McCall 1991.

11. It would appear that by the term *sodomy* Maqueda refers to the practice of anal sex. The term and its multiple meanings in early modern Spain are detailed in Chapter Two.

12. The conversion of prostitutes into penitents and the institution of the Magdalen house in sixteenth- and seventeenth-century Seville is discussed in Perry 1985 (152–56). For an update on the process and meaning of counter-reformist female spiritual conversion in Spain, see Sánchez Ortega 1995.

13. In a 2005 article, "La amorosa pestilencia y los celos renacentistas," Lidia Falcón discusses the disastrous effects of excessive passion in *Don Quixote,* concluding that Cervantes advocates prudent, sensible love as a proper basis for marriage.

14. On the foundational relationship between the female picaresque and prostitution, see A. Cruz's "Sexual Enclosure: Textual Escape" (1989a), updated in her *Discourses of Poverty* (1999). For the fullest treatment of the origins and sociology of the Celestinesque theme in literature, see Márquez Villanueva 1993 and Rouhi 1999.

15. See Chauvin 1983 on the history of Christianity's mercurial relationship with prostitution.

16. See Martínez-Góngora 1999 (66–72) on Antonio de Guevara's insistence on the social and political necessity of excluding women from public discourse.

17. Regarding "rogue females," Peter Dunn concludes that they go beyond the canon and that, however we look at them, "they have, in effect, been neutered by their separation from a society that is both patrilineal and matrifocal. Power and creativity (intellectual, cultural, economic) are ascribed to the male, veneration to the chaste (including the dedicatedly reproductive) female" (1993, 250–51).

18. This is particularly evident if we compare *La tía fingida* to another Golden Age text centered on prostitution, *La Lozana andaluza.* Francisco Delicado's 1528 text was also historically marginalized by critics who rejected its explicit eroticism on moral grounds. In contrast to *La tía fingida,* however, it has been recovered and, since the 1950s, has received renewed and serious critical attention (see Delicado 1969). Alongside Lozana and her text, Esperanza and hers seem chaste indeed.

19. Throughout the early modern period, multiple city ordinances were created to regulate outdoor dress for prostitutes. For example, a 1425 Seville ordinance required that "las mugeres mundarias trayan un prendedero de oropel en la cabeça, encima.de las tocas, en manera que parezca, porque sean conocidas" (quoted in Vázquez García and Moreno Mengíbar 1997, 293 n. 23) [prostitutes wear a tinsel brooch on the head, on top of their headdress, so that it is visible and they are known]. Other ordinances from Seville (1553) and Ronda (1570) decreed, "Mandamos de aquí adelante

que ninguna de las dichas mugeres de la dicha mancebía no puedan traer ni traigan mantos, ni sombreros, ni guantes, ni pantufos, como algunas suelen calzar, y solamente traigan cubiertas mantillas amarillas cortas sobre las sayas" (quoted in Vázquez García and Moreno Mengíbar 1997, 293 n. 23). [We decree that from now on none of the said women from the said brothel may wear cloaks, hats, gloves, or slippers, as some do, and that they wear only short yellow mantillas over their skirts.] Such laws had to be modified periodically to accommodate changes in women's fashion. For example, when the color yellow became popular in the mid-sixteenth century, the regulation yellow headdresses were changed to black.

20. These are the words of the Donoso Poeta Entreverado in his poem to Sancho Panza, which is included among the preliminary verses in part 1 of *Don Quixote*.

21. Márquez Villanueva (2005) has examined the illicit relationships that the Cervantes women cultivated with gentlemen of certain means and social position. Although Márquez Villanueva affirms that the "Cervantas" were, in fact, courtesans, he argues that their conduct cannot be sanctioned in terms of morality, since their tainted blood as *conversas* [from a lineage of converted Jews], combined with their lack of dowry, effectively made them unmarriageable. Regarding the suspicious circumstances surrounding Cervantes's daughter and granddaughter, see Javier Blasco Pascual's 2005 biography of the author (151–55).

22. Unless otherwise noted, all quotations from *Don Quijote de la Mancha* are from Cervantes 2004, with part and chapter indicated; English renderings are from Cervantes 2003.

23. José Ramón Fernández de Cano y Martín (1990) studies the anatomy and function of ugly women in *Don Quijote de la Mancha,* affirming that *tuertas* (one-eyed women) are paradigmatic of the ugly woman at the time. He concludes that Maritornes's ugliness provides the necessary humorous distance by which Cervantes subverts the eroticism in the encounter scene (Cervantes 2004, pt. 1:16) at the inn (298).

24. Particularly surprising, for example, is Falcón's omission of any mention of Maritornes in her 1997 study *Amor, sexo y aventura en las mujeres del Quijote*. Needless to say, except for a brief appearance in Hsu's 2002 study, *La tía fingida*'s Esperanza has been totally neglected in this regard.

25. Heath Dillard, however, discusses the precarious situation of prostitutes in the small towns of medieval Spain, who were subject to physical abuse by their clients and unequal protection under the law (rarely were men punished for raping prostitutes). Women accused of harlotry could be required to prove their innocence or guilt by submitting to the ordeal of the hot iron: The woman would be forced to carry a burning hot iron rod for a

distance of nine paces. If her palm was charred, she was convicted (see Dillard 1989, 196–99).

26. He continues, "Even leaving aside the flood-tides of poverty that increased the numbers of available women on all the high roads of the land, vagabond whores, with or without their 'ruffian' protectors, went from village to village to swell the ranks of the handful of 'women common to all' already there. They adapted their itinerary to the calendar of fairs and markets, pilgrimages, or the busiest seasons for agricultural labour. In remote barns, hired farm hands and tenant farmers who shared living quarters would share a whore as well, for several days or several weeks" (Rossiaud 1988, 3).

27. In their study on prostitution in Catalonia, Carrasco and Almazán (1994) also point to the scarcity of historical data on rural areas; they focus instead on small communities located on the outskirts of larger cities.

28. The lengthiest study to date on La Tolosa and La Molinera is Isabel Colón Calderón's 2005 essay in *El* Quijote *en clave de mujer/es.*

29. According to Pierre Alzieu, Robert Jammes, and Yvan Lissorgues, "Marica" is almost a folkloric character, who appears in many proverbs as a loose woman (see examples in *Poesía erótica del Siglo de Oro* [1984, 156–57]).

30. It is also possible that Tolosa is a toponym, since prostitutes often used their place of origin as a surname (Graullera 1994, 71).

31. See several examples of this usage in the poems collected in *Poesía erótica del Siglo de Oro* (Alzieu, Jammes, and Lissorgues 1984).

32. Regarding this ambiguous door scene, Colón Calderón cites the advice that Justina's mother gives to the female rogue as to how one young prostitute should be stationed at the front door of an inn as an advertisement and a hook for clients (2005, 315). This custom is reflected in Cervantes's novella *El licenciado Vidriera* [The Glass Licentiate], in the denunciation of the practice made by the protagonist, Tomás Rodaja: "Pasando un día por la casa llana y venta común, vio que estaban a la puerta della muchas de sus moradoras, y dijo que eran bagajes del ejército de Satanás, que estaban alojados en el mesón del infierno" (2001, 279–80). [Passing by the brothel one day, he saw several girls at the door and called them baggage of Satan's army and lodgers in Hell's inn.]

33. Teresa Aveleyra notes in "El erotismo de don Quijote" (1977) that the innkeeper's daughter is the most authentic and outstanding female figure in the novel and the only one that the aging bachelor allows himself to desire.

34. Don Quijote proudly proclaims his celibacy later in the novel, when he presents his hand to Maritornes before the hayloft trick, telling her, "Tomad esa mano, digo, a quien no ha tocado otra de mujer alguna, ni aun la de aquella que tiene entera posesión de todo mi cuerpo" (pt. 1:43). ["Takest thou this hand, I say, untouched by the hand of any woman, not e'en the hand of she who hath entire possession of this, my body" (380)].

35. Don Quijote's, or Alonso Quijano's, repressed sexuality and the reasons for it have been re-created and explored from a psychoanalytical perspective by Carroll Johnson in *Madness and Lust* (1983) and Ruth El Saffar, "Sex and the Single Hidalgo: Reflections on Eros in *Don Quixote*" (1989). Updated psychoanalytical readings of the novel can be found in *Quixotic Desire* (El Saffar and Armas Wilson 1993).

36. González points out a similarity between Maritornes and the portrait of Clara Perlerina presented by the farmer from Miguel Turra in the Insula Barataria episode: "Si va a decir la verdad, la doncella es como una perla oriental, y mirada por el lado derecho parece una flor del campo: por el izquierdo no tanto, porque le falta aquel ojo, que se le saltó de viruelas; y aunque los hoyos del rostro son muchos y grandes, dicen los que la quieren bien que aquéllos no son hoyos, sino sepulturas donde se sepultan las almas de sus amantes. Es tan limpia, que por no ensuciar la cara trae las narices, como dicen, arremangadas, que no parece sino que van huyendo de la boca" (Cervantes 2004, pt. 2:47). ["If truth be told, the maiden is like an Oriental pearl, and looked at from the right side she seems a flower of the field; from the left side it's a different story, because she lost that eye when she had smallpox; and though she has many large pockmarks on her face, those who love her dearly say that those aren't pockmarks but the graves where the souls of her suitors are buried. She's so clean that in order not to dirty her face her nose, as they say, is so turned up that it looks like it's running away from her mouth" (Grossman, 763)].

37. For example, in Valladolid in 1604, one year prior to the publication of part 1 of *Don Quixote*, legislation was passed to regulate streetwalkers. Around the time of the publication of the novel, laws regulating brothels and restricting prostitutes to them had increased (Colón Calderón 2005, 311).

CHAPTER TWO

1. Michael Ruse, perusing Sartre's views on homosexuality, concludes that Sartre "is mainly interested in using the refusal to accept homosexual identity as an example of bad faith" (1995, 123).

2. See, for example, the essays included in Blackmore and Hutcheson 1999 (particularly Blackmore's essay "The Poets of Sodom," in which he studies—from a perspective similar to my own—the power dynamics involved in sodomitical texts in the medieval Galician-Portuguese satirical *cantigas d'escarnho e mal dizer*) and Delgado and Saint-Saëns 2000.

3. Unfortunately, Louis Crompton's *Homosexuality and Civilization* limits Spanish homosexuality to the context of the Inquisition, constructing yet another dismissive Black Legend in its limited scope. Crompton opens his

chapter on Spain as follows: "[Spain] was the nation of Christian Europe where hatred for homosexuals ran deepest and persecution was most intense. Political absolutism, historical racial conflicts, and the popular superstition all conspired to fuel the fires of prejudice. In Castilian Madrid and Andalusian Seville, action by the secular authorities was merciless and swift. And in half the new state—in the provinces of Aragon, Valencia, and Catalonia—homosexual conduct was in the course of the century brought under the jurisdiction of Renaissance Europe's most formidable instrument of oppression, the Spanish Inquisition. Spain's Siglo de Oro, its splendid Golden Century, the zenith of its culture, wealth, and influence, was for homosexuals a Siglo de Terror" (2003, 291).

4. In *Homosexuality and Civilization,* Crompton recognizes that "to adopt Foucault's view that the homosexual did not exist 'as a person' until this time [1869] is to reject a rich and terrible past" (2003, xiv).

5. See an excellent discussion of Foucault's contribution to the field of sexuality in Bristow 1997 (168–218).

6. See, in this regard, the discussion in Díez Fernández's *La poesía erótica de los Siglos de Oro* (2003, ch. 2).

7. Crompton 2003 relies heavily on Carrasco 1985 for information about homosexuality in early modern Spain.

8. Pedro de León (1981, 437–38) also writes of the identifying dress, hairstyle, demeanor, speech, and secret signs used by homosexuals in Seville.

9. Regarding the different types of eunuchs (castrated palace servants, men who were born eunuchs or were medically castrated) and methods of castration, see Oltra Tomás 1996 (157–58 n. 14).

10. *El jardín de Venus* is included in *PESO* and in Labrador Herraiz, DiFranco, and Bernard 1989. See María Cristina Quintero's 1996 analysis of misogyny in these poems, "The Rhetoric of Desire and Misogyny in *Jardín de Venus.*"

11. This said, in *La poesía erótica de los Siglos de Oro,* J. Ignacio Díez Fernández discusses how Juan de Arguijo's sonnet (a translation of another by Girolamo Fracastoro) on the myth of Ganymede, "No temas, o bellísimo troyano," provides a non-negative view of homosexuality. Although the poem does not explicitly defend sodomitical practices, it does relate the abduction of Ganymede in sensual terms. See Díez Fernández's discussion of this sonnet and others that relate Ganymede to sodomy (2003, 236–39).

12. See Boswell 1980 (207–66) regarding homosexuality in medieval Christian literature. Norman Roth (1982) explores the "boy-love" theme in the works of the greatest Hebrew poets of medieval Spain: Samuel Ibn Nagrillah, Solomon Ibn Gabirol, Moses Ibn Ezra, and Judah ha-Levi.

13. See the analysis of Sor Violante del Cielo's poems in Martín 1997. A selection of her poems is anthologized in Olivares and Boyce 1993.

14. This same character is also the protagonist of Quevedo's interlude *La vieja Muñatones*. The playlet centers on the old procuress's advice to her prostitutes on the best ways to extract money from their clients.

15. The linking of sodomy and heresy, sexual and religious deviance, is studied in Karlen 1971, Bullough 1974, and Caro Baroja 1978.

16. For politics as a theme of satire, see Highet's classic work (1962, 73–77, passim), keeping in mind his general definition that "its vocabulary and the texture of its style are difficult to mistake" (18) and that its motives can involve "real" persons (238–44). Pollard's (1970) overview concentrates on the satirist's intentions, yet it does not delineate the function of politics in human experience. In Fowler's more contemporary reading, satire is examined as a catalyst for generic mixture (1982, 180–90), which is not really the same as the invective role it often played in the Spanish Renaissance. Along these lines, Margaret Rose's study examines satire from an intertextual perspective, differentiating it from parody (1993, 80–86). It is clear that the mercurial textuality of satire still challenges criticism.

17. The full epigraph on one manuscript is "Epitafio de Quevedo a Julio el librero." Another reads, "Epitafio al sepulcro de un caballero italiano que se llamaba Julio Bolti, y era muy inclinado al mal vicio, que lo son los demás de su nación italiana. Es extremado" (Quevedo 1969–81, 2:109–10) [Epitaph on the tomb of an Italian gentleman called Julio Bolti, who was very inclined to the evil vice, as are the rest of the Italian nation. It is extreme].

18. Góngora would also typically make the connection between Italians (especially the Genoese) and effeminates. See his poems "Las no piadosas martas ya te pones" (1967, 548), "Musas, si la pluma mía" (329–32), and "Vuela, pensamiento, y diles" (300–302). Additional texts that equate homosexuals with Italians can be found in Herrero García 1966 (349–52). For a discussion of Ganymede and *lindo* as paradigmatic metaphors for homosexuals, see Martín 1995 (159–61). The figure of the *lindo* is discussed in depth in Cartagena-Calderón 2000. See also Heiple 1997 and Vélez-Quiñones 1999.

19. For a discussion of Quevedo's textual obsession with the anus and excrement, which in a sense replicates with erudition what is patently clear to his critical and general readers, see Profeti 1982 and 1984 and Goytisolo 1978.

20. The palm frond as symbol of virginity appears in chapter 69, part 2, of *Don Quijote de la Mancha* when Altisidora, supposedly dead, is laid out with "un ramo de amarilla y vencedora palma" (Cervantes 2004) [a yellowed palm branch of victory] in her hands.

21. Discussion of ethnicity is always also by implication a discussion of gender and sexuality. Marc Daniel discusses the reality of homosexuality in Islamic society as well as the teachings of the Koran regarding sexual deviance (see Martín 1995).

22. Raimondi's engravings were based on drawings done by Renaissance

artist Giulio Romano; public reaction to "I modi" landed Raimondi in prison and caused Romano to flee to Mantua (Waddington 2004, 23). Illustrations of the engravings and the text of the sonnets are included in Talvacchia 1999.

23. See the usage "con la pija arrecha" in the sonnet "—¿Qué me quiere señor?—Niña, hoderte" (*PESO*, 213).

24. Similarly, in *Grandeza y miseria en Andalucía* Pedro de León relates the execution of "Machuco el negro," a freed slave who was notorious for procuring boys for noblemen (1981, 438–39). All Seville apparently turned out to view the spectacle of Machuco wearing a painted breastplate on which he appeared holding the hand of two young boys, all three with curled hair.

25. For a discussion of the false hermit and his unpious ways in Golden Age satire, see Martín 1991 (85–88).

26. Many Golden Age authors considered sodomy to be common practice among Arabs. See, for example, Bunes Ibarra 1989 (236–39) and Herrero García 1966 (543–45). A pertinent embodiment of this assumption about Muslim males is the pedophilic Cadí in Cervantes's Algerian plays (see Martín 1995).

27. I should clarify that the poems in this chapter did not appear grouped together on any manuscripts.

28. In many of his poetic diatribes against Góngora, Quevedo, hardly the one to criticize, satirizes the Cordoban poet's tendency to write about sodomites and anuses. See the personal satires against Góngora collected in Quevedo 1963 (1186–209). Two brief examples are these: the ballad "Poeta de *¡Oh, qué lindicos!*" wherein Quevedo calls Góngora "poeta de bujarrones / y sirena de los rabos, / pues son ojos de culo / todas tus obras o rasgos" (1191) [poet of buggers, siren of asses, since all your works or traits are assholes] and in the *décimas* "Ya que coplas componéis," which say, "De vos dicen por ahí / Apolo y todo su bando/que sois poeta nefando / pues cantáis culos así" (1186). [Apollo and all his band say that you are a nefarious poet, since you sing about asses.] See my discussion in Martín 2002.

29. According to Juan and Isabel Millé y Giménez (see Góngora 1967) the version that appears in *Quaderno de varias poesías de Don Luis de Góngora* from the Biblioteca de la Universidad de Barcelona has the epigraph cited previously. In manuscript 10920 of the Biblioteca Nacional de Madrid, the epigraph to the poem reads, "A tres hombres, que se llamaban Carrión, Tordesillas y Olivares, indiciados de pecado nefando" [To three men called Carrión, Tordesillas, and Olivares, accused of the nefarious sin]. Millé and Millé do not analyze the poem but simply point out that certain passages are obscene. Unfortunately, such editorial prudery is typical for this type of verse. Díez Fernández 2003 and Vélez Quiñones 1999 discuss this poem briefly.

30. Illuminating in this regard is the case of Francisco de Salazar, bishop of Salamina, whose trial for the *pecado nefando* was personally micromanaged

by Philip II in a political move to assert the Crown's power over Rome. See Francisco Núñez Roldan's excellent microhistory, *El pecado nefando del Obispo de Salamina: Un hombre sin concierto en la corte de Felipe II* (2002).

31. The complete title of León's work, of which four copies apparently exist, is *Compendio de algunas experiencias en los ministerios de que usa la Compañía de Jesús, con que prácticamente se muestra con algunos acontecimientos y documentos el buen acierto en ellos, por orden de los superiores, por el Padre Pedro de León, de la misma Compañía*. It provides a wealth of sociohistorical data on criminals, their crimes and punishments, and the conditions in the Seville jail in the early seventeenth century. The text is available in a 1981 edition, *Grandeza y miseria en Andalucía*.

32. The most famous exception is the fraile de la Merced from *Lazarillo de Tormes*. Nonetheless, the subject is treated with sublety there, and the author of the novel avoids the obscenity found in the poetry under study here. Regarding the "cosillas" that occurred with the friar that Lázaro refuses to detail, see Shipley 1996, and regarding boy prostitution, see Carrasco 1985. Other sodomites who populate picaresque novels are the cardinal in *Guzmán de Alfarache* and the man in Quevedo's *El buscón* who was jailed for "cosas de atrás . . . por puto" (1982, 222) [things from behind . . . as a faggot]. These examples notwithstanding, it would seem that satire focuses criticism of the clergy on their connections with prostitution (as in Francisco Rojas's *La Celestina* and Fernando de Delicado's *La Lozana andaluza,* the latter containing a wealth of detail on the Roman clergy's intimacy with the world of prostitution). As the proverb says, "Putas y frailes andan a pares" (Correas 2000, 666). [Whores and friars go together.]

33. Other examples of *çirio,* meaning "penis," are found in *PESO*; see poems 42, verse 10; 59, verse 13; and 131, verse 10.

34. See Díez Fernández 2003 (218–24) on Cornejo's erotic verse.

35. See the introduction to J. Goldberg 1994 and Katz 1994 on sodomy as a sociopolitical designation generally mobilized in the face of perceived threats to the social order.

36. Consequently, a fairly large proportion of the poems that deal with sodomy are burlesque epitaphs. See further discussion of this extremely popular poetic mode in Martín 1991 (149) and, with respect to Quevedo, Mas 1957 (186).

37. With specific reference to Quevedo, Ignacio Navarrete affirms that the homosexuality theme is a double violation of poetic decorum, since both the obscene lexicon used and the social attitudes represented have no place in the Petrarchist tradition (1994, 236–37).

CHAPTER THREE

1. Castle's book includes, typically, two brief poems by the Mexican poet Sor Juana Inés de la Cruz.

2. Lesbian desire was recognized as a particular risk in the convent. In several works Saint Teresa of Avila (among others) expresses concerns about the dangers to communal life posed by "special friendships" *intra muros*. See Martín 1997 (65–67).

3. Again, Pedro de León's *Grandeza y miseria en Andalucía* is a fascinating source of information on the Seville jail and its remarkable functioning.

4. See Perry 1989 for further discussion of the attitudes held toward crimes against nature in early modern Spain. The same mentality crossed the Atlantic, as is seen in Pilar Gonzalbo Aizpuru's "Del bueno y del mal amor en el siglo XVIII novohispano" in López-Baralt and Márquez Villanueva 1995b (139–58).

5. Very little is known about this rather mysterious woman. See the preliminary study and the text of San Jerónimo's *Razón y forma de la Galera* in Isabel Barbeito's edition of *Cárceles y mujeres en el siglo XVII* (1991).

6. Tradition had it that the best artificial penises were manufactured in Mileto and exported all over the world. They had many names in as many languages—for example, *olisbo, baubon, gaude-mihi, godemiché, disletto,* and *dildo*. For a very brief history of their presence in literature, see Malo 1985 (13–14).

7. I quote here from Michael Solomon's bilingual edition and translation, but the treatise has been translated into Spanish in a 2000 edition by Teresa Vicens.

8. In *Frontiers of Heresy*, William Monter mentions cases of women convicted of sodomy in Spain. In 1560 several women were accused of lesbian practices performed without using a false phallus. The Supreme Council of the Inquisition, when consulted, determined that this behavior did not constitute sodomy (Monter 1990, 281–82). In the mid-1650s a widow and a laundress were convicted of sodomy by the Aragon tribunal, based on the testimony of neighbors; their sentence is unknown although Monter states that no one was executed for sodomy by the Inquisition after 1633 (316–17). Crompton also mentions the case of two women from Castile who were sentenced to death in the 1620s. Their sentence was reduced, on appeal, to 400 lashes and banishment, and they were subsequently pardoned (2003, 299).

9. See Traub 2002 (41–44) for the broader context of patterns of legal prosecution for female sodomy in pre–eighteenth century Europe and colonial North America.

10. Another far less aesthetically accomplished and more openly obscene poem collected in *PESO* further extolls the virtues of the *baldrés*; see "*¿Si habrá en este baldrés*" (110–11). Serna and his works are discussed in more detail in Chapter Five.

11. In Fisher 2006 (59–82), the codpiece is analyzed as a constituent component of early modern masculine attire and identity.

12. See Alonso 1990 (9–11) for an extended analysis of the medicinal and erotic qualities of Belardo's garden.

13. On priapic poetry, see Díez Fernández 2003 (289–324) and Richlin 1992 (116–27).

14. The composition (which appears in manuscript 2803 of the Biblioteca Real de Madrid and has been published in José J. Labrador Herraiz and Ralph A. DiFranco's 1989 edition of *Cancionero de poesías varias: Manuscrito 2803 de la Biblioteca del Palacio Real de Madrid*) is modernized and reprinted in Martín and Díez Fernández 2003 (83–99); all textual quotations are from the 2003 edition. See also the limited-run (250 copies) edition edited by Luis Montañés in 1976 and illustrated with etchings by José Luis Ferrer, held in the Princeton University Library and the Biblioteca Nacional de Madrid (see Serna 1976).

15. See Fisher 2006 regarding beards, masculinity, and the role of facial hair in sexual transformation.

16. As is well-known, aspects of Laqueur's approach have been challenged by several historians, who assert that he has disregarded early modern medical paradigms that differed from the one-sex model. See, for example, Park and Nye 1991, Cadden 1993, and Schleiner 2000.

17. See also the discussion in Díez Fernández 2003 (196–98) about possible explanations for Teodora's miraculous transformation.

18. This is the type of impersonation known as the bed trick (see the discussion in Chapter Five).

19. Sherry Velasco also discusses briefly the Julio-Julieta-Melisa love triangle in her article "Mapping Selvagia's Transmutable Sexuality in Montemayor's *Diana*" (1997, 407–9).

20. The links between the monastery, the university, and erotic-burlesque literature that inform Serna's verse novellas are explored in Chapter Five.

21. As Asunción Rallo points out in her edition (Villalón 1990), the tale also closely approximates the story of the twins Riciardeto-Bradamante and the beautiful Flor-de-Espina from Canto 25 of Ludovico Ariosto's *Orlando Furioso*.

22. Throughout this section, I quote from Villalón 1990.

23. Throughout this section, I quote from Asunción Rallo's 1991 edition of Montemayor's *Los siete libros de la Diana*.

24. Sherry Velasco has analyzed what she calls "transmutable sexuality" in the episode, concluding that Selvagia is a "potentially subversive model for female sexuality that presents a variety of gender and sexual combinations involving both women and men as the objects of desire for other women" (1997, 412).

25. This said, it is also recognized that the pastoral mythological sphere is the world of lesbian themes and love and erotic exploration in general. For this reason early modern artists (such as Titian) mined provocative scenes from classical mythology to create erotic art, mainly (although not exclusively) through the female nude. This is evident in the paintings hung in the private chambers of Spanish royalty during the Golden Age. See Portús Pérez 1998.

26. My discussion of the *doncella guerrera* ballad in Chapter Four analyzes female eyes and hands as gender determinants within the semiotics of femininity.

27. On Neoplatonic love theory, see the works of Nesca Robb (1935), Edouard Meyland (1938), Jean Festugière (1941), John Charles Nelson (1958), Paul Oskar Kristeller (1964), and A.C. Lloyd (1990).

28. The principal Renaissance texts governed by Neoplatonism would be León Hebreo's *Diálogos de amor*, Marsilio Ficino's *De amore*, the third book of Pietro Bembo's *Asolani*, the fourth book of Baldassarre Castiglione's *The Courtier*, and Petrarch's lyric. It is important to keep in mind that these texts that divulged Neoplatonic theory distanced themselves from the more ambivalent understanding of the physical world that typified the Middle Ages.

29. I paraphrase from María Grazia Profeti, "La escena erótica de los siglos áureos" (1992: 57–89), in which she adds, "En la prosa la escena erótica, si aparece, no se acogerá por cierto a la mención desvergonzada o a la directa representación, sino a las más sutiles modalidades de la alusión" (1992: 69). [In prose the erotic scene, if it appears at all, will certainly not include shameful mentions or direct representation, but instead the most subtle modes of allusion.] *Mutatis mutandi*, this is what occurs in each erotic episode in *La Diana*.

30. Here I paraphrase from Guy Hocquenghem's *Homosexual Desire* (1993, 49). A varied selection of feminist critical conceptualizations of this idea can be found in *Feminisms: An Anthology of Literary Theory and Criticism* (Warhol and Herndl 1991). See, for example, the articles by Nancy Armstrong, Hélène Cixous, Luce Irigaray, Ann Rosalind Jones, Linda S. Kauffman, Helena Michie, Leslie W. Rabine, Barbara Smith, Jane Tompkins, and Susan Willis. The specific Spanish context is addressed in the section "Una mirada española," in *Del Renacimiento a la Edad Moderna*, volume 3 of *Historia de las mujeres en Occidente* (Duby and Perrot 1992).

31. Recent editions do not include the study of Montemayor's reception in the twentieth century initiated by Genouy 1928. For an update see Teixeira Anacleto 1994 and, especially, Fosalba 1994. For the relationship with religious history and devout literature, see Rhodes 1992.

32. In this regard I disagree with Renato Poggioli, who asserts that in pastoral literature love can be in conflict with social laws but not with natural laws; therefore, it does not become perversion. He explains the absence of what he calls "unnatural love" as follows: "Even in the Renaissance, the paganism of both the culture and the mores was still so permeated with the ethos of Christianity as to prevent, in spite of the slavish imitation of the ancients, any characterization patterned after Virgil's Corydon" (1975, 62). The relationship between homosexuality and Christianity is examined in detail in Boswell 1980, Bullough 1974, and Crompton 2003.

33. Goodheart 1991 (113–41) puts the discourse of desire into perspective in terms of the academy, general culture, and its utopical tyranny.

34. "Pastoral characters express an inner voice which has been traditionally ascribed to 'the feminine,' but which need not be relegated by quality or quantity to biological sexual categories" (Rhodes 1992, 17).

35. Of course, male homosexuality and bisexuality were present in the classical bucolic tradition, especially in Virgil's *Eclogues*, in particular the *Corydon*.

CHAPTER FOUR

1. More recently Louise Vasvári has written on the ballad from the perspective of queer theory in her article "Queering the *Donçella Guerrera*" (2006).

2. There are also many south Slavic versions: Serbian, Croatian, Macedonian, Bulgarian, and Slovenian. López Estrada attributes the persistence of the ballad in folklore and its multiplicity of variants to its great capacity for reinvention and reshuffling of the elements that compose the basic plot structure (1985, 409).

3. Jorge Ferreira de Vasconcellos quotes a couple of verses in Spanish in his Portuguese *Aulegraphia* (act 3, scene 1), which dates from 1619. However, the oldest extant text of the ballad is a Hungarian translation from the Serbo-Croatian dating from 1570 (Vargyas 1967, 79).

4. Numerous folk motifs and tales incorporate the theme of a woman in male disguise. See, among other discussions, Stith Thompson's K1837: Disguise of woman in man's clothes in *Motif-Index of Folk-Literature* (1989) and Antti Aarne's Tale Type 884B in *The Types of the Folktale* (1961).

5. It is worth remembering that the poem is, above all else, a song to

be performed before an audience of listeners, presumably with appropriate gestures.

6. Stephen Greenblatt has analyzed the sexually provocative nature of clothing on the Elizabethan stage in his "Erotische Provokation im Elizabethanischen Theater" (1988).

7. Regarding the cultural history of shoes throughout the centuries, see the essays in Riello and McNeil 2006.

8. Stith Thompson (1989) has a separate category for sex tests (Motif H1578.1: Test of sex of girl masking as man), which are designed to unmask transvestite women. Two that are related to the trials employed in this ballad are (1) to throw a ball into a person's lap (the woman spreads her legs, whereas the man brings his legs together) and (2) to place a spinning wheel nearby (a woman will express interest in it, whereas a man will not).

9. See Salmón and Cabré 1998 regarding the poisonous properties of menstrual blood and its relationship to fascination (the evil eye) in academic medical discussions in early modern Spain.

10. Niccoli also notes that the menstruating woman was considered maximally impure and that relations with her were considered damaging: "At her touch flowers withered, the strings of musical instruments snapped, beer went sour, sauces boiled over" (1990, 9).

11. Roses are also associated with men in a Sicilian folk motif collected by Stith Thompson (1989). In Motif H1578.1.3: Test of sex of girl masking as man: choosing flowers, a woman will choose a carnation, but a man will choose a rose. This might also be the significance behind placing a fresh rose in the room of the soldier/*doncella*.

12. See da Costa Fontes 2000.

13. This also explains the spinning wheel test described in note 8.

14. In *Cross Dressing, Sex, and Gender,* Vern L. and Bonnie Bullough point out that "cross dressing and impersonation, or playing with gender, was an increasingly important theme in the sixteenth and seventeenth centuries, emphasizing that gender differences were more flexible than they appeared" (1993, 74).

15. Regarding the white horse as a particularly noteworthy phallic symbol, see Slater 1979. In Bahian versions the horse is a magic animal that counsels the girl on how to pass the tests imposed by the mother. As Slater notes, "The Donzela must rely on the horse because she lacks the masculine principle which he represents. It is revealing that in one variant the horse actually transforms himself into a man who brings the maiden a letter from home before changing back into the steed on which she goes galloping off" (174).

16. Both of these ballads are included in Menéndez Pidal 1965. See the discussion of women's vital and active role as a stabilizing and humanizing force in the *romancero* in Odd 1983. A markedly different solution for the

dishonored woman is provided in the "Doña Antonia of Lisbon" ballads. In these songs Antonia, the protagonist, willingly surrenders her virginity to Don Pedro, her lover. When Don Pedro abandons her for another woman, however, Antonia dons male disguise, defeats him in a sword fight, cuts off his head, and hangs it on his new lover's door. See several versions of this ballad in Armistead and Silverman 1977 (130–38).

17. Sherry Velasco's book *The Lieutenant Nun* (2000) analyzes the utilization of Erauso in various cultural "texts" from the seventeenth century through the twentieth century.

18. Because of the accessibility, updated bibliography, and modernized spelling and punctuation of Esteban's critical edition, all quotations from the primary text are from Erauso 2002; secondary materials are taken from Vallbona 1992.

19. Perry finds this information in "Noticias y casos" (No. 1 of the *efemérides* [records of notable events]) of the Municipal Archive in Seville. She also reports that Erauso was referred to as Catalina de Crusa or Catalina de Eranso. To date, Perry's 1980 work provides the fullest social and historical contextualization for Erauso's return to Spain. Her subsequent work in this regard (1987a, 1987b, and 1999) adds to our historicized understanding of Erauso.

20. Pacheco's portrait is reproduced in several editions of Erauso's autobiography, including Ferrer 1829, Vallbona 1992, and Velasco 2000. Interestingly, in the 1631 inventory of artworks that belonged to one of baroque Spain's greatest still-life painters, Juan Van der Hamen y León (1596–1631), Pacheco's portrait of Erauso is listed as one of twenty portraits of illustrious men (including Francisco de Quevedo, Luis de Góngora, Lope de Vega, and Juan Ruiz de Alarcón). At the time, the painting was appraised at four ducats, whereas the portraits of the writers were appraised at three. In his doctoral dissertation on the artist, William Jordan attributes the portrait to Van der Hamen y León rather than to Pacheco (1967, 362–64). Two other portraits of Erauso exist: one painted by Francisco Crescencio in Rome (1626) and one painted by J. L. Villar in 1941 (Villar's portrait is featured on the cover of Erauso 2002). An illustration of an engraving that belongs to the Biblioteca Nacional de Madrid and that Antoine Fauchery made from the 1630 portrait is included in Velasco 2000 (79).

21. Several still shots of María Félix in the role of the *monja alférez* are reproduced in Velasco 2000.

22. Her lack of more abundant facial hair also distinguishes her from male soldiers of the time, who conventionally wore a large mustache or goatee (Valcárcel 2005, 66).

23. The most daring critic is Manuel Serrano y Sanz (1975, 388–92), who, calling the book a pseudoautobiography, posits that it was written in

the nineteenth century, perhaps by Cándido María Trigueros. Trigueros, who worked for Juan Bautista Muñoz (author of *Historia del Nuevo Mundo*), was an imitator and transcriber of early modern texts who owned the Seville manuscript that Ferrer used for his edition.

24. With respect to the alleged research by Burke, see Berruezo 1959 (13–14) and Castresana 1968 (11–12).

25. This having been said, Isabel Valcárcel (2005) provides information regarding women soldiers in the Hispanic world.

26. Asunción Lavrin's "Introduction: The Scenario, the Actors, and the Issues" in *Sexuality and Marriage in Colonial Latin America* (1989) provides a fuller context for the period. The issue of gender vis-à-vis the discourse of discovery is still unexplored for the Spanish context.

27. Vallbona (1992, 52 n. 4) describes the episode with the young girl as picaresque and Boccaccian, along the lines of *Tirant lo Blanc*. However, the protagonist's history does not fully reinforce an alliance with conventionally picaresque developments (see Dunn 1993). Humor, for example, is notably absent from the *Historia*.

28. Medina confirms that a 1595 decree by Philip II extended the frequent punishment of expulsion from the Indies to all those who had been condemned and punished by the Holy Office. They were to be embarked at sea and could remain in America only during completion of the sentence imposed by the Holy Office (1952, 132). Three recent complementary overviews are Pinto Crespo 1983, Kamen 1985 (an update of Henry Kamen's previous work), and Alberro 1987 (which concentrates on women in New Spain).

29. For example, in what can be deemed a very chaste footnote to the *Historia*, Ferrer prefers to ignore the homoerotic implications of the scene between Erauso and Solarte's sister-in-law. He opts, instead, to interpret Erauso's "caprice" of enamoring virgins as an indication either that she accepted the illusion that she was a man or that she perceived the behavior as a way of disguising her true sex even further (1829, 24).

30. It is obvious that there is a resemantization of the gender ascribed not only to Erauso but also to her deeds. Thus, she is not only a "conqueror" or a "soldier" but also a "heroine." Regarding this last aspect, see Tejera 1988, in which the author views Erauso's *Vida* as a picaresque novel, considering de Quincey's 1847 version to be more attractive and "wordy" (298).

31. Dekker's and van de Pol's study is, to date, the fullest with respect to women who passed as men. They document 119 cases in the Netherlands and 50 cases in Great Britain between the years 1550 and 1839.

32. All Spanish quotations from the *Libro de buen amor* are from J. Ruiz 1988; all translations are from J. Ruiz 1972.

33. On the meaning of the word *camino* [way, path] to indicate vagina, see Vasvári 1977, 1567–1570.

34. See, in this regard, Burke 1973.

35. See the versions collected in Hernández Hernández and Martínez Terrón 1993.

36. This is the manner in which the *serrana de la Vera* is depicted in a rather charming and larger-than-life-sized statue that can be found today on the country road that leads from Garganta la Olla to the Monastery of Yuste. Evidently, the legend is still alive in this region of Extremadura.

37. I do not include Lope de Vega's version of *La serrana de la Vera* in this discussion, since his character is merely a lady from Plasencia who disguises herself as a *serrana*. The plot is summarized in Vélez de Guevara 1916 (131–34).

38. I quote from Vélez de Guevara 2002; all translations are my own.

39. According to Giorgio Vasari in his study of the lives of famous artists, Fra Bartolommeo di Pagholo's painting of Saint Sebastian was so erotically stimulating that the friars in the convent where it was displayed reported that the women who looked at it during confession were moved to sin (1981–89, 5:12).

40. Ruano de la Haza explains that the corridors of the *corral* were often used to accommodate *apariencias,* such as Gila pierced with arrows, because they were intended to be shown in an elevated position (2000, 236).

CHAPTER FIVE

1. Although a number of articles on erotic aspects of specific texts or fragments of texts have been published in recent decades, cohesive book-length studies, especially in Anglo-American criticism, are still few.

2. For a brief overview of medieval erotic literature and its historical context, see Aparicio Maydeu 1992.

3. Regarding the inquisitorial crackdown on sexually explicit literature that occurs in subsequent centuries, see Palacios Fernández 2006.

4. For an outline of the pedagogical issues involved in the study of erotic Golden Age poetry, see Martín 2005.

5. See Hurtado de Mendoza 1995, 111–15.

6. See Donald McGrady's edition of Tamariz 1974.

7. The details of Serna's biography and literary works are updated in the essays included in Martín and Díez Fernández 2003.

8. See Labrador Herraiz and DiFranco 1989; see also Labrador Herraiz, DiFranco, and Bernard 1997 and 2001 These works include a substantial selection of erotic compositions written by Serna.

9. "Novela del cordero," or "Cuento del pintor," appears in a manuscript from the Biblioteca Nazionale Vittorio Emanuele III Naples (Brancacciana V-A-16), published as *Romancero de la Biblioteca Brancacciana* by R. Foulché Delbosc in volume 65 of *Revue Hispanique* in 1925. In his edition of Tamariz's *Novelas y cuentos en verso* (1956), Rodríguez Moñino attributes the work to Tamariz. It also appears as anonymously written in Fradejas Lebrero 1985 (293–99). The editorial history of "El sueño de la viuda de Aragón" is more extensive. The work appeared, without a byline, in *Cancionero de obras de burlas provocantes a risa,* edited by Eduardo Lustonó and published in Madrid in 1872; in Luis Montañés's edition of *Sueño de la viuda* (Serna 1976), a very limited edition illustrated with etchings by José Luis Ferrer; in *Jardín de flores y ramillete de sonetos eróticos del Siglo de Oro: Fray Melchor de la Serna y otros* (1977), also edited by Montañés and with etchings by Esther Ortego; and in Labrador Herraiz and DiFranco 1989 (207–21). An abbreviated versión appears in *Poesías del Maestro León y de Fr. Melchor de la Serna y otros (s. XVI): Códice núm. 961 de la Biblioteca Real de Madrid* (1991), edited by C. Ángel Zorita, Ralph A. DiFranco, and José J. Labrador Herraiz, with a prologue by Dietrich Briesemeister. It also appears in Labrador Herraiz, DiFranco, and Bernard 2001 (58–74), with a prologue by José Lara Garrido. Labrador Herraiz and DiFranco (1989, xxix) list other manuscript versions of *El sueño,* to which we can add the one on EP CXIV-3 (this final note has been provided by *BIPA,* the database of Golden Age poetry prepared by DiFranco and Labrador Herraiz under the auspices of the National Endowment for the Humanities). "Novela de la mujer de Gil" appears in Labrador Herraiz, DiFranco, and Bernard 1997 (99–104). "Novela de las madejas," appears in Biblioteca Nacional de Madrid manuscript 3168 (folios 106–8) and Biblioteca Nacional de Madrid manuscript 3915 (folios 302–6v). Because it is the oldest, the text of Biblioteca Nacional de Madrid manuscript 3168 was published in Lissorgues 1978. It was subsequently published in Labrador Herraiz, DiFranco, and Bernard 1997 (114–18) and 2001 (100–108). See also Cerezo 2001 (207–9) for a recent bibliography of Serna's novellas.

10. Proof that a rich melding of narrative and verse is still possible in our time is Vikram Seth's 1986 novel, *The Golden Gate,* which is written entirely in sonnets.

11. McGrady credits Tamariz with the idea of versifying the Italian novellas and views him as a precursor of baroque playwrights such as Lope de Vega, who combined plots inspired by Italian novellas with verse form (see Tamariz 1974, 22).

12. In other versions of this novella, the verse reads, "Guárdense de mi voz, no las encante" (hence, my translation "bewitch").

13. An implicitly female audience is also evoked in the poetry written by

Catalina Clara Ramírez de Guzmán, an accomplished burlesque poet born into the provincial aristocracy in Llerena (Badajoz). Her verse is, in many aspects, a genial poetics of everyday life as experienced by women. Ramírez de Guzmán produced a great deal of specifically academic poetry: verse with a decidedly protofeminist slant intended for reading aloud at literary salons. Some may find it surprising that Ramírez de Guzmán, a woman who lived her entire life in the provinces (under the shadow of the important Llerena Inquisition tribunal), was able to achieve her apparent level of education. Clearly, it is time to revise past assumptions regarding not only women's reading practices but also the accessibility of literary salons to cultivated women. Ramírez de Guzmán's verse is collected in her *Obras poéticas* (2004).

14. For example, the episode of the friar's underpants is one case of several, in as many literatures, in which a friar or priest leaves his pants behind in his lover's bedroom. See the fabliau "Des braies au Cordelier" [The Franciscan's Britches] (bilingual French/English text in Eichmann and DuVal 1984) and several tales listed in Rotunda 1942 (under the motif K1526, Friar's trousers on adulteress's bed). In the eighteenth century, Félix María de Samaniego reworked the motif in his verse tale "Los calzones de San Francisco" (see Samaniego 2004, 261–63). Samaniego's tale is both less ingenious and more scatological than Serna's, since his Franciscan friar's *calzones* are both sweaty and soiled. McGrady (1981) has studied the Italian origins of Samaniego's tale, but neither he nor Palacios Fernández (see Samaniego 2004) mentions Serna's superior version.

15. The names used in erotic literature are rarely gratuitous; they generally carry particular connotations within specific contexts, as noted in Chapter One with respect to María/Marica/Maritornes and as noted with respect to Gil from this poem. According to Margit Frenk (1992), the name Pedro, and its derivatives—such as Perucho, Perico, and Periquito—indicate a proverbial character with a specific although varied profile: servant, farmer, shepherd, cuckold (if married). Given the typically roguish comportment of the Pedro character as a trickster and seducer of women, several proverbs warn against admitting a Pedro into the household. See, for example, "Ni moço ni Pedro en casa" in Frenk 1992. Many poems with Pericos—especially the lusty erotic *letrilla* "Dámelo, Periquito, perro. / Periquito, dámelo" (Alzieu, Jammes, and Lissorgues 1984, 151–52), whose tone is similar to Serna's narrative poem—are included in *PESO*.

16. On the centrality of the (female) body in Golden Age erotic literature, see Damiani and Imperiale 1991.

17. See the eighth story of the eighth day, "A story concerning two close friends, of whom the first goes to bed with the wife of the second. The second man finds out, and compels his wife to lock the first man in a chest, on which

he makes love to his friend's wife whilst he is trapped inside" (Boccaccio 1995, 610–15).

18. Of course, the concealment motif has a long history in folklore and its literature. See the many examples connected with adulterous deceptions registered in S. Thompson 1989 (K1300–99, Seduction or deceptive marriage, and K1500–99, Deceptions connected with adultery), in H. Goldberg 1998, and in Rotunda 1942.

19. One of the more linguistically ingenious of these poems is "Caldero y llave, madona, / jura Di, pero vos amar, / je voléu vos adobar" (145) [I swear to God, my lady, I would like to prepare you a pot and key in order to love you], narrated by a wandering French hawker whose skills are patently erotic.

20. On this motif in English theater, see Desens 1994.

21. It should be remembered that to sneeze can also mean to ejaculate.

22. See Julián Olivares's introduction to his edition of Zayas y Sotomayor's *Novelas amorosas y ejemplares* (2000, 92).

Works Cited

Aarne, Antti. 1961. *The Types of the Folktale.* Trans. Stith Thompson. Helsinki: Suomalainen Tiedeakatemia/Academia Scientarum Fennica.

Alatorre, Antonio. 2003. *El sueño erótico en la poesía española de los Siglos de Oro.* Mexico City: Fondo de Cultura Económica.

Alberro, Solange. 1987. "Herejes, brujas y beatas: Mujeres ante el Tribunal del Santo Oficio de la Inquisición en la Nueva España." In *Presencia y transparencia: La mujer en la historia de México.* Ed. Carmen Ramos Escandón et al. Mexico City: El Colegio de México, 79–94.

Alonso, José Luis. 1990. "Claves para la formación del léxico erótico." *Edad de Oro* 9:7–17.

Althusser, Louis. 1976. *Essays on Ideology.* London: Verso.

Alzieu, Pierre, Robert Jammes, and Yvan Lissorgues, eds. 1984. *Poesía erótica del Siglo de Oro [PESO].* Barcelona: Crítica.

Aparicio Maydeu, Javier. 1992. "Carnaval vence a Cuaresma: Algunos apuntes para una ojeada erótica a la Edad Media." In *Discurso erótico y discurso transgresor en la cultura peninsular: Siglos XI al XX.* Ed. Myriam Díaz-Diocaretz and Iris M. Zavala. Madrid: Tuero, 11–27.

Apráiz, Julián. 1906. *Juicio de "La tía fingida."* Madrid: Sucesores de Hernando.

Arellano, Ignacio. 1995. *Historia del teatro español del siglo XVII.* Madrid: Cátedra.

Aretino, Pietro. 1994. *Dialogues.* Trans. Raymond Rosenthal. New York: Marsilio.

Armistead, Samuel G. 1978. *El romancero judeo-español en el Archivo Menéndez Pidal (catálogo-índice de romances y canciones).* 3 vols. Madrid: Cátedra-Seminario Menéndez Pidal.

Armistead, Samuel G., and Joseph H. Silverman, eds. 1977. *Romances judeo-españoles de Tanger recogidos por Zarita Nahón.* Madrid: Cátedra-Seminario Menéndez-Pidal.

Astrana Marín, Luis. 1953. *Vida ejemplar y heroica de Miguel de Cervantes Saavedra.* Madrid: Reus.

Avalle-Arce, Juan Bautista, ed. 1982. *Novelas ejemplares,* by Miguel de Cervantes. Madrid: Castalia.

Aveleyra, Teresa. 1977. "El erotismo de don Quijote." *Nueva Revista de Filología Hispánica* 26:468–79.

Aylward, E. T. 1982. "'Rinconete y Cortadillo,' 'El celoso extremeño,' and 'La tía fingida': A Question of Authorship." Chapter 1 of *Cervantes: Pioneer and Plagiarist.* London: Tamesis.

Barbeito, Isabel, ed. 1991. *Cárceles y mujeres en el siglo XVII.* Madrid: Castalia.

Barthes, Roland. 2001. "The Death of the Author." In *The Norton Anthology of Theory and Criticism.* Ed. Vincent B. Leitch. New York: W. W. Norton, 1466–70.

Bartra, Roger. 2001. *Cultura y melancolía: Las enfermedades del alma en la España del Siglo de Oro.* Madrid: Anagrama.

Bataille, Georges. 1989. *The Tears of Eros.* Trans. Peter Connor. San Francisco: City Lights Books.

Bautista C., Álvaro. 1997. "Maritornes: Doncella y coima: Una lectura del capítulo XVI de '*El Quijote*.'" *Alba de América* 15:412–17.

Beauvoir, Simone de. 1974. *The Second Sex.* 1949. Reprint, New York: Vintage Books.

Benmayor, Rina, ed. 1979. *Romances judeo-españoles de Oriente: Nueva recolección.* Madrid: Cátedra-Seminario Menéndez Pidal/Gredos.

Bergeron, David M. 1991. *Royal Family, Royal Lovers: King James of England and Scotland.* Columbia: University of Missouri Press.

Berruezo, José. 1959. "La monja alférez Doña Catalina de Erauso." Prologue to *Historia de la monja alférez Doña Catalina de Erauso, escrita por ella misma.* Pamplona, Spain: Editorial Gómez.

Bezler, Francis. 1994. *Les pénitentiels espagnols: Contribution à l'étude de la civilisation de l'Espagne chrétienne du Haut Moyen Age.* Münster, Germany: Aschendorff.

Blackmore, Josiah. 1999. "The Poets of Sodom." In *Queer Iberia.* Ed. Josiah Blackmore and Gregory S. Hutcheson. Durham, N.C.: Duke University Press, 195–221.

Blackmore, Josiah, and Gregory S. Hutcheson, eds. 1999. *Queer Iberia.* Durham, N.C.: Duke University Press.

Blasco Pascual, Javier. 2005. *Miguel de Cervantes Saavedra: Regocijo de las musas.* Valladolid, Spain: Universidad de Valladolid.

Boccaccio, Giovanni. 1995. *The Decameron.* Trans. G. H. McWilliam. 2nd ed. London: Penguin Books.

Borges, Jorge Luis. 1974. *Obras completas.* Buenos Aires: Emecé Editores.

Boswell, John. 1980. *Christianity, Social Tolerance, and Homosexuality.* Chicago: University of Chicago Press.

Bray, Alan. 1982. *Homosexuality in Renaissance England.* London: Gay Men's Press.

Bredbeck, Gregory W. 1991. *Sodomy and Interpretation: Marlowe to Milton.* Ithaca, N.Y.: Cornell University Press.

Bristow, Joseph. *Sexuality.* 1997. London: Routledge.

Brown, Judith C. 1986. *Immodest Acts: The Life of a Lesbian Nun in Renaissance Italy.* New York: Oxford University Press.

Bubnova, Tatiana. 1996. "Estado, iglesia, universidad: Prostitución y proxenetismo como problema de conciencia en la vida cotidiana y en la expresión literaria." In *Caballeros, monjas y maestros en la Edad Media.* Ed. Lillian von der Walde, Concepción Company, and Aurelio González. Mexico City: Universidad Nacional Autónoma de México, 415–31.

Bullough, Vern L. 1974. "Heresy, Witchcraft, and Sexuality." *Journal of Homosexuality* 1.2:183–201.

Bullough, Vern L., and Bonnie Bullough. 1993. *Cross Dressing, Sex, and Gender.* Philadelphia: University of Pennsylvania Press.

Bunes Ibarra, Miguel Angel de. 1989. *La imagen de los musulmanes y del norte de África en la España de los siglos XVI y XVII.* Madrid: Consejo Superior de Investigaciones Científicas.

Burke, James F. 1973. "Juan Ruiz, the Serranas, and the Rites of Spring." *Journal of Medieval and Renaissance Studies* 5.1 (Spring): 13–35.

Butler, Judith. 1990. *Gender Trouble: Feminism and the Subversion of Identity.* New York: Routledge.

Cadden, Joan. 1993. *Meanings of Sex Difference in the Middle Ages: Medicine, Science, and Culture.* Cambridge, England: Cambridge University Press.

Cady, Joseph. 1993. "Renaissance Awareness and Language for Heterosexuality: 'Love' and 'Feminine Love.'" In *Renaissance Discourses of Desire.* Ed. Claude J. Summers and Ted-Larry Pebworth. Columbia: University of Missouri Press, 143–58.

Cardaillac, Louis, and Robert Jammes. 1985. "Amours et sexualité à travers les 'Memoires' d'un inquisiteur du XVIIe siècle." In *Amours légitimes: Amours illégitimes en Espagne (XVIe–XVIIe siècles).* Ed. Augustin Redondo. Paris: Publications de la Sorbonne, 183–94.

Caro Baroja, Julio. 1978. *Las formas complejas de la vida religiosa.* Madrid: Akal.
———. 1974. *Ritos y mitos equívocos.* Madrid: Istmo.

Carrasco, Eva, and Ismael Almazán. 1994. "Prostitución y criminalidad en Cataluña en la época moderna." In *La prostitution en Espagne de l'époque des Rois Catholiques à la IIe République.* Ed. Raphaël Carrasco. Paris: Les Belles Lettres, 23–65.

Carrasco, Rafael. 1985. *Inquisición y represión sexual en Valencia: Historia de los sodomitas (1565–1785).* Barcelona: Laertes.

Carreira, Antonio, ed. 1994. *Nuevos poemas atribuidos a Góngora.* Barcelona: Quaderns Crema.

Cartagena-Calderón, José R. 2000. "Entre telones masculinos: Teatro, literatura y construcción de masculinidades en la España aurisecular." Ph.D. diss., Harvard University.

Castle, Terry, ed. 2003. *The Literature of Lesbianism*. New York: Columbia University Press.

Castresana, Luis de. 1968. *Catalina de Erauso: La monja alférez*. Madrid: Afrodisio Aguado.

Castro, Américo. 1924. "'Romance de la mujer que fué a la guerra.' (Esbozos de historia literaria.)" In *Lengua, enseñanzas y literatura (esbozos)*. Madrid: Victoriano Suárez, 259–80.

Castro Pires de Lima, Fernando de. 1958. *A mulher vestida de homem*. Lisbon: Fundação Nacional para a Alegria no Trabalho.

Cátedra, Pedro M., and Anastasio Rojo. 2004. *Bibliotecas y lecturas de mujeres, Siglo XVI*. Salamanca, Spain: Instituto de Historia del Libro y de la Lectura.

Cela, Camilo José. 1988. *Diccionario del erotismo*. Barcelona: Grijalbo.

Cerezo, José Antonio. 2001. *Literatura erótica en España: Repertorio de obras, 1519–1936*. Madrid: Ollero y Ramos.

Cernuda, Luis. 2005. "No decía palabras." In *Poesía completa*. Vol. I of *Obra completa*. 5th ed. Ed. Derek Harris and Luis Maristany. Madrid: Siruela, 178.

Cervantes, Miguel de. 2004. *Don Quijote de la Mancha*. Ed. Francisco Rico. Edition of the Instituto Cervantes, 1605–2005. Barcelona: Galaxia Gutenberg, Círculo de Lectores, Centro para la Edición de los Clásicos Españoles.

———. 2003. *Don Quixote*. Trans. Edith Grossman. New York: Ecco/HarperCollins.

———. 2001. *Novelas ejemplares*. Ed. Jorge García López. Barcelona: Cátedra.

———. 1982. *Novelas ejemplares*. Ed. Juan Bautista Avalle-Arce. Madrid: Castalia.

———. 1980. *El viejo celoso: Entremeses*. Ed. Eugenio Asensio. Madrid: Castalia.

———. 1919. *La tía fingida*. Ed. José Toribio Medina. Santiago, Chile: Minerva.

Chauvin, Charles. 1983. *Les Chrétiens et la prostitution*. Paris: Editions du Cerf.

Chaves, Cristóbal de. 1983. *Relación de la cárcel de Sevilla*. Madrid: Clásicos el Arbol.

Colón Calderón, Isabel. 2005. "La Tolosa y la Molinera (*Quijote*, 1, 2–3) en el marco de la prostitución de comienzos del siglo XVII." In *El* Quijote *en clave de mujer/es*. Ed. Fanny Rubio. Madrid: Editorial Complutense, 305–28.

Correas, Gonzalo. 2000. *Vocabulario de refranes y frases proverbiales (1627)*. Ed. Louis Combet. Rev. Robert Jammes and Maïté Mir-Andreu. Madrid: Castalia.

Cortés Vázquez, Luis. 1989. *La vida estudiantil en la Salamanca clásica*. Salamanca, Spain: Ediciones Universidad de Salamanca.

Cossío, José María de. 1942. "Notas al romancero: Caracteres populares de la feminidad en 'La doncella que va a la guerra.'" *Escorial: Revista de cultura y letras* 6.17:413–23.

Costa Fontes, Manuel da. 2000. "Knitting and Sewing Metaphors and a Maiden's Honor in *La Celestina*," Chapter 4 of *Folklore and Literature*. Albany: State University of New York.

Creel, Bryant. 1990. "Aesthetics of Change in a Renaissance Pastoral: New Ideals of Moral Culture in Montemayor's *Diana*." *Hispanófila* 99 (May): 1–27.

Criado de Val, Manuel. 1953. *Análisis verbal del estilo: Indices verbales de Cervantes, de Avellaneda y del autor de "La tía fingida."* Madrid: Consejo Superior de Investigaciones Científicas.

Crompton, Louis. 2003. *Homosexuality and Civilization*. Cambridge, Mass.: Harvard University Press.

———. 1980–81. "The Myth of Lesbian Impunity: Capital Laws from 1720 to 1791." *Journal of Homosexuality* 6.1/2 (Fall/Winter): 11–25.

Crusius, Timothy W. 1989. *Discourse: A Critique and Synthesis of Major Theories*. New York: Modern Language Association.

Cruz, Anne J. 1999. *Discourses of Poverty: Social Reform and the Picaresque Novel in Early Modern Spain*. Toronto: University of Toronto Press.

———. 1996. "La búsqueda de la madre: Psicoanálisis y feminismo en la literatura del Siglo de Oro." In *Historia silenciada de la mujer: La mujer española desde la época medieval hasta la contemporánea*. Ed. Alain Saint-Saëns. Madrid: Editorial Complutense, 39–64.

———. 1989a. "Sexual Enclosure, Textual Escape: The *Pícara* as Prostitute in the Spanish Female Picaresque Novel." In *Seeking the Woman in Late Medieval and Renaissance Writings: Essays in Feminist Contextual Criticism*. Ed. Sheila Fisher and Janet Halley. Knoxville: University of Tennessee Press, 135–59.

———. 1989b. "Studying Gender in the Spanish Golden Age." In *Cultural and Historical Grounding for Hispanic and Luso-Brazilian Feminist Literary Criticism*. Ed. Hernán Vidal. Minneapolis, Minn.: Institute for the Study of Ideologies and Literature, 193–222.

Cruz, Sor Juana Inés de la. 1985. "Hombres necios que acusáis." In *Poesía de la Edad de Oro*. Vol. 2, *Barroco*. Ed. José Manuel Blecua. Madrid: Castalia, 405.

Curtius, Ernst Robert. 1973. *European Literature and the Latin Middle Ages*. Trans. Willard R. Trask. Princeton, N.J.: Princeton University Press.

Damiani, Bruno, and Joan Cammarata. 1994. "La composición mitológica de *La Diana*." *Quaderni Ibero-Americani* 76 (December): 5–34.

Damiani, Bruno, and Louis Imperiale. 1991. "El erotismo en la literatura del Siglo de Oro." *Monographic Review/Revista Monográfica* 7:23–37.

D'Amico, Robert. 1982. "What Is Discourse?" *Humanities in Society* 5.3/4 (Summer/Fall): 201–12.

Daniel, Marc. 1994. "Arab Civilization and Male Love." In *Reclaiming Sodom*. Ed. Jonathan Goldberg. Trans. Winston Leyland. New York: Routledge, 59–65.

Daston, Lorraine, and Katharine Park. 1985. "Hermaphrodites in Renaissance France." *Critical Matrix* 1.5:1–19.

Dean, Tim. 2000. *Beyond Sexuality.* Chicago: University of Chicago Press.

Dekker, Rudolf M., and Lotte C. van de Pol. 1989. *The Tradition of Female Transvestism in Early Modern Europe.* Basingstoke, England: Macmillan Press.

Delamarre, Catherine, and Bertrand Sallard. 1992. *La femme au temps des conquistadores.* Paris: Stock/Pernoud.

Delgado, María José, and Alain Saint-Saëns, eds. 2000. *Lesbianism and Homosexuality in Early Modern Spain.* New Orleans: University Press of the South.

Delicado, Francisco. 1969. *La Lozana andaluza.* Ed. Bruno Damiani. Madrid: Castalia.

Delpech, François. 1986. "La 'doncella guerrera': Chansons, contes, rituels." In *Formas breves del relato.* Ed. Yves-René Fonquerne and Aurora Egido. Zaragoza, Spain: Universidad de Zaragoza, 57–86.

———. 1979. "La leyenda de la Serrana de la Vera: Las adaptaciones teatrales." In *La mujer en el teatro y la novela del siglo XVII.* Toulouse: Institut d'Études Hispaniques et Hispano-Americaines, Université de Toulouse-LeMirail, 23–36.

De Maio, Romeo. 1988. *Mujer y renacimiento.* Trans. Margarita Vivanco Geffaell. Madrid: Mondadori.

Derrida, Jacques. 1972. *La dissémination.* Paris: Seuil.

Desens, Marliss. 1994. *The Bed-Trick in English Renaissance Drama.* Newark: University of Delaware Press.

Deyermond, Alan. 1977. "Hilado-Cordón-Cadena: Symbolic Equivalence in *La Celestina.*" *Celestinesca* 1.1:6–12.

Díaz-Diocaretz, Myriam, and Iris M. Zavala, eds. 1992. *Discurso erótico y discurso transgresor en la cultura peninsular: Siglos XI al XX.* Madrid: Tuero.

Díez Fernández, J. Ignacio. 2003. *La poesía erótica de los Siglos de Oro.* Madrid: Laberinto.

———. 1995. Introduction to *Poesía erótica,* by Diego Hurtado de Mendoza. Málaga, Spain: Ediciones Aljibe, 21–98.

Díez, J. Ignacio, and Adrienne L. Martín, eds. 2006. *Venus venerada: Tradiciones eróticas de la literatura española.* Madrid: Editorial Complutense.

Dillard, Heath. 1989. *Daughters of the Reconquest: Women in Castilian Town Society, 1100–1300.* 1984. Reprint, Cambridge, England: Cambridge University Press.

Doniger, Wendy. 2000. *The Bedtrick: Tales of Sex and Masquerade.* Chicago: University of Chicago Press.

Duby, Georges, and Michelle Perrot. 1992. *Historia de las mujeres en Occidente.* Vol. 3, *Del Renacimiento a la Edad Moderna.* Ed. Arlette Farge and Natalie Zemon Davis. Trans. Marco Aurelio Galmarini. Madrid: Taurus.

Dugaw, Dianne. 1989. *Warrior Women and Popular Balladry, 1650–1850.* Cambridge, England: Cambridge University Press.

Dunn, Peter N. 1993. *Spanish Picaresque Fiction: A New Literary History.* Ithaca, N.Y.: Cornell University Press.

Eichmann, Raymond, and John DuVal, ed. and trans. 1984. *The French Fabliau B.N. Ms. 837.* New York: Garland Publishing.

Eisenbichler, Konrad, and Jacqueline Murray. 1992. Introduction to *On the Beauty of Women,* by Agnolo Firenzuola. Trans. and ed. Konrad Eisenbichler and Jacqueline Murray. Philadelphia: University of Pennsylvania Press, xiii–xli.

El Saffar, Ruth. 1989. "Sex and the Single Hidalgo: Reflections on Eros in *Don Quixote.*" In *Studies in Honor of Elias Rivers.* Ed. Bruno M. Damiani and Ruth El Saffar. Potomac, Maryland: Scripta Humanistica, 76–93.

———. 1971. "Structural and Thematic Discontinuity in Montemayor's *Diana.*" *Modern Language Notes* 86.2:182–98.

El Saffar, Ruth Anthony, and Diana de Armas Wilson, eds. 1993. *Quixotic Desire: Psychoanalytic Perspectives on Cervantes.* Ithaca, N.Y.: Cornell University Press.

Entwistle, William J. 1939. *European Balladry.* Oxford, England: Clarendon Press.

Erauso, Catalina de. 2002. *Historia de la monja alférez escrita por ella misma.* Ed. Ángel Esteban. Madrid: Cátedra.

Ericson, Kai. 1964. "Notes on the Sociology of Deviance." In *The Other Side: Perspectives on Deviance.* Ed. Howard Becker. New York: Free Press, 9–21.

Faderman, Lillian. 1981. *Surpassing the Love of Men.* New York: William Morrow.

Falcón, Lidia. 2005. "La amorosa pestilencia y los celos renacentistas: Belleza, amor cortés, sexualidad y tentación mágica." In *El* Quijote *en clave de mujer/es.* Ed. Fanny Rubio. Madrid: Editorial Complutense, 207–22.

———. 1997. *Amor, sexo y aventura en las mujeres del Quijote.* Madrid: Vindicación Feminista; Barcelona: Editorial Hacer.

Ferber, Michael. 1999. "Mountain." In *A Dictionary of Literary Symbols.* Cambridge, England: Cambridge University Press, 129–31.

Fernández de Cano y Martín, José Ramón. 1990. "Carirredonda y chata (una aproximación—honesta—a las feas del *Quijote*)." In *Actas del III Coloquio Internacional de la Asociación de Cervantistas.* Barcelona: Anthropos, 289–98.

Ferré, Rosario. 1983. "Celestina en el tejido de la *cupiditas.*" *Celestinesca* 7.1:3–16.

Ferrer, Joaquín María de, ed. 1829. *Historia de la monja alférez, Doña Catalina de Erauso, escrita por ella misma, é ilustrada con notas y documentos.* Paris: Julio Didot.

Festugière, Jean. 1941. *La philosophie de l'amour de Marsile Ficin.* Paris: Librairie Philosophique J. Vrin.

Ficino, Marsilio. 1985. *Commentary on Plato's Symposium on Love.* Trans. Sears Jayne. Dallas, Tex.: Spring Publications.

Filios, Denise. 2005. *Performing Women in the Middle Ages: Sex, Gender, and the Iberian Lyric.* New York: Palgrave Macmillan.

Firenzuola, Agnolo. 1992. *On the Beauty of Women.* Ed. and trans. Konrad Eisenbichler and Jacqueline Murray. Philadelphia: University of Pennsylvania Press.

Fisher, Will. 2006. *Materializing Gender in Early Modern English Literature and Culture.* Cambridge, England: Cambridge University Press.

Flügel, John Carl. 1966. *The Psychology of Clothes.* London: Hogarth Press.

Fosalba, Eugenia. 1994. *La Diana en Europa: Ediciones, traducciones e influencias.* Barcelona: Department de Filología Espanyola, Universitat Autonoma de Barcelona.

Foucault, Michel. 1990a. *An Introduction.* Vol. 1 of *The History of Sexuality.* New York: Vintage Books.

———. 1990b. *The Use of Pleasure.* Vol. 2 of *The History of Sexuality.* New York: Vintage Books.

———. 1980. "Truth and Power." In *Power/Knowledge: Selected Interviews and Other Writings.* Ed. Colin Gordon. Trans. Colin Gordon, Leo Marshall, John Mepham, and Kate Soper. Brighton, England: Harvester Press, 109–33.

———. 1977a. "A Preface to Transgression." In *Language, Counter-Memory, Practice.* Ed. Donald F. Bouchard. Trans. Donald F. Bouchard and Sherry Simon. Ithaca, N.Y.: Cornell University Press, 29–52.

———. 1977b. "What Is an Author?" In *Language, Counter-Memory, Practice.* Ed. Donald F. Bouchard. Trans. Donald F. Bouchard and Sherry Simon. Ithaca, N.Y.: Cornell University Press, 113–38.

———. 1972. "The Discourse on Language." In *The Archaeology of Language and the Discourse on Language.* Trans. A. M. Sheridan Smith. New York: Pantheon Books.

Foulché-Delbosc, Raymond. 1899. "Étude sur *La tía fingida.*" *Revue Hispanique* 6.17:256–306.

Fowler, Alastair. 1982. *Kinds of Literature: An Introduction to the Theory of Genres.* Cambridge, Mass.: Harvard University Press.

Fradejas Lebrero, José. 1985. *Novela corta del siglo XVI.* Barcelona: Plaza y Janés.

Frank, Manfred. 1989. "Sur le concept de discours chez Foucault." In *Michel Foucault philosophe: Rencontre Internationale Paris, 9, 10, 11 Janvier 1988.* Ed. Georges Canguilhem. Paris: Editions du Seuil, 125–36.

Frenk, Margit. 1992. "Mucho va de Pedro a Pedro (polisemia de un personaje proverbial)." In *Scripta philologica in honorem Juan M. Lope Blanch.* Ed. Elizabeth Luna Traill. Vol. 3. Mexico City: Universidad Nacional Autónoma de México, 203–20.

———. 1987. *Corpus de la antigua lírica popular hispánica (siglos XV a XVII): Nueva Biblioteca de Erudición y Crítica.* 2nd ed. Madrid: Castalia.

Frow, John. 1986. *Marxism and Literary History.* Cambridge, Mass.: Harvard University Press.

Fuente, Vicente de la. 1884–89. *Historia de las universidades, colegios y demás establecimientos de enseñanza en España*. 4 vols. Madrid: Imprenta de la Viuda e Hija de Fuente-Nebro.

Galán Sánchez, Ángel, and María Teresa López Beltrán. 1984. "El status teórico de las prostitutas del reino de Granada en la primera mitad del siglo XVI (las ordenanzas de 1536)." In *Las mujeres en las ciudades medievales*. Ed. Cristina Segura Graíño. Madrid: Universidad Autónoma de Madrid, 161–69.

García López, Jorge, ed. 2001. *Novelas ejemplares,* by Miguel de Cervantes. Barcelona: Cátedra.

Garber, Marjorie. 1992. *Vested Interests: Cross-Dressing and Cultural Anxiety.* New York: Routledge.

García Barrientos, José Luis. 2004. *Teatro y ficción*. Madrid: Fundamentos.

Genouy, Hector. 1928. *L'Arcadia de Sidney dans ses rapports avec l'Arcadia de Sannazaro et* La Diana *de Montemayor.* Paris: Didier.

Gibert Cardona, Jorge María. 1986. "Del romance de la doncella guerrera a la escenificación de Rafael Dieste." In *La juglaresca*. (Actas del I Congreso Internacional sobre la Juglaresca.) Ed. Manuel Criado de Val. Madrid: EDI-6, 495–502.

Gilbert, Arthur N. 1980–81. "Conceptions of Homosexuality and Sodomy in Western History." *Journal of Homosexuality* 6.1/2 (Fall/Winter): 57–68.

Gilbert, Sandra. 1982. "Costumes of the Mind: Transvestism as Metaphor in Modern Literature." In *Writing and Sexual Difference*. Ed. Elizabeth Abel. Chicago: University of Chicago Press, 193–219.

Girard, René. 2000. *The Girard Reader*. Ed. James G. Williams. New York: Crossroad Publishing.

Goldberg, Harriet. 1998. *Motif-Index of Medieval Spanish Folk Narratives*. Tempe, Ariz.: Medieval and Renaissance Texts and Studies.

Goldberg, Jonathan, ed. 1994. *Reclaiming Sodom*. New York: Routledge.

Gómez Canseco, Luis, Pablo L. Zambrano, and Laura P. Alonso, eds. 1997. *El sexo en la literatura*. Huelva, Spain: Universidad de Huelva.

Góngora, Luis de. 1975. *Sonetos completos*. Ed. Biruté Ciplijauskaité. Madrid: Castalia.

———. 1967. *Obras completas*. Ed. Juan Millé y Giménez and Isabel Millé y Giménez. 6th ed. Madrid: Aguilar.

González, José Emilio. 1993. *De aventura con Don Quijote (ensayos y exploraciones)*. Río Piedras: Editorial de la Universidad de Puerto Rico.

González Echevarría, Roberto. 2005. *Love and the Law in Cervantes*. New Haven, Conn.: Yale University Press.

Goodheart, Eugene. 1991. "Desire and Its Discontents." In *Desire and Its Discontents*. New York: Columbia University Press, 113–41.

Gossy, Mary S. 1993. "'The Pretended Aunt': Misreading and the Scandal of the Missing Mothers." In *Quixotic Desire*. Ed. Ruth Anthony El Saffar and Diana de Armas Wilson. Ithaca, N.Y.: Cornell University Press, 255–63.

———. 1989. "Voyeurism and Paternity: Reading *La tía fingida*," In *The Untold Story: Women and Theory in Golden Age Texts*. Ann Arbor: University of Michigan Press, 83–109.

Gotor, José Luis. 1980. "Fray Melchor de la Serna, poeta 'ovidiano' inédito del siglo XVI." In *Codici della trasgressività in area ispanica: Atti del Convegno di Verona*. Verona: Università degli Studi di Padova, Facoltá di Economia e Commercio, 143–65.

Goytisolo, Juan. 1978. "Quevedo y la obsesión excremental." In *Disidencias*. Barcelona: Seix Barral, 117–35.

Graña Cid, María del Mar. 1999. "Palabra escrita y experiencia femenina en el siglo XVI." In *Escribir y leer en el siglo de Cervantes*. Ed. Antonio Castillo. Prol. Armando Petrucci. Barcelona: Gedisa, 211–42.

Graullera Sanz, Vicente. 1994. "Delincuencia y vida cotidiana en el burdel de Valencia del siglo XVI." In *La prostitution en Espagne de l'époque des Rois Catholiques à la IIe République*. Ed. Raphaël Carrasco. Paris: Belles Lettres, 67–80.

Greenberg, David F. 1988. *The Construction of Homosexuality*. Chicago: University of Chicago Press.

Greenblatt, Stephen. 1988. "Erotische Provokation im Elizabethanischen Theater." *Shakespeare Jahrbuch* 124:56–61.

Grosz, Elizabeth. 1994. *Volatile Bodies: Toward a Corporeal Feminism*. Bloomington: Indiana University Press.

Gruzinski, Serge. 1986. "Las cenizas del deseo: Homosexuales novohispanos a mediados del siglo XVII." In *De la santidad a la perversión o de porqué no se cumplía la ley de Dios en la sociedad novohispana*. Ed. Sergio Ortega. Mexico City: Grijalbo, 255–81.

Halperin, David M. 1990. *One Hundred Years of Homosexuality*. New York: Routledge.

Handy, Otis. 1983. "The Rhetorical and Psychological Defloration of Melibea." *Celestinesca* 7.1:17–27.

Hebreo, León. 1953. *Diálogos de amor*. Trans. David Romano. Barcelona: José Janés Editor.

Heiple, Daniel L. 1997. "*El lindo don Diego* and the Question of Homosexual Desire." In *Hispanic Essays in Honor of Frank P. Casa*. Ed. A. Robert Lauer and Henry W. Sullivan. New York: Peter Lang, 306–15.

Hernández Hernández, Delfín, and Luis Martínez Terrón. 1993. *La Serrana de la Vera: Antología y romancero*. Cáceres, Spain: Asociación Cultural "Amigos de la Vera."

Herrero García, Miguel. 1966. *Ideas de los españoles del siglo XVII*. Madrid: Gredos.

Highet, Gilbert. 1962. *The Anatomy of Satire*. Princeton, N.J.: Princeton University Press.

Hocquenghem, Guy. 1993. *Homosexual Desire.* Trans. Daniella Dangoor. Durham, N.C.: Duke University Press.

Horn, Pierre L., and Mary Beth Pringle. 1984. *The Image of the Prostitute in Modern Literature.* New York: Frederick Ungar.

Hsu, Carmen. 2002. *Courtesans in the Literature of the Spanish Golden Age.* Kassel, Germany: Reichenberger.

Huerta Calvo, Javier. 1995. *El nuevo mundo de la risa: Estudios sobre el teatro breve y la comicidad en los siglos de oro.* Palma de Mallorca, Spain: Oro Viejo.

———. 1990. "Risa y eros: Del erotismo en los entremeses." *Edad de Oro* 9:113–23.

Hurtado de Mendoza, Diego. 1995. *Poesía erótica.* Ed. J. Ignacio Díez Fernández. Málaga, Spain: Ediciones Aljibe.

Hutchinson, Steven. 2001. *Economía ética en Cervantes.* Alcalá de Henares, Spain: Centro de Estudios Cervantinos.

Icaza, Francisco A. de. 1916. *De cómo y por qué "La tía fingida" no es de Cervantes y otros nuevos estudios cervantinos.* Madrid: Imprenta Clásica Española.

Jacquart, Danielle, and Claude Thomasset. 1989. *Sexualidad y saber médico en la Edad Media.* Trans. José Luis Gil Aristu. Barcelona: Labor.

Jammes, Robert. 1980. "La risa y su función social en el Siglo de Oro." In *Risa y sociedad en el teatro español del Siglo de Oro.* Paris: Centre National de la Recherche Scientifique, 3–11.

Jauralde Pou, Pablo, ed. 1990. *El erotismo y la literatura clásica española. Edad de Oro* 9.

Jelinek, Estelle C. 1987. "Disguise Autobiographies: Women Masquerading as Men." *Women's Studies International Forum* 10.1:53–62.

Johnson, Carroll B. 1995. "*Amor aliqua vincit:* Erotismo y amor en *La Diana.*" In *Erotismo en las letras hispánicas: Aspectos, modos y fronteras.* Ed. Luce López Baralt and Francisco Márquez Villanueva. Mexico City: Colegio de Mexico, 165–81.

———. 1983. *Madness and Lust: A Psychoanalytical Approach to "Don Quixote."* Berkeley and Los Angeles: University of California Press.

Joly, Monique. 1982. *La bourle et son interprétation: Recherches sur le passage de la facetie au roman (Espagne, XVIe—XVIIe siècles).* Lille, France: Université de Lille III.

Jones, Ann Rosalind, and Peter Stallybrass. 2000. *Renaissance Clothing and the Materials of Memory.* Cambridge, England: Cambridge University Press.

Jordan, William B., Jr. 1967. "Juan Van der Hamen y León." Ph.D. diss., New York University.

Kamen, Henry. 1985. *Inquisition and Society in Spain in the Sixteenth and Seventeenth Centuries.* Bloomington: Indiana University Press.

Karlen, Arno. 1971. "The Homosexual Heresy." *Chaucer Review* 6 (Summer): 44–63.

Katz, Jonathan Ned. 1994. "The Age of Sodomitical Sin, 1607–1740." In *Reclaiming Sodom*. Ed. Jonathan Goldberg. New York: Routledge, 43–58.

Kettering, Alison McNeil. 2004. Selection on "Gallant Conversation." In *Gerard ter Borch*. Ed. Arthur K. Wheelock, Jr. With contributions by Alison McNeil Kettering, Arie Wallert, and Marjorie E. Wieseman. Catalog of an exhibition held at the National Gallery of Art, Washington, D.C., and at the Detroit Institute of Arts, 2004–2005. Washington, D.C.: National Gallery of Art/ New York: American Federation of Arts, 114–17.

Kristeller, Paul Oskar. 1964. *The Philosophy of Marcilio Ficino*. Trans. Virginia Conant. Gloucester, Mass.: Peter Smith.

Kristeva, Julia. 1980. *Desire in Language: A Semiotic Approach to Literature and Art*. Ed. and trans. Leon Roudiez. New York: Columbia University Press.

Labrador Herraiz, José J. 1989. "La novela en verso en los cancioneros manuscritos del siglo XVI." *Reales Sitios* 36.100:49–64.

Labrador Herraiz, José J., and Ralph A. DiFranco, eds. 1989. *Cancionero de poesías varias: Ms. 2803 de la Biblioteca del Palacio Real de Madrid*. Prol. Maxime Chevalier. Madrid: Editorial Patrimonio Nacional.

Labrador Herraiz, José J., Ralph A. DiFranco, and Lori A. Bernard, eds. 2001. *Poesías de Fray Melchor de la Serna y otros poetas del siglo XVI: Códice 20.028 de la Biblioteca Nacional de Madrid*. Prol. José Lara Garrido. Málaga, Spain: Analecta Malacitana.

———. 1997. *Manuscrito Fuentelsol (Madrid, Palacio II-973)*. Cleveland: Cleveland State University.

Lacarra, María Eugenia. 1993. "La evolución de la prostitución en la Castilla del siglo XV y la mancebía de Salamana en tiempos de Fernando de Rojas." In *Fernando de Rojas and* Celestina. Ed. Ivy A. Corfis y Joseph T. Snow. Madison, Wis.: Hispanic Seminary of Medieval Studies, 33–78.

Laqueur, Thomas. 1990. *Making Sex: Body and Gender from the Greeks to Freud*. Cambridge, Mass.: Harvard University Press.

Lavrin, Asunción, ed. 1989. *Sexuality and Marriage in Colonial Latin America*. Lincoln: University of Nebraska Press.

León, Fray Luis de. 1992. *La perfecta casada*. Ed. Javier San José Lera. Madrid: Espasa Calpe.

León, Nicolás. 1973. *Aventuras de la monja alférez*. Mexico City: Complejo Editorial Mexicano.

León, S. J., Pedro de. 1981. *Grandeza y miseria en Andalucía: Testimonio de una encrucijada histórica (1578–1761)*. Ed. Pedro Herrera Puga, S. J. Prol. Antonio Domínguez Ortiz. Granada, Spain: Universidad de Granada, Facultad de Teología.

Lissorgues, Yvan. 1978. "Obras de burlas de Fray Melchor de la Serna: I—La novela de las madejas." *Criticón* 3:1–27.

Lloyd, A. C. 1990. *The Anatomy of Neoplatonism*. Oxford, England: Clarendon Press.

Lockyer, Roger. 1981. *Buckingham: The Life and Political Career of George Villiers, First Duke of Buckingham, 1592–1628.* London: Longman.

López, Gregorio. 1829–31. *Las siete partidas del sabio rey Don Alonso el Nono, nuevamente glosadas por el licenciado Gregorio López.* 1565. Reprint, Salamanca, Spain: A. de Portonaris.

López-Baralt, Luce, and Francisco Márquez Villanueva. 1995a. Introduction to *Erotismo en las letras hispánicas: Aspectos, modos y fronteras.* Mexico City: Colegio de México, 9–16.

————, eds. 1995b. *Erotismo en las letras hispánicas: Aspectos, modos y fronteras.* Mexico City: Colegio de México.

López Beltrán, María Teresa. 1987. "Evolución de la prostitución en el reino de Granada a través de las ordenanzas de la mancebía de Ronda." In *Realidad histórica e invención literaria en torno a la mujer.* Ed. María Teresa López Beltrán et al. Málaga, Spain: Servicio de Publicaciones, Diputación Provincial de Málaga, 9–23

López Estrada, Francisco. 1985. "El romance de la doncella guerrera en el Cancionero de Antequera." In *Serta gratulatoria in honorem Juan Régulo I.* La Laguna, Spain: Universidad de La Laguna, 405–9.

MacDonell, Diane. 1986. *Theories of Discourse.* Oxford, England: Basil Blackwell.

Madrigal, José Luis. 2003. "De cómo y por qué *La tía fingida* es de Cervantes." *Artifara* 2 (January–June). Available at *www.artifara.com/Rivisa2/testi/tiafingida.asp.*

Malo, Fray [pseud.]. 1985. *Chapitu de Baratiyo; Ramillete breve de diversas flores compuesto para adorno en el altar de Príapo.* Ed. Pedro Roso and Esteban Díaz. Córdoba, Spain: Cuadernos de Albenda.

Margouliès, G. 1928. "Deux poèmes sur la jeune fille partie a la guerre pour remplacer son père." *Revue de Littérature Comparée* 8:304–9.

Marino, Nancy. 1987. *La serranilla española: Notas para su historia e interpretación.* Potomac, Md.: Scripta Humanistica.

Márquez Villanueva, Francisco. 2005. "La cuestión del judaísmo de Cervantes." In *Don Quijote en el reino de la fantasía: Realidad y ficción en el universo mental y biográfico de Cervantes.* Ed. Rogelio Reyes Cano. Seville, Spain: Fundación Focus Abengoa, 51–73.

————. 1993. *Orígenes y sociología del tema celestinesco.* Barcelona: Anthropos.

————. 1990. "*La tía fingida:* Literatura universitaria." In *On Cervantes: Essays for L.A. Murillo.* Ed. James A. Parr. Newark, Del.: Juan de la Cuesta, 119–48.

————. 1987. "Pan 'pudendum muliebris' y 'Los españoles en Flandes.'" In *Hispanic Studies in Honor of Joseph H. Silverman.* Newark, Del.: Juan de la Cuesta, 247–69.

Martín, Adrienne L. 2005. "Challenges and Rewards of Teaching Erotic Poetry." *Calíope* 11.2:81–90.

————. 2002. "Góngora, 'poeta de bujarrones.'" *Calíope* 8.1:141–60.

_____. 1999. "Rereading *El amante liberal* in the Age of Contrapuntal Sexualities." In *Cervantes and His Postmodern Constituencies.* Ed. Anne J. Cruz and Carroll B. Johnson. New York: Garland Publishing, 151–69.

———. 1998. "Hacia el Cervantes del siglo que termina." In *Estudios sobre literatura española de los siglos XIX y XX: Homenaje a Juan María Díez Taboada.* Ed. José Carlos de Torres Martínez and Cecilia García Antón. Madrid: Consejo Superior de Investigaciones Científicas, 617–22.

———. 1997. "The Rhetoric of Female Friendship in the Lyric of Sor Violante del Cielo." *Calíope* 3.2:56–71.

———. 1995. "Images of Deviance in Cervantes's Algiers." *Cervantes* 15.2:5–15.

———. 1991. *Cervantes and the Burlesque Sonnet.* Berkeley and Los Angeles: University of California Press.

_____, ed. 2006. *La poesía erótica del Siglo de Oro: Crítica y antología. Calíope* 12.2.

Martín, Adrienne L., and J. Ignacio Díez Fernández, eds. 2007. *Venus venerada II: Literatura erótica y modernidad en España.* Madrid: Editorial Complutense.

_____. 2003. *La poesía erótica de Fray Melchor de la Serna. Canente Revista Literaria* (Málaga, Spain) 5–6.

Martínez-Góngora, Mar. 1999. *Discursos sobre la mujer en el humanismo renacentista español: Los casos de Antonio de Guevara, Alfonso y Juan de Valdés y Luis de León.* York, S.C.: Spanish Literature Publications.

Martínez-López, Enrique. 1995. "Erotismo y ejemplaridad en *El viejo celoso* de Cervantes." In *Erotismo en las letras hispánicas: Aspectos, modos y fronteras.* Ed. Luce López Baralt and Francisco Márquez Villanueva. Mexico City: Colegio de México, 335–85.

Mas, Amédée. 1957. *La caricature de la femme du mariage et de l'amour dans l'oeuvre de Quevedo.* Paris: Ediciones Hispano-Americanas.

Maurer, Christopher. 1990. "'Soñé que te . . . ¿Dirélo?' El soneto del sueño erótico en los siglos XVI y XVII." *Edad de Oro* 9:149–67.

McCall, Andrew. 1991. *The Medieval Underworld.* 1979. Reprint, New York: Dorset Press.

McFarlane, Cameron. 1997. *The Sodomite in Fiction and Satire,1660–1750.* New York: Columbia University Press.

McGrady, Donald. 1981. "El origen italiano de 'Los calzones de San Francisco' por Samaniego." *Dieciocho* 4.2:167–73.

———. 1978. *The Story of the Painter and His Little Lamb.* Bogotá, Colombia: Instituto Caro y Cuervo.

———. 1968. "Sources and Significance of the Novelas del Licenciado Tamariz." *Romanic Review* 59:10–15.

Medina, José Toribio. 1970. "La historia de América como fuente del teatro antiguo español." In *Estudios sobre literatura colonial de Chile*. Vol. 2. Ed. Guillermo Feliu Cruz. 1915. Reprint, Santiago, Chile: Fondo Histórico y Bibliográfico José Toribio Medina, 35–169.

———. 1952. "Modo de proceder del Santo Oficio." In *Ensayos*. Santiago, Chile: Editorial del Pacífico, 119–35.

Menéndez Pidal, Ramón. 1976. *Flor nueva de romances viejos*. Madrid: Espasa-Calpe.

———. 1968. *Romancero hispánico*. 2 vols. Madrid: Espasa Calpe.

Menéndez y Pelayo, Marcelino. 1961. *Orígenes de la novela*. Ed. Enrique Sánchez. 4 vols. Madrid: Consejo Superior de Investigaciones Científicas.

———. 1900. *Suplemento a la "Primavera y flor de romances" de Wolf*. In *Antología de poetas líricos castellanos*. Vol. 10. Madrid: Hernando.

Menjot, Denis. 1994. "Prostitutas y rufianes en las ciudades castellanas a fines de la Edad Media." *Temas Medievales* 4:189–204.

Merrim, Stephanie. 1994. "Catalina de Erauso: From Anomaly to Icon." In *Coded Encounters: Writing, Gender, and Ethnicity in Colonial Latin America*. Ed. Francisco Cevallos et al. Amherst: University of Massachusetts Press, 177–205.

Meyerson, Mark. 1991. *The Muslims of Valencia in the Age of Fernando and Isabel*. Berkeley and Los Angeles: University of California Press.

Meyland, Edouard F. 1938. "L'evolution de la notion d'amour platonique." *Humanisme et Renaissance* 5:418–22.

Mignolo, Walter. 1982. "Cartas, crónicas y relaciones del descubrimiento y la conquista." In *Historia de la Literatura Hispanoamericana*. Vol. 1, *Epoca colonial*. Ed. Luis Iñigo Madrigal. Madrid: Cátedra, 57–116.

———. 1981. "El metatexto historiográfico y la historiografía indiana." *Modern Language Notes* 96.2 (March): 358–402.

Molina Molina, Ángel Luis. 1998. *Mujeres públicas, mujeres secretas*. Murcia, Spain: Editorial KR.

Montemayor, Jorge de. 1991. *Los siete libros de la Diana*. Ed. Asunción Rallo. Madrid: Cátedra.

Monter, William. 1990. *Frontiers of Heresy: The Spanish Inquisition from the Basque Lands to Sicily*. Cambridge, England: Cambridge University Press.

Morales, Gregorio. 1998. *Antología de la literatura erótica*. Madrid: Espasa Calpe.

Moreno Mengíbar, Andrés, and Francisco Vázquez García. 1999. *Crónica de una marginación: Historia de la prostitución en Andalucía (siglos XII–XX)*. Cádiz, Spain: Junta de Andalucía.

Nalle, Sara T. 1989. "Literacy and Culture in Early Modern Castile." *Past and Present* 125 (November): 65–96.

Navarrete, Ignacio. 1994. *Orphans of Petrarch*. Berkeley and Los Angeles: University of California Press.

Nelson, John Charles. 1958. *Renaissance Theory of Love*. New York: Columbia University Press.

Nelson, William. 1973. *Fact or Fiction: The Dilemma of the Renaissance Storyteller.* Cambridge, Mass.: Harvard University Press.

Niccoli, Ottavia. 1990. "'Menstruum Quasi Monstruum': Monstrous Births and Menstrual Taboo in the Sixteenth Century." In *Sex and Gender in Historical Perspective.* Ed. Edward Muir and Guido Ruggiero. Baltimore: Johns Hopkins University Press, 1–25.

Norton, Rictor. 1997. *The Myth of the Modern Homosexual.* London: Cassell.

Núñez Roldán, Francisco. 2002. *El pecado nefando del Obispo de Salamina: Un hombre sin concierto en la corte de Felipe II.* Seville, Spain: Universidad de Sevilla.

Odd, Frank L. 1983. "Women of the *Romancero:* A Voice of Reconciliation." *Hispania* 66.3 (September): 360–68.

Oehrlein, Josef. 1993. *El actor en el teatro español del Siglo de Oro.* Trans. Miguel Ángel Vega. Madrid: Castalia.

Olivares, Julián. 2000. Introduction to *Novelas amorosas y ejemplares,* by María de Zayas y Sotomayor. Ed. Julián Olivares. Madrid: Cátedra, 9–135.

Olivares, Julián, and Elizabeth S. Boyce, eds. 1993. *Tras el espejo la musa escribe: Lírica femenina de los Siglos de Oro.* Madrid: Siglo Veintiuno de España.

Oltra Tomás, José Miguel. 1996. "Bromas y ¿veras? Sobre el sexo heterodoxo en el siglo XVII." In *Los territorios literarios de la historia del placer: Primer Coloquio de Erótica Hispana (Montilla, Casa del Inca, 18–20, junio, 1993).* Ed. José Antonio Cerezo, Daniel Eisenberg, and Víctor Infantes. Madrid: Huerga y Fierro, 151–73.

Orozco y Berra, Manuel. 1853–56. *Gran diccionario universal.* Mexico City: Tipografía de R. Rafael.

O'Sullivan-Beare, Nancy. ca. 1956. *Las mujeres de los conquistadores: La mujer española en los comienzos de la colonización americana (aportaciones para el estudio de la trasculturación).* Madrid: Compañía Bibliográfica Española.

Ovid. 1984. *Metamorphoses.* Trans. Frank Justus Miller. 2 vols. 1916. Reprint, Loeb Classical Library. Cambridge, Mass.: Harvard University Press.

———. 1982. *The Erotic Poems.* Trans. Peter Green. London: Penguin Books.

Pagden, Anthony. 1993. "The Principle of Attachment." In *European Encounters with the New World.* New Haven, Conn.: Yale University Press, 17–49.

Palacios Fernández, Emilio. 2006. "Panorama de la literatura erótica del siglo XVIII." In *Venus venerada: Tradiciones eróticas de la literatura española.* Ed. J. Ignacio Díez and Adrienne L. Martín. Madrid: Editorial Complutense, 191–239.

Park, Katharine, and Robert A. Nye. 1991. "Destiny Is Anatomy." *New Republic,* 18 February, 53–57.

Parker, Alexander A. 1985. *The Philosophy of Love in Spanish Literature, 1480–1680.* Edinburgh: Edinburgh University Press.

Pellicer, José. 1965. *Avisos históricos.* Madrid: Taurus.

Pérez, Janet, and Genaro J. Pérez. 1991. *Hispanic Marginal Literatures: The Erotic, The Comics, Novela Rosa. Monographic Review/Revista Monográfica* 7.

Perry, Mary Elizabeth. 1999. "From Convent to Battlefield: Cross-Dressing and the Self in the New World of Imperial Spain." In *Queer Iberia.* Ed. Josiah Blackmore and Gregory S. Hutcheson. Durham, N.C.: Duke University Press, 394–419.

———. 1990. *Gender and Disorder in Early Modern Seville.* Princeton, N.J.: Princeton University Press.

———. 1989. "The 'Nefarious Sin' in Early Modern Seville." In *The Pursuit of Sodomy: Male Homosexuality in Renaissance and Enlightenment Europe.* Ed. Kent Gerard and Gert Hekma. New York: Haworth Press, 67–89.

———. 1987a. "The Manly Woman: A Historical Case Study." *American Behavioral Scientist* 31.1 (September–October): 86–100.

———. 1987b. "*La monja alférez:* Myth, Gender, and the Manly Woman in a Spanish Renaissance Drama." In *La Chispa '87: Selected Proceedings.* Ed. Gilbert Paolini. New Orleans: Tulane University, 239–49.

———. 1985. "Deviant Insiders: Legalized Prostitutes and a Consciousness of Women in Early Modern Seville." *Comparative Studies in Society and History* 27:138–58.

———. 1980. *Crime and Society in Early Modern Seville.* Hanover, N.H.: University Press of New England.

———. 1978. "Lost Women in Early Modern Seville: The Politics of Prostitution." *Feminist Studies* 4.1 (February): 195–214.

Petrov, Krinka Vidakovic. 1993. "La Doncella Guerrera." *Jewish Folklore and Ethnology Review* 15.2:23–28.

Pinto Crespo, Virgilio. 1983. Inquisición y control ideológico en la España del siglo XVI. Madrid: Taurus.

Poggioli, Renato. 1975. *The Oaten Flute.* Cambridge, Mass.: Harvard University Press.

Pollard, Arthur. 1970. *Satire.* London: Methuen.

Portús Pérez, Javier. 1998. *La sala reservada del Museo del Prado y el coleccionismo de pintura de desnudo en la corte española, 1554–1838.* Madrid: Museo del Prado.

Prince, Gerald. 1988. "The Disnarrated." *Style* 22.1:1–8.

Profeti, Maria Grazia. 1994. "Mujer libre—mujer perdida: Una nueva imagen de la prostituta a fines del siglo XVI y principios del XVII." In *Images de la femme en Espagne aux XVIe et XVIIe siècles.* Ed. Augustin Redondo. Paris: Presses de la Sorbonne Nouvelle, 195–205.

———. 1992. "La escena erótica de los siglos áureos: Poesía novela teatro." In *Discurso erótico y discurso transgresor en la cultura peninsular: Siglos XI al XX.* Ed. Myriam Díaz-Diocaretz and Iris M. Zavala. Madrid: Ediciones Tuero, 57–89.

———. 1984. *Quevedo: La scrittura e il corpo.* Rome: Bulzoni.

————. 1982. "La obsesión anal en la poesía de Quevedo." In *Actas del VII Congreso de la Asociación Internacional de Hispanistas.* Rome: Bulzoni, 837–45.

————. 1980. "Il corpo attraente-il corpo repellente." In *Codici della trasgressività in area ispanica: Atti del Convegno di Verona.* Verona: Università degli Studi di Padova, Facoltá di Economia e Commercio, 95–115.

Puig, Angelina, and Nuria Tuset. 1986. "La prostitución en Mallorca (s. XVI): ¿El estado un alcahuete?" In *Ordenamiento jurídico y realidad social de las mujeres: Siglos XVI a XX.* Ed. María Carmen García-Nieto Paris. Madrid: Ediciones de la Universidad Autónoma de Madrid, 71–82.

Pumar Martínez, Carmen. 1988. *Españolas en Indias: Mujeres-soldado, adelantadas y gobernadoras.* Madrid: Ediciones Anaya.

Quevedo, Francisco de. 1991. *Gracias y desgracias del ojo del culo.* Alicante, Spain: Alcodre Ediciones.

————. 1990. *Poesía original completa.* Ed. José Manuel Blecua. Barcelona: Planeta.

————. 1982. *La vida del Buscón, llamado Don Pablos.* Ed. Domingo Ynduráin. Madrid: Cátedra.

————. 1969–81. *Obra poética.* Ed. José Manuel Blecua. 4 vols. Madrid: Castalia.

————. 1963. *Obras completas.* Vol. 1. Ed. José Manuel Blecua. Barcelona: Planeta.

Quintero, María Cristina. 2003. "La musa maculada de Fray Melchor de la Serna." *La poesía erótica de Fray Melchor de la Serna. Canente Revista Literaria.* (Málaga, Spain) 5–6:197–210.

————. 1996. "The Rhetoric of Desire and Misogyny in *Jardín de Venus.*" *Calíope* 2.2:51–69.

Ramírez de Guzmán, Catalina Clara. 2004. *Obras poéticas.* 1929. *Poesías de doña Catalina Clara Ramírez de Guzmán.* Ed. Joaquín de Entrambasaguas y Peña. Badajoz, Spain: Imprenta de Antonio Arqueros. Reprint, Brenes (Sevilla), Spain: Muñoz Moya Editores Extremeños.

Redondo, Augustin, ed. 1985. *Amours légitimes: Amours illégitimes en Espagne (XVIe–XVIIe siècles).* Paris: Sorbonne.

————. 1983. "De molinos, molineros y molineras: Tradiciones folklóricas y literatura en la España del Siglo de Oro." In *Literatura y folklore: Problemas de intertextualidad.* Ed. J. J. Alonso Hernández. Salamanca, Spain: Universidad de Salamanca, 101–15.

Rey Hazas, Antonio. 1990. "Cervantes, el *Quijote* y la poética de la libertad." In *Actas del I Coloquio Internacional de la Asociación de Cervantistas.* Barcelona: Anthropos, 369–80.

Reyes Peña, Mercedes de los. 1998. "En torno a la actriz Jusepa Vaca." In *Las mujeres en la sociedad española del Siglo de Oro: Ficción teatral y realidad histórica.* Granada, Spain: Universidad de Granada, 81–114.

Rhodes, Elizabeth. 1992. *The Unrecognized Precursors of Montemayor's "Diana."* Columbia: University of Missouri Press.

———. 1987. "Skirting the Men: Gender Roles in Sixteenth-Century Pastoral Books." *Journal of Hispanic Philology* 11.2 (Winter): 131–49.

Richlin, Amy. 1992. *The Garden of Priapus: Sexuality and Aggression in Roman Humor.* Rev. ed. New York: Oxford University Press.

Riello, Giorgio, and Peter McNeil, eds. 2006. *Shoes: A History from Sandals to Sneakers.* Oxford, England: Berg.

Robb, Nesca A. 1935. *Neoplatonism of the Italian Renaissance.* London: Allen and Unwin.

Rodríguez Moñino, Antonio. 1968. *Critical Reconstruction vs. Historical Reality of Spanish Poetry in the Golden Age.* Trans. Lesley Byrd Simpson. Berkeley, Calif.: Lawton and Alfred Kennedy. (Translation of *Construcción crítica y realidad histórica en la poesía española de los siglos XVI y XVII.* Madrid: Castalia, 1965.)

———, ed. 1956. *Novelas y cuentos en verso del Licenciado Tamariz (Siglo XVI).* Valencia, Spain: "… la fonte que mana y corre."

Rodríguez Puértolas, Julio, ed. 1984. *Poesía crítica y satírica del siglo XV.* Madrid: Castalia.

Rosales, Luis. 1960. *Cervantes y la libertad.* 2 vols. Madrid: Sociedad de Estudios y Publicaciones.

Rose, Margaret A. 1993. *Parody: Ancient, Modern, and Post-Modern.* Cambridge, England: Cambridge University Press.

Rose, Mary Beth. 1986. "Gender, Genre, and History: Seventeenth-Century English Women and the Art of Autobiography." In *Women in the Middle Ages and the Renaissance.* Syracuse, N.Y.: Syracuse University Press, 245–78.

Rossiaud, Jacques. 1988. *Medieval Prostitution.* Trans. Lydia G. Cochrane. New York: Basil Blackwell.

Roth, Norman. 1982. "'Deal Gently with the Young Man': Love of Boys in Medieval Hebrew Poetry of Spain." *Speculum* 57.1 (January): 20–51.

Rotunda, Dominic Peter. 1942. *Motif-Index of the Italian Novella in Prose.* Bloomington: Indiana University Press.

Rouhi, Leyla. 1999. *Mediation and Love: A Study of the Medieval Go-Between in Key Romance and Near-Eastern Texts.* Leiden, Netherlands: Brill.

Rowson, Everett K. 1991. "The Categorization of Gender and Sex Irregularity in Medieval Arabic Vice Lists." In *Body Guards: The Cultural Politics of Gender Ambiguity.* Ed. Julia Epstein and Kristina Straub. New York: Routledge, 50–79.

Ruano de la Haza, José María. 2000. *La puesta en escena en los teatros comerciales del Siglo de Oro.* Madrid: Castalia.

Ruggiero, Guido. 1985. *The Boundaries of Eros: Sex Crime and Sexuality in Renaissance Venice.* New York: Oxford University Press.

Ruiz, Juan (Arcipreste de Hita). 1988. *Libro de buen amor*. Ed. G. B. Gybbon-Monypenny. Madrid: Castalia.

———. 1972. *Libro de buen amor*. Ed., intro. and trans. Raymond S. Willis. Princeton, N.J.: Princeton University Press.

Ruiz, Teofilo F. 2001. *Spanish Society, 1400–1600*. Harlow, England: Longman.

Ruse, Michael. 1995. "Is Homosexuality Bad Sexuality?" In *Philosophical Perspectives on Sex and Love*. Ed. Robert M. Stewart. New York: Oxford University Press, 113–24.

Salmón, Fernando, and Montserrat Cabré. 1998. "Fascinating Women: The Evil Eye in Medical Scholasticism." In *Medicine from the Black Death to the French Disease*. Ed. Roger French, et al. Aldershot, England: Ashgate, 53–84.

Samaniego, Félix María de. 2004. *El jardín de Venus*. Ed. Emilio Palacios Fernández. Madrid: Biblioteca Nueva.

Sánchez Ortega, María Helena. 1995. *Pecadoras de verano, arrepentidas en invierno*. Madrid: Alianza.

San Jerónimo, Magdalena de, and Teresa Valle de la Cerda. 1991. *Cárceles y mujeres en el siglo XVII: Razón y forma de la Galera. Proceso Inquisitorial de San Plácido*. Ed. Isabel Barbeito. Madrid: Castalia.

Sanponts y Barba, Ignacio, Ramón Martí de Eixalá, and José Ferrer y Subirana, eds. 1843–44. *Las siete partidas del rey Don Alfonso el IX con las variantes de más interés, y con la glosa de Gregorio López; vertida al castellano y estensamente adicionada con nuevas notas y comentarios y unas tablas sinópticas comparativas, sobre la legislación española, antigua y moderna, hasta su actual estado*. 4 vols. Barcelona: A. Bergnes.

Sanz Hermida, Jacobo. 1996. "Ensoñación y transformismo: La parodia erótica en *El sueño de la viuda* de fray Melchor de la Serna." In *Studia Aurea: Actas del III Congreso de la AISO*. Vol. 1. Pamplona, Spain: GRISO; Toulouse, France: Université de Toulouse, 513–23.

Saslow, James M. 1988. "'A Veil of Ice between My Heart and the Fire': Michelangelo's Sexual Identity and Early Modern Constructs of Homosexuality." *Genders* 2 (Summer): 77–90.

Schleiner, Winfried. 2000. "Early Modern Controversies about the One-Sex Model." *Renaissance Quarterly* 53:180–91.

———. 1994. "'That Matter Which Ought Not to Be Heard Of': Homophobic Slurs in Renaissance Cultural Politics." *Journal of Homosexuality* 26.4:41–75.

Schwartz, Regina, and Valeria Finucci. 1994. Introduction to *Desire in the Renaissance: Psychoanalysis and Literature*. Ed. Valeria Finucci and Regina Schwartz. Princeton, N.J.: Princeton University Press, 3–15.

Sedgwick, Eve Kosofsky. 1990. *Epistemology of the Closet*. Berkeley and Los Angeles: University of California Press.

———. 1985. *Between Men: English Literature and Male Homosocial Desire*. New York: Columbia University Press.

Serna, Fray Melchor de la. 1976. *Sueño de la viuda*. Ed. Luis Montañés. Madrid: Gisa Ediciones.

Serralta, Frédéric. 1990. "Juan Rana homosexual." *Criticón* 50:81–92.

Serrano y Sanz, Manuel. 1975. *Apuntes para una biblioteca de escritoras españolas.* Pt. 2, vol. 1. Madrid: Atlas.

Shell, Marc. 1993. *The Economy of Literature*. Baltimore: Johns Hopkins University Press.

Shipley, George. 1996. "'Otras cosillas que no digo': Lazarillo's Dirty Sex." In *The Picaresque: Tradition and Displacement.* Ed. Giancarlo Maiorini. Minneapolis: University of Minnesota Press, 40–65.

Short, John Rennie. 1991. *Imagined Country: Environment, Culture and Society.* London: Routledge.

Sieber, Harry. 1978. *Language and Society in "La vida de Lazarillo de Tormes."* Baltimore: Johns Hopkins University Press.

Slater, Candace. 1979. "The *Romance* of the Warrior Maiden: A Tale of Honor and Shame." In *The Hispanic Ballad Today: History, Comparativism, Critical Bibliography.* Madrid: Cátedra Seminario Menéndez Pidal, 167–82.

Solé-Leris, Amadeu. 1980. *The Spanish Pastoral Novel*. Boston: Twayne.

Solomon, Michael, ed. and trans. 1990. *The Mirror of Coitus: A Translation and Edition of the Fifteenth-Century "Speculum al foderi."* Madison, Wis.: Hispanic Seminary of Medieval Studies.

Soons, Alan. 1970. "Characteristics of the Late Medieval *Facetia* in *La tía fingida*." *Annali: Sezione Romanza* 12:275–79.

Souviron López, Begoña. 1997. *La mujer en la ficción arcádica.* Frankfurt, Germany: Vervuert Iberoamericana.

Stagg, Geoffrey. 1984. "The Refracted Image: Porras and Cervantes." *Cervantes* 4:139–53.

Stallybrass, Peter, and Allon White. 1986. *The Politics and Poetics of Transgression.* Ithaca, N.Y.: Cornell University Press.

Stroud, Matthew D. 2000. "Homo/Hetero/Social/Sexual: Gila in Vélez de Guevara's *La serrana de la Vera*." *Calíope* 6.1–2:53–69.

Summers, Claude J. 1992. "Homosexuality and Renaissance Literature, or the Anxieties of Anachronism." *South Central Review* 9.1:2–23.

Taibo, Paco Ignacio, II. 1985. "A María le sienta bien el pantalón." In *María Félix: Cuarenta y siete pasos por el cine.* Mexico City: Joaquín Mortiz, 55–62.

Talvacchia, Bette. 1999. *Taking Positions: On the Erotic in Renaissance Culture.* Princeton, N.J.: Princeton University Press.

Tamariz, Cristóbal de. 1974. *Novelas en verso*. Ed. Donald McGrady. Charlottesville, Va: Biblioteca Siglo de Oro.

Tejera, Dionisia. 1988. "Catalina de Erauso: Heroína barroca interpretada en el romanticismo inglés." In *Veinticinco años de Filosofía y Letras*. Vol. 1, *Estudios de lengua y literatura.* Ed. Roberto Pérez. Bilbao, Spain: Universidad de Deusto, 285–308.

Tena, Pedro. 1990. "El retablo maravilloso de *La tía fingida*." In *Actas del I Coloquio Internacional de la Asociación de Cervantistas*. Barcelona: Anthropos, 283–94.

Teixeira Anacleto, Marta. 1994. *Aspectos da recepcão de* Los siete libros de la Diana *em França: As traducões de Nicolas Colin (1578) e S. G. Pavillon (1603)*. Coimbra, Portugal: Universidade de Coimbra, Faculdade de Letras.

Thompson, Peter E. 2006. *The Triumphant Juan Rana*. Toronto: University of Toronto Press.

Thompson, Stith. 1989. *Motif-Index of Folk-Literature*. Bloomington: Indiana University Press.

———. 1946. *The Folktale*. New York: Holt, Rinehart and Winston.

Tomás y Valiente, Francisco. 1990. "El crimen y pecado contra natura." In *Sexo barroco y otras transgresiones premodernas*. Ed. F. Tomás y Valiente et al. Madrid: Alianza, 33–55.

Traub, Valerie. 2002. *The Renaissance of Lesbianism in Early Modern England*. Cambridge, England: Cambridge University Press.

Trumbach, Randolph. 1977. "London's Sodomites: Homosexual Behaviour and Western Culture in the Eighteenth Century." *Journal of Social History* 11.1 (Fall): 1–33.

Unamuno, Miguel de. 1988. *Vida de Don Quijote y Sancho*. Ed. Alberto Navarro. Madrid: Cátedra.

Valcárcel, Isabel. 2005. *Mujeres de armas tomar*. Prol. Asunción Doménech. Madrid: Algaba Ediciones.

Vallbona, Rima-Gretchen R. de., ed. 1992. *Vida i sucesos de la monja alférez: Autobiografía atribuida a Doña Catalina de Erauso*. Tempe, Arizona: Center for Latin American Studies, Arizona State University.

———. 1981. "Historic Reality and Fiction in 'Vida y sucesos de la monja alférez.'" Ph.D. diss., Middlebury College.

van der Meer, Theo. 1992. "Tribades on Trial: Female Same-Sex Offenders in Late Eighteenth-Century Amsterdam." In *Forbidden History: The State, Society, and the Regulation of Sexuality in Modern Europe*. Ed. John C. Fout. Chicago: University of Chicago Press, 189–210.

Vargas Llosa, Mario. 1986. "Bataille o el rescate del mal." In *Contra viento y marea*. Vol 2. Barcelona: Seix Barral, 9–29.

Vargyas, Lajos. 1967. *Researches into the Medieval History of the Folk Ballad*. Trans. Arthur H. Whitney. Budapest: Akademiai Kiado.

Vasari, Giorgio. 1981–89. *Les vies des meilleurs peintres, sculpteurs et architectes*. Ed. and trans. André Chastel. 12 vols. Paris: Berger-Levrault.

Vasvári, Louise. 2006. "Queering the *Donçella Guerrera*." *Calíope* 12.2:93–117.

———. 1999. *The Heterotextual Body of the* Mora Morilla. London: Queen Mary and Westfield College, Department of Hispanic Studies.

———. 1983. "La semiología de la connotación: Lectura polisémica de 'Cruz Cruzada Panadera.'" *Nueva Revista de Filología Hispánica* 32.2:299–324.

————. 1977. "Peregrinaciones por topografías pornográficas en el *Libro de buen amor.*" In *Actas del VI Congreso Internacional de la Asociación Hispánica de Literatura Medieval.* Ed. José Manuel Lucía Megías. Vol. 2. Alcalá de Henares, Spain: Universidad de Alcalá, 1563–72.

Vázquez García, Francisco, and Andrés Moreno Mengíbar. 1997. *Sexo y razón: Una genealogía de la moral sexual en España (siglos XVI–XX).* Madrid: Akal.

Velasco, Sherry. 2000. *The Lieutenant Nun: Transgenderism, Lesbian Desire, and Catalina de Erauso.* Austin: University of Texas Press.

————. 1997. "Mapping Selvagia's Transmutable Sexuality in Montemayor's *Diana.*" *Revista de Estudios Hispánicos* 31:403–17.

Vélez de Guevara, Luis. 2002. *La serrana de la Vera.* Ed. William R. Manson and C. George Peale. Newark, Del.: Juan de la Cuesta.

————. 1916. *La serrana de la Vera.* Ed. Ramón Menéndez Pidal y María Goyri de Menéndez Pidal. Madrid: Sucesores de Hernando.

Vélez-Quiñones, Harry. 1999. "Capones, Italianos, Ermitaños y Lindos: Towards a Queer Subjectivity in Golden Age Poetry." *Calíope* 5.1:35–45.

Vicens, Teresa. 2000. *Speculum al joder: Tratado de recetas y consejos sobre el coito.* 1978. Reprint, Palma de Mallorca, Spain: Medievalia.

Victorio, Juan. 1995. "El erotismo en la lírica tradicional." In *Erotismo en las letras hispánicas: Aspectos, modos y fronteras.* Ed. Luce López-Baralt and Francisco Márquez Villanueva. Mexico City: Colegio de México, 501–14.

Vidal, César. 1999. *Enciclopedia del Quijote.* Barcelona: Planeta.

Vidal, Jean-Pierre. 1975. "Le mythe de la 'serrana' ou les avatars de la 'mere-ogresse.'" *La Pensée, Revue du Rationalisme Moderne* 183 (October): 75–92.

Vigil, Mariló. 1987. "La importancia de la moda en el barroco." In *Actas de las Cuartas Jornadas de Investigación Interdisciplinaria: Literatura y vida cotidiana.* (Seminario de Estudios de la Mujer.) Ed. María Angeles Durán and José Antonio Rey. Zaragoza, Spain: Universidad Autónoma de Madrid, 187–200.

Villalón, Cristóbal de. 1990. *El Crótalon de Cristóforo Gnofoso.* Ed. Asunción Rallo. Madrid: Cátedra.

Vives, Juan Luis. 1947. *Formación de la mujer cristiana: Obras completas.* Vol. 1. Trans. Lorenzo Riber. Madrid: Aguilar.

Waddington, Raymond B. 2004. *Aretino's Satyr: Sexuality, Satire, and Self-projection in Sixteenth-Century Literature and Art.* Toronto: University of Toronto Press.

Ward, John Powell. 1981. *Poetry and the Sociological Idea.* Brighton, England: Harvester Press.

Wardropper, Bruce W. 1951. "The *Diana* of Montemayor: Revaluation and Interpretation." *Studies in Philology* 48.2:126–44.

Warhol, Robyn R., and Diane Price Herndl, eds. 1991. *Feminisms: An Anthology of Literary Theory and Criticism.* New Brunswick, N.J.: Rutgers University Press.

Weeks, Jeffrey. 1986. *Sexuality.* London: Routledge.

Wellek, René, and Austin Warren. 1977. *Theory of Literature.* 3rd ed. 1949. Reprint, New York: Harcourt Brace Jovanovich.

Williams, Raymond. 1973. *The Country and the City.* New York: Oxford University Press.

Zayas y Sotomayor, María de. 2000. *Novelas amorosas y ejemplares.* Ed. Julián Olivares. Madrid: Cátedra.

Index